Laws and Trials
That Created History

Salem woman is accused of being a witch.

Laws and Trials That Created History

by Brandt Aymar and Edward Sagarin

Crown Publishers, Inc., New York

We appreciate permission to use certain excerpts and portions of actual trial testimony from the following: The Viking Press, Inc., for *Eichmann in Jerusalem*, by Hannah Arendt, © 1963, by Hannah Arendt; Simon and Schuster, Inc., for *Attorney for the Damned*, by Arthur Weinberg, © 1957, by Arthur Weinberg; Holt, Rinehart and Winston, Inc., for *The Sacco-Vanzetti Case: Transcript of the Record*, edited by Newton D. Baker, *et al.*; Alfred A. Knopf, Inc., for *The Era of Construction* by Kenneth M. Stampp, and *The Record: The Trial of Adolf Eichmann for the Crimes Against the Jewish People and Against Humanity*, by Lord Russell of Liverpool; and a quotation from *The Legacy of Sacco and Vanzetti*, by Louis Joughin and Edmund M. Morgan.

We also appreciate the very valuable help that so many people gave us in the preparation of this book: Daniel J. Foley; Virginia Daiker, Library of Congress; Lieutenant Colonel Gene Gurney; Lieutenant Colonel Robert Webb and Colonel Grover Heiman, Book and Magazine Division, United States Department of Defense; Dr. Hans Trefousse, professor of history, Brooklyn College, New York; D. E. J. MacNamara, criminologist, the City University of New York; Ezekiel Lifschitz, Yivo Institute for Jewish Research; Martin H. Bush, Carnegie Library, Syracuse University; Mary B. Gifford, Fall River Historical Society; Louis Torres, Federal Hall National Memorial, New York; Ellen Shaffer, the Free Library of Philadelphia; Rachel Minick, New-York Historical Society; Marion K. Conant, Dedham Historical Society; Dr. and Mrs. H. Ewing Bowmar; Kendall J. Cram, Tennessee State Library and Archives; Edith Gregor Halpert, Downtown Gallery, New York; Eugene D. Becker, Minnesota Historical Society; Treves di Bonfili; Will Edell, Wide World Photos; Maurice Davey, United Press International; and the invaluable reference sources of the New York Public Library, the Library of Congress, and the National Archives.

Many of the illustrations in this book are from well-known periodicals: *Frank Leslie's Weekly, Harper's Weekly, Harper's Monthly, Illustrated London News, The Graphic, Police Gazette, Illustrated American, Vanity Fair,* and others.

We have made every effort to credit the illustrations and the text references to the proper sources. If we have inadvertently omitted any, we shall be happy to add this information in subsequent printings.

Contents

Introduction

THE HISTORY OF ALL SOCIETIES COULD BE written as a story of wars and of trials, and indeed they constitute two of the most dramatic occurrences where man opposes his fellowman. In the courtroom, as on the battlefield, the struggle is often one of life and death, and out of each such battle there emerge not only a victor and a vanquished (or sometimes two sides that are vanquished), but a new world that is not quite what it had been before.

Trials are probably as old as Homo sapiens, or at least date back to the time when man began to live with other human beings in a community that was the model of what is today called a society. The guilt or innocence of an accused was once decided by his ability to withstand torture, and at other times by revelation from supernatural forces. The right to decide the fate of an accused has been vested in witch doctors, tribal chiefs, learned judges, and juries of one's peers. Whatever the system, the miscarriages of justice were many, and their end is not in sight.

Trials record the history of law, social change, and crime; of man's struggle against those who transgress, as well as of courtroom procedures and the effort to protect the rights of the accused. And at the same time, through many historic trials man has left evidence of some of his noblest struggles: the fight for ever-widening freedom; or against OPPRESSION OF A STATE, GENOCIDAL EXTERMINATION, and virulent racism.

The interest of men and women in courtroom procedures is unceasing; it is attested today by newspaper headlines of situations that will be forgotten tomorrow. But though forgotten, many of these trials will leave their mark on society, sometimes changing, if only slightly, man's outlook, attitudes, and procedures, and sometimes redirecting the course of a nation.

Hundreds of trials could be named—criminal and civil—of significance in the life and development of nations. Here we have dipped into a few, and of necessity overlooked many others. In the twenty-four trials we have chosen, we have sought to capture the spirit of many types of courts: those of many nations, civilian and military, and trials of the lowly and the mighty.

We start with Socrates, one of the noblest to challenge the old order, and end with Philip Berrigan and Angela Davis, who continue that challenge in our own day. Between them we have military trials: those of Alfred Dreyfus, where the French military and France herself was on trial before world opinion; of Billy Mitchell, who sought court-martial as part of his effort to obtain a dialogue in which he could espouse his cause of greater air strength; of Edith Cavell whose life and death were utilized by the Allies as part of the propaganda struggle against Germany.

Royalty has fallen and history has been changed through significant trials: those of Catherine of Aragon and of Charles I. Centuries earlier, Joan of Arc stood trial in France and was burned at the stake, accused of leading her people against the authorities; and in our own times, Jomo Kenyatta, facing a situation that might be called parallel, was found guilty and went off to prison, only to emerge and become head of his liberated nation.

No history of trials is complete without impeachment, and no impeachment trial matched the significance of that of Andrew Johnson, the President who, but for one vote, would have lost his job. Trials are also often the story of man against government and of government against man; this will be seen in the cases of Zenger, Scopes, and others. They are likewise the story of man's struggle for intellectual freedom, for the right of heresy, as will be seen in the stories of Socrates, Joan, and Galileo.

Trials illustrate a variety of facts, situations, and circumstances. In Nuremberg and again in Israel, we have ex post facto law, with the defendants accused of crimes of such enormity that, even if they were not illegal, they were nevertheless criminal. The significance of these trials for the future of international relations can hardly be exaggerated.

We have narrated some trials that have been told many times before. That of Sacco and Vanzetti, it seems to us, is never told too often; and Scottsboro stands in grave danger of being forgotten by young people today. The trial of the Chicago Eight, who became the Chicago Seven, has, for all its circus atmosphere, a chilling character for millions of Americans deeply concerned about the rights of the accused.

The trials have their lessons: in human liberty, in human error, and in the superhuman effort to bring to the courtroom an ever more precise method of judging the guilty· and acquitting the innocent; but above all in their effect on human history. These are trials that not only have a place in history: they changed the course of history.

Ideally, the narrator should be impartial, but this is an impossible requirement. Partiality is shown by the choice of one fact to narrate rather than another, as well as by the manner in which the material is arranged. No reader of the Dreyfus case can be other than outraged at the crude frame-up, but in other cases sympathies may differ. We are more sympathetic to the managers who sought Johnson's impeachment than almost all other modern writers have been; we cannot, after reading the testimony, help but doubt whether the defendants at Scottsboro received a fair trial; and we find most unconvincing those who state not only that Sacco was guilty but also that he received a fair trial before an impartial judge.

We hope, however, that our views have not interfered with the task of presenting these events as we understood them and in some instances lived through them, and that the reader will find not only the excitement and drama that these courtroom scenes inherently possess but will also see the many important lessons that history has to teach us.

Laws and Trials
That Created History

Socrates

399 B.C.

THE ATHENIAN COURTS OF JUSTICE IN Socrates' day bore little if any resemblance to our modern courts of justice. There were no judges, no prosecutors, no defense counselor. There was only a jury, but not of twelve good men and true. An Athenian jury might consist of 101 citizens of Athens, or 501, or 1,001. The odd number was a guarantee that there could not be a tie, for a simple majority was all that was needed to convict or acquit.

The court before which Socrates was tried was known as the Court of the Heliasts. It had jurisdiction over all public cases other than homicide. Any Athenian citizen of sound mind, age thirty or more and not afflicted with any disabilities, and a full citizen of Athens, could become a member of this court. At the beginning of each judicial year citizens offered themselves voluntarily, and a list was drawn up of all those who qualified. Perhaps six thousand in all were accepted for the year. Each was paid a small sum of three obols (about nine cents a day); so it at once becomes obvious that only those in need of money were attracted to such duty. These six thousand were divided into ten sections known as dicasteries, and each dicastery consisted of some five hundred or more citizens. Each day a case was tried before a dicastery, and all cases had to be concluded in the space of one day, and the verdict rendered, thus dispensing almost instant justice.

ANY ATHENIAN CITIZEN WHO ENJOYED the full rights of citizenship could bring an accusation against his neighbor and have him tried in this court of law. But there was a safeguard against unwarranted and purely malicious attacks. A plaintiff in such a private suit had to pay all court costs if he lost. Moreover, if one-fifth of the jurors did not support his charge, he was fined heavily, as much as one thousand drachmas (about $1,-000). There was no appeal from the Court of the Heliasts, either for the prosecutor or for the defendant.

In his charge the accuser also named the penalty he wished imposed. Here again the defendant was not entirely at the mercy of his accuser. If he was declared guilty, and a bare majority of one was sufficient to bring this about, he could then propose an alternate penalty, which, if accepted by the jurors, would be his punishment.

There were several procedures necessary for an accuser to bring a criminal charge against another person. First, he had to put the accusation in writing and take it to the office of the king-archon, where he presented it to a magistrate, along with the name of the accused, his address, and a description of his person. If the magistrate considered the accusation trivial or involving no violation of the law, he then and there threw the case out. But if there seemed grounds for the complaint, he set a date for a preliminary

"Socrates," by Paul Pontius. THE NEW YORK PUBLIC LIBRARY

dicastery consisted of 501 judges, or jurors. Presiding over the court was the king-archon himself. He had no judicial duties to perform and nothing to say in regard to the case itself. He simply conducted the trial, and oversaw the voting procedures by which jurors dropped guilty or not guilty tokens into the proper receptacle. When all the judges, spectators, accusers, and accused had assembled on the appointed day, the king-archon solemnly opened the trial and informed the jurors that the case to be tried on this day was that of Meletus against Socrates. A clerk then read the indictment.

Meletus, the son of Meletus, of Pitthea, impeaches Socrates, the son of Sophroniscus of Alopece, to wit: Socrates is guilty on the ground that he does not recognize the gods recognized by the state, but introduces other new divinities; he is further guilty on the ground that he corrupts the youth. The penalty is death.

Thus Socrates was accused of the grave crimes of impiety and of corrupting Athenian youth. Corrupting in this sense meant influencing youths to question the wisdom of their parents and the leaders of Athenian society. How did it happen that the greatest philosopher and thinker of his day, known throughout the civilized world for his wit and wisdom, found himself in the dire predicament of fighting for his life before those very fellow citizens among whom he had lived for all his seventy years? Partly it was due to his unfortunate past political alliances, and partly to his infuriating superiority in exposing the ignorance and lack of true knowledge on the part of all his contemporaries, whether they were senators or peasants. As the Delphic oracle had spoken, "No man is wiser than Socrates." The leading citizens of Athens resented it.

From the time he was a young man,

hearing with accuser and accused. It was the accuser's duty to find the accused, inform him of the charge before two witnesses, and advise him to appear at the preliminary hearing on a certain day. At this hearing both parties put in writing their declarations and supported them with evidence. Unless such evidence had been given at this hearing it could not be introduced at the actual trial before the Court of the Heliasts. The magistrate then fixed the day upon which the case would be tried.

In the trial of Socrates in 399 B.C., the

Socrates' international fame as a person of outstanding intellectual power had been established. Even in his student days, his curiosity led him to delve into the greatest thinking of the times, sometimes embracing one school briefly, questioning it, and then abandoning it as logically unsatisfactory. He was well known to the sophists (professional teachers of rhetoric) of his day, and often disagreed with Protagoras, their eminent leader.

About 431 B.C., the oracle at Delphi pronounced Socrates the wisest man in Greece. Although amazed, Socrates became convinced that his calling was to search for wisdom about right conduct by which he might guide the intellectual and moral improvement of the Athenians. Neglecting, therefore, his own affairs, he spent his time discussing virtue, justice, and piety wherever his fellow citizens congregated.

At the outbreak of the Peloponnesian War, Socrates had many friends in high circles, the most famous of whom was Alcibiades. Alcibiades was well known in Athenian democracy, a beautiful youth who led his country to many victories, only to turn traitor. He then fled to Sparta, where he fought against his fellow Athenian citizens. Although he was many years younger than Socrates, the two formed a deep attachment for each other. It is hinted that Anytus, one of Socrates' accusers at his trial, was jealous of this relationship; he may also have been disturbed that his own son was one of Socrates' followers.

For a number of years now, the once proud and invincible Athens had been fighting and losing wars. In 413 B.C., the Athenians fought against Syracuse. The war ended in the complete collapse of the old moral, political, and economic order of Ath-

"Socrates and Alcibiades," by L. Lipparini. Alcibiades in his teens had formed a passionate attachment to Socrates, but later, at the time of this painting, he has become a dilettante, while Socrates has turned to the preaching of his moral philosophy. COURTESY RACCOLIA TREVES DE BONFILI, VENICE

ens. The following years were no less militarily unkind to the city-state, and she capitulated in 404 to Lysander. The Spartans, having no use for democracy, pressured Athens into replacing her form of government with an oligarchy ruled by a Commission of Thirty. The rule of this body was marked by arbitrary executions and property confiscations so odious that in 403 the commission was expelled, and Athens returned once again to democratic rule. Unfortunately for the reputation of Socrates, two of his close associates were prominent in the Commission of Thirty: Critias, a cousin of Plato's mother, and Charmides, her brother. Thus it again appeared, as in the case of Alcibiades, that Socrates was educating traitors. It was also well known that Socrates was not in sympathy with the democratic form of government. As might be expected of an eminent philosopher, whose sole mission in life was the quest for knowledge, Socrates believed in a rule of the intellectuals. Those who qualified in knowledge should lead the citizens of Athens, not those elected by popular acclaim. Thus, his political affiliations and philosophy alienated a large number of influential Athenians, and led directly to the trial. These enemies wanted him banished from the country. They had no wish for his death, only for his removal from their society. But Socrates had other plans.

At the opening of the trial, the accusers spoke first, each one of the three presenting his view and evidence of Socrates' apparent guilt. Since the charge was originated by Meletus, he spoke first, and concerned himself with Socrates' speculations in physical science, which resulted, so he claimed, in the rejection of the recognized gods of the state. Since it was no crime in Athens at that time to worship any gods one wished, it is difficult to see how this constituted a crime

"Socrates and His Friends," by John La Farge. MINNESOTA HISTORICAL SOCIETY

of impiety. Nor was there any illegality in Socrates' "divine sign" or "divine voice," which Meletus accused him of obeying. The citizens of Athens were well aware of Socrates' self-proclaimed mission. Meletus was more accurate when he charged that Socrates had ridiculed the poets, an unpopular pastime, since poets were regarded as divine seers and true teachers of the people.

The second accuser was Lycon, a rhetorician, who entranced the jurors with his knowledge of the law. He cited previous cases where impiety had been the charge, and stressed the importance of enforcing the law. He ended by implying that Socrates had continually ridiculed the rhetoricans.

It is hard to see why a respected leader such as Anytus could have become embroiled in the trial of Socrates, yet he probably was the prime instigator, a man intensely jealous of Socrates. Socrates had caused Anytus' own son to question his father's wisdom and his qualifications. Stung to the quick by Socrates' many attacks on politicians and statesmen, Anytus stressed this antipathy in his charge. He made many telling points against the prisoner, accusing him of criticizing public life but refusing to partake in any public functions, which to an Athenian was the moral obligation of every citizen. (Socrates was to go to great lengths in the *Apology* to explain his reasons for leading a private, not a public life.) And, of course, Anytus charged Socrates with teaching the young to disrespect their parents and to criticize many of the democratic institutions, such as the use of the lot in appointing men to office. Because he had been instrumental in formulating the Amnesty of 404–403 for any criminal acts committed before its enactment, he referred only obscurely to Socrates' close friendships with Alcibiades and Critias. But even an obscure reference was clear enough to the jurors, who were very familiar with the former associates and pupils of Socrates.

The accusers ended their speeches and now the philosopher was to answer their charges. Socrates had refused the help of a professional to formulate his defense, preferring instead to go before the court and tell the truth in his own words. That he had little expectation of being acquitted is suggested by his casual manner of speaking, as if he were engaging in a private conversation, and in his apparent disregard of what the jurors thought, as long as he could speak the truth as usual.

Socrates began his defense by asking his judges to forgive the way he spoke in court. "At the age of more than seventy years, I am now for the first time appearing before a court of justice, so that I am an utter stranger to the manner of speaking here." He then went on to say that the real reason for his being tried was not the two formal charges now being put against him by Meletus, Lycon, and Anytus, but the many enemies he had acquired over the years and the false rumors they had spread about him. "These I fear more than Anytus and his friends. . . . Those who, getting hold of you for the most part while you were yet children, have persuaded you to believe this false accusation, that there is a certain Socrates, a wise man, who speculates on things in the heavens and searches into all things under the earth, and makes the worse appear the better reason."

Socrates defending himself before his judges. From a relief by Antonio Canova.

He then told the court that the oracle at Delphi had said he was the wisest man in the world, and how he set out to refute it by finding a man wiser than himself. One of those he questioned was a leading Athenian statesman. "It seemed to me that this man had the appearance of being wise in the eyes of many others, and most of all in his own, but in reality was not wise. Whereupon I tried to convince him that he only thought himself wise but was not really so, and consequently I became an object of hatred to him and to many of those who were present." Such was the way Socrates infuriated the leaders of Athenian society.

Socrates then called Meletus to answer some questions in regard to his charge of impiety, and quickly tricked Meletus into accusing him of being an atheist. "But tell me, in the name of Zeus, do you really think that I believe there is no God?"

Meletus cried out, "By Zeus, I swear that you believe there is no God at all." It was a telling point by Socrates, for Meletus' charge was that Socrates had introduced gods other than those recognized by the state, so how could he possibly have been an atheist?

Socrates countered, "Nobody will believe that, Meletus, and I doubt whether you do yourself." The entire charge of impiety was so nebulous that the accusers themselves did not know what it meant, and the jurors had even less notion of its meaning. Thus, on any legal basis, the first charge in the indictment was invalid.

Socrates told the court that by putting him to death they would only harm themselves. He referred to himself as God's gift to Athenian society.

Such a man, citizens, you will not easily find again, and if you take my advice you will spare me. . . . And that I am such a gift of God to the state you can see from this my conduct; for it is not in the ordinary course of human nature that I should have been thus neglectful of my own affairs, and have suffered my household interests to be uncared for these many years, while I was continually busying myself with yours, going about to each one of you individually, like a father or an elder brother, and trying to take thought for virtue.

He then went to some lengths to justify why he never gave his advice in public before the senate but only in private conversations. The one time he was in the senate he held out against all the others for law and order, even against a threat of prison or death.

Our tribe had chief direction of state affairs on that occasion when the ten generals who had not picked up the men after the naval combat were brought to trial. You wished to try them all in a body, which was contrary to law, as you all afterwards admitted; but I then alone, out of the whole body of fifty Prytanes, was opposed to doing anything against the laws and voted in opposition. . . . Do you really think, then, that I could have lived for so many years if I had led a public life, and, acting as an honest man, had stood by the right and held this, as I ought, above every other consideration?

Then Socrates turned to the charge against him of corrupting the youth of Athens.

I have never been a teacher to any man, but if any one, whether young or old, wished to hear me speak while carrying out my mission, I never grudged him the opportunity. Nor is it my habit to discourse when I am paid, and refuse to discourse when I am not; but I hold myself ready to be questioned alike by rich and poor; or if any one prefers that I should question him, I let him first answer me and then hear what I have to say. And whether any of my hearers become better or worse, for that I cannot justly be made answerable. . . . If I am corrupting some of the young men, and have corrupted others, surely some of those who are now grown up, and have come to know that when young they received bad advice from me, ought now to appear in court in order to accuse me and have me punished. Or if they themselves were unwilling to do this, some of their kinsfolk, fathers or brothers, or others belonging to them, should, if members of their family had received any harm at my hands, remember it now against me and seek my punishment.

Socrates then brought his defense to a close. "Well, citizens, these facts and perhaps others of the same nature make up about all the defense I can offer." He stated that he would not ask his judges for mercy or implore them with many tears or bring his children to court to plead for him. Such would not be honorable and, the world knowing him to surpass most men, it would be unworthy.

It does not seem to me right either to owe one's escape to entreaties or to supplicate a judge rather than to enlighten and convince him. For the judge sits in court to give judgment, not to award justice by favor; and he has not sworn to grant favors to whomsoever he pleases, but to judge according to the laws. . . . For if I were to persuade you and by force of entreaties overpower your oaths, I should clearly be teaching you not to believe in gods, and accusing myself of not believing in them while in the very act of defending myself against this accusation. But far from this, O men of Athens, I do believe in them as does not one of my accusers; and to you and to God I leave it to judge my case as shall be best for me as well as for yourselves.

Thus spoke Socrates.

The judges now turned to voting on his guilt or innocence. Each of the 501 advanced to the urns and deposited his verdict. Upon counting, it was found that by sixty votes the majority was against the accused.

Since Meletus had proposed the death penalty, it was now Socrates' turn to make a counterproposal for penalty. All present

A group of jurors in a court of Athens.

expected Socrates to propose banishment for himself, which would have been immediately accepted and his life spared. But they had not reckoned with the absolute integrity of the philosopher. He had no intention of outwitting the death penalty, and almost jokingly suggested that he be supported in the Prytaneum at public expense for the rest of his life. Then he continued discussing more serious alternatives, ending with a fine. Although very poor, he suggested, "I might possibly pay one mina of silver; therefore, I propose that amount. But Plato here, O men of Athens, and Crito and Critobulus and Apollodorus bid me say thirty minas, and offer to be my sureties. This, then, I propose; and for the payment of the money they will be ample security to you."

The judges now voted on the two proposed penalties, and chose death.

Socrates took the remainder of his time, while the clerks were gathering up all their materials, to discourse on death as a good thing. "Death must be one of two things: either he who is dead becomes naught, and has no consciousness of anything; or else, as men say, there is a certain change and removal of the soul from this place to some other." If the former, it would be like the most wonderful dreamless sleep a man ever had. If the latter, what greater good than thus being set free from so-called judges and being able to face the true judges of Hades and meet all the great men of the past. Socrates told them that for him to die now was best. He looked forward to being released from wordly affairs. In farewell he said, "But now it is time for us to go away, I to die, you to live. Which of us is going to a better fate is unknown to all save God."

The custom in Athenian criminal law was for a condemned man to be turned over at once to a law body known as the Eleven, whose duty it was to see that the execution took place within twenty-four hours. Socrates was an exception.

Each year a boat was dispatched, after a sacred ceremoney, to the shrine of Apollo in Delos, in memory of the deliverance by Theseus from the annual tribute of seven lads and seven maidens to Minos of Cnossus, from whence they never returned. Until this ship came back, no executions were allowed to be carried out. The religious ceremonies had begun the day before the trial of Socrates took place, so the Eleven were faced with the problem of what to do with him until the ship arrived. As it happened, contrary winds forced the ship's delay, and it was a month before it finally reached Athens. Socrates' wealthy friend Crito begged the court to let him remain free until that time, but his plea was refused. Consequently, the condemned philosopher was put in the prison of the Eleven, but was allowed a certain amount of freedom in receiving and passing the day with friends and admirers. Several friends from abroad came to Athens to be with him until the end. For the first time in his life, he took to writing poetry, composing a paean to Apollo and putting into verse Aesop's fables.

During the month's wait Crito and some of his other friends raised enough money to bribe the proper officials and effect an escape. This would have met with the approval of the Athenians, who wanted only banishment, not death. But Socrates refused, seeing in such an escape a renunciation of all the principles he had advocated in his lifetime. However wrong Anytus and Meletus had been in accusing him, and however unfair the verdict against him, it was the legal finding of the court, and to escape would be a crime against the state. For Socrates to commit a crime after advocating a life of virtue and conduct according to the laws was unthinkable. In reasoning with Crito on his entreaty to escape, Socrates argued:

Do we then hold that we ought in no way intentionally to commit injustice, or that we may commit it in one way, and not in another; or do we still, as in former times, admit that to act unjustly is in no case good and honorable? And all the principles which we have acknowledged within these last few days to be now thrown away, and have we, Crito, at our age, been thus long and earnestly reasoning among ourselves, unconscious all the while that we are no better than children? Or rather, whether the mass of men acknowledge it or not, and whether a sterner or milder fate is in store for us, is not what we said before still true, that to do injustice is in every way a disgrace and an evil to the doer of it? Do we admit this or not?

To which Crito replied, "We do."

Socrates then recited to Crito what he believed the state would logically say if he did escape. The state is speaking.

As it is now, if you depart hence [that is, take the hemlock], you go as one wronged, not by us, the laws, but by men; but if you take to flight, thus disgracefully rendering back injustice and injury by breaking the covenants and agreements which you yourself made with us, and working evil against those whom least of all you ought to injure—your own self as well as your friends, your country and ourselves —we shall be angry with you here while you are yet alive, and our brothers, the laws in Hades, will not receive you kindly, knowing that you sought, so far as in you lay, to destroy us. So do not, we beg you, let Crito persuade you to follow his advice rather than ours.

Then, ending his argument, he urged Crito to accept his logic.

These, you must know, my dear friend Crito, are the words which I seem to hear, even as the Corybantes imagine that they hear the sound of flutes; and their echo resounding within me makes me unable to hear aught besides. Know, therefore, that if you say anything contrary to this, you will but speak in vain. Nevertheless, if you think that anything will be gained thereby, say on.

But Crito was now convinced. "No, Socrates, I have nothing more to say."

"Then so let it rest, Crito: and let us follow in this way, since in this way it is that God leads."

When the ship arrived from Delos, the Eleven informed Socrates to be ready for death that day. Phaedo and other friends of the philosopher learned of this early in the morning when they arrived at the prison. When they reached Socrates' cell they found that he had been freed from his shackles and that his wife Xanthippe, carrying their infant son, was with him. Seeing his friends enter, she burst into tears and, at Socrates' request, was taken home.

The rest of the day was spent by Socrates answering many questions that were disturbing his friends.

To you, my judges, I want to declare my reason for thinking that a man who has really given up his life to the pursuit of philosophy should take courage when about to die, and be of good hope that, after leaving this life, he will attain to the greatest good yonder. And how this may be, Simmias and Cebes, I will try to tell you.

It is apt to escape the notice of others, that they who are rightly following philosophy are devoting themselves solely to the study of dying and death. Now, if this be true, and they have been their whole life long eagerly anticipating this one thing alone, it would surely be absurd for them to be distressed when that to which they had been looking forward with a devotion of a lifetime had at length arrived.

At this unassailable logic Simmias laughed. Socrates then continued with a discussion of how at death the soul was released from the body and at the same time purified of the unworthy desires and tendencies of living and endowed with courage, temperance, and wisdom. The subject of immortality itself consumed several hours.

Now the sun was almost setting, and Socrates left his friends to take a bath. After this, his children and the women of his household came to bid him farewell and hear his last directions. When they had gone, Socrates returned to his friends, where they all sat quietly, saying very little. Soon the servant of the Eleven arrived to inform him that it was time to drink the poison and to tearfully bid him good-bye. Socrates was ready. "Let the poison be brought if it is already mixed; if not, let the man mix it."

A servant standing nearby was sent to get

the hemlock, and, when he returned with it, Socrates said, "Well, my friend, I must ask you, since you have had experience in these matters, what I ought to do."

"Nothing," replied the servant, "but walk about after drinking until you feel a heaviness in your legs, and then, if you lie down, the poison will take effect of itself."

With a prayer to the gods, Socrates then took the libation and lightly tossed it down. His friends could stand it no longer, and all broke into tears. Socrates was amazed. "What are you doing, you strange people? My chief reason for sending away the women was that we might be spared such discordance as this; for I have heard that a man ought to die in solemn stillness. So pray be composed, and restrain yourselves!"

Socrates rose and began his last walk around in his cell. Soon, feeling the heaviness coming on, he lay down and covered his face with the sheet. From time to time the man who had given him the poison felt his legs and pressed hard on them. Socrates said he could not feel anything. Higher and higher the numbness rose until it reached his waist. At this point he looked out from under the sheet and said to Crito, "We owe a cock to Aesculapius. Pay the debt, and do not neglect it." Crito replied, "It shall be done, Socrates. But think if you have nothing else to say."

There was no answer, for the poison had reached the heart, and Socrates was dead.

In the history of mankind, the meaning of morality differs according to time and place; and Athenian society was a far cry from Anglo-Saxon puritanism. For Socrates, morality had a deeper meaning: living by estab-

"The Death of Socrates," by Jacques Louis David. He takes the fatal hemlock as his friends break down weeping, for which he chides them, saying that that is why he has sent away the womenfolk. THE METROPOLITAN MUSEUM OF ART, WOLFE FUND, 1931

lished values without deviating from them for the sake of opportunism, as witness his refusal to escape from prison, even when it had been neatly and financially arranged.

What are these established values? Socrates was the first to create the concept of the *soul*, which has ever since dominated the thinking of the majority of people of the Western world. Man's supreme reason for being was to cultivate the soul, make the best of it, and finally answer for its state when at last upon death it went to Hades. It was this philosophy that was ready-made for the coming Christianity. Man was master of his own soul, and could shape its personality in any way he wished, wise or foolish, virtuous or vicious, according to how he wished to live. It was unavoidably bound up with an individual's personal intelligence and character. Socrates "brought philosophy down from heaven to earth," and taught that it was man's primary duty to tend his soul and make it as good as possible. Thus his "divine mission" was to make others realize how ignorant they were and how unjustified in doing and believing as they did. He admonished them to live, not by opinions or fancy assumptions, but by reason arrived at through logic and knowledge. A tyrant, for instance, thinking himself above the laws, might subjugate property and personal freedoms to his own whims, but this did not bring him the happiness he wanted because what he was doing was wrong; his soul was diseased. This is not to say that hedonism was wrong, that good and pleasure could not be the same thing. But the pleasure had to be real, and not the imagined results of evildoing.

Just as Athenians did not distinguish between public and private life, Socrates did not distinguish between the actions of private individuals and the state in the application of his moral philosophy. Here he came

violently in conflict with the leaders of democratic Athens, from Themistocles to Pericles, whom he accused of lacking the knowledge of good and who were therefore unfit to rule. Even though they made Athens wealthy and powerful, they did nothing for the moral values of the people. Such criticism of national heroes was one of the chief reasons for Socrates being prosecuted. His theory of rule by intellectuals was decidedly antidemocratic.

Socrates was the first man in the world consciously to question the relationship of scientific objects with their moral values. Today, we question the status of our scientific discoveries, and still wonder just what is a moral ideal. It is the heritage of Socrates that man in his intellectual pursuits questions, doubts, and demands answers.

It would be ironical if one were to discover overwhelming evidence that there was no Socrates, that he was a creation primarily of Plato, as a few have contended. This is unlikely; but though the evidence points to the man, much of his philosophy seems to be Plato's, and many events of his life may be fictitious. Was he tried by the Athenians, and condemned? Was he offered an escape that he refused? These are matters that it is difficult today to state with certainty. One need only apply to the questions the Socratic method of skeptical challenging and searching.

But through his life and the trial (or Plato's version of it), there is a Socratic legacy. For Plato, Socrates was "truly the wisest, and justest, and best of all the men I have ever known." If one were to summarize the trial of Socrates in a few words, he was condemned, not for offering answers, but for posing questions. Into the minds of youth he instilled doubt: this alone, Athenian power could not face.

Joan of Arc

1431

ON MAY 7, 1429, THE FRENCH, UNDER THE leadership of a young girl of seventeen, drove the mighty English army out of the once impregnable fortress of Les Tourelles outside Orléans, and thus brought about a complete reversal of the military and political situation in France and reestablished the sagging morale of the French army. It was the culminating victory for Joan of Arc, known as La Pucelle (the maiden or the virgin), who had welded a wretched French army, whose only creed was greed, into a potent fighting force simply through her inspiring leadership and her belief in God's will. The voices of St. Catherine, St. Margaret, and St. Michael spoke to her, she believed, and encouraged her to drive the English from France and restore the dauphin, Charles VII, to his rightful throne.

On the morning of Sunday, July 16, 1429, at a colorful ceremony in the cathedral at Rheims, Joan of Arc had her fondest wish granted. In full armor, standing close to the king, she saw two of the ecclesiastical peers lift up the chair on which Charles sat, while others held the crown over his head. By this simple act Charles VII was crowned king. Joan knelt before him, embraced his knees, and with tears running down her cheeks said, "Gentle king, now has God's pleasure been accomplished Who willed that I should raise the siege of Orléans and lead you to this city of Rheims for your coronation, thus MANIFESTING THAT YOU ARE THE TRUE KING to whom this realm of France by right belongs."

For her deeds of valor in restoring the monarchy of France to its rightful ruler, she paid with her life, as a result of a conspiracy between King Henry VI of England and the Church of Rome, and was virtually abandoned by the very king she had set on the throne.

Once crowned, Charles ignored her advice to march on Paris, take it, and thus forestall further effective action by his two enemies: the Burgundians under Philip and the English under the Duke of Bedford. Instead, Charles's advisers counseled the concluding of a peace treaty. Through their efforts a general truce, established the previous Christmas, was extended into April 1430. This was just what the Duke of Burgundy and his English allies needed to get ready to retake Orléans. For months he had been urging Charles to take some concrete action to implement the truce, namely, the turning over to him of the city of Compiègne. The brave people of Compiègne adamantly refused to be a pawn in this maneuver, and wrote Charles that they were his loyal subjects and would serve only him. Inspired by their fortitude, Joan, unbeknown to the king, headed for that city, rallying around her the irregular forces in the area, who were constantly harassing the Burgundians and the English. By provoking clashes she prevented the enemy from gaining any permanent footholds from which they might launch a successful attack on Compiègne, which Joan thought would lead to an attack on Paris.

On Easter Sunday, April 17, four thousand Burgundians and fifteen hundred English, together with a strong force of artillery, siege engines, and sappers marched toward Compiègne. The truce was ended. For weeks now, using Compiègne as her base, Joan with her army of two thousand men had moved around the countryside, fighting the enemy in many places. On May 23 Joan rode out of Compiègne with five hundred men to launch a surprise attack on the town of Margny. Although they took the Burgundians by surprise, they had been spotted by Jean de Luxembourg and his friends, who were approaching the town on horseback. Luxembourg sent for more troops, hoping to prevent Joan's forces from returning to Compiègne. In the ensuing battle most of Joan's forces succeeded in retreating into the fortress of Compiègne; but, unknown to Joan, those inside Compiègne, fearing the entry of the enemy, had raised the bridge and lowered the portcullis. Joan was trapped outside the fortification. She fought heroically, until an enemy bowman grabbed hold of her and pulled her from her horse. She surrendered to an archer, a nobleman in the ranks of the Bastard of Wandomme. She was now the prisoner of its feudal overlord, Jean de Luxembourg.

The English were anxious to destroy her influence. Joan of Arc must be burned at the stake, if the English were ever to be effective again in their conquest of France. Joan's very presence at the head of the French forces made them almost supernaturally invincible. Never again could she be allowed to lead them.

Joan meeting Charles VII.

But the English did not own the prisoner. She had been captured in the Bastard of Wandomme's territory and was a prisoner of Jean de Luxembourg, who in turn was a vassal to Philip of Burgundy. The English decided to buy Joan from the Burgundians. Philip of Burgundy agreed to turn her over to the English for ten thousand gold pounds, plus a regular income paid to Jean de Luxembourg. The English leader, the Duke of Bedford, knew the only way to get her burned at the stake was by ecclesiastical trial, conducted with every canonical guar-

After her many victories on behalf of her king, Joan is finally captured at Compiègne, when the gates to the town were lowered, leaving her outside, at the mercy of the English.

antee. A trial was necessary if Joan was to be sentenced to death, and a Church trial was the best means of silencing criticism.

Joan was captured within the diocese of Pierre Cauchon, the bishop of Beauvais, a greedy, power-hungry man who had already conspired with the English, and been admirably rewarded. He was, therefore, delighted to help Bedford arrange a Church trial. Cauchon would claim Joan as a prisoner of the Church and condemn her; but, even better, he would get her to confess her alliance with the forces of evil and to denounce the very coronation of Charles VII she had fought so hard to achieve. But the confession must be made *of her own free will*, if anyone was to believe it. And the Church must be responsible for the foregone verdict of guilty. Accordingly, Cauchon

would quickly call for judges to be drawn from the University of Paris, the Inquisition, and the Bench of Bishops.

Meanwhile, Joan had been taken from Noyon to the castle of Beaulieu, where she made her first unsuccessful attempt at escape. From there she was transferred to Beaurevoir, where she was nearly killed after jumping from her seventy-foot tower. At Beaurevoir she was treated kindly by the wife and the aunt of her captor. She was then moved about constantly—to Arras, to the castle of Drugy, to Le Crotoy, where she could look out over the English Channel. She was sustained in those days by two considerations: she was treated fairly and honorably as a prisoner of war, and her "voices" were still speaking to her and encouraging her. On November 24 she was transferred by barge to Vinieu, thence taken to Saint-Valéry, to Eu, to Dieppe, and finally to Rouen. It was nearly Christmas, 1430, when she arrived at the castle of Rouen and was put in chains in its tower, attended now by boorish male guards who attempted at every opportunity to rape and abuse her. It was in this cell that she was visited by the earls of Stafford and Warwick. To them she said, "I know well that these English will do me to death, thinking when I am dead to gain the kingdom of France, but if they were a thousand godons more than they are now, they shall not have the kingdom." This so enraged Stafford that he drew his sword to kill her, but was restrained by Warwick.

Cauchon made devious plans during these months preceding the trial. Although the University of Paris wanted Joan brought there for trial, Cauchon, at the bidding of the English, succeeded in having Rouen chosen as its locale. He had sent emissaries everywhere to unearth incriminating facts that he could use against Joan. He found few, and promptly suppressed all reports that tended to exonerate her. Thus, he began her trial with very little legal evidence.

On January 3, 1431, Henry VI of England came to visit Warwick in the castle of Rouen, where Joan was imprisoned in one of its towers. He issued the letters necessary to start the proceedings against Joan. In them he only "lent" her to the ecclesiastical judges for them to decide whether or not she was to be punished by death, and he made it clear that the English retained full authority over her.

These letters ordered that "La Pucelle shall be delivered over to the bishop of Beauvais, for the purpose of her being tried, according to God and reason; and orders are issued to all to give to the prelate aid, defence, protection, and comfort. It is therein also expressly reserved, at all events, that Jeanne shall still be retained—even in case she is found not guilty."

By the middle of February Cauchon was ready to proceed with the trial. On February 19 it was stated that on the basis of preliminary investigations there was good reason to try the Maid and convict her on religious grounds. To complete his court Cauchon inveigled the vicar of the Inquisition, Jean Lemaître, to sit as cojudge. He was reluctant to serve, not believing in Joan's guilt, and did so only on orders of his superior, Graverend. He was there only for a small part of the trial, but voted for her death in order to save his own life. He had been threatened with execution unless he did. Many members of the court objected to the legality of the proceedings and to Cauchon's fraudulent practices of tampering with the evidence. They advised Joan to appeal directly to the Pope, but they were of no avail against Cauchon's unrelenting fury and domination. Cauchon had brought in six members of the all-powerful University of Paris, which had triumphed over kings and popes alike but which in recent years had lost its men of stature. The two younger ones, who still possessed a sense of justice, took one look at the setup and returned to Paris for good. Including judges, lawyers, and assessors, the court consisted of 117 persons. Against this formidable array, writes Lucien Fabre, "isolated, without anyone to advise or support her, seated on a high stool, dressed in black hose and a black tunic, with her dark hair cropped to the shape of an inverted basin ending just above the ears, her eyes bright with fever and fatigue, emaciated, but burning with the fire of the spirit, and having God within her —Joan." Her public trial, or more precisely, her public questioning, began on Wednesday, February 21, 1431. The judges knew well what was expected of them by the English.

The questioning lasted over three weeks. The first day the bishop of Beauvais stated his credentials for presiding at the trial, and, when Joan was brought in, explained to her that she was being tried by this court for her unorthodox actions both in this province and others throughout France. She was urged to tell the truth and asked to take an oath. To this she agreed with one reservation. She would say nothing of her secret communications with King Charles VII, whom she had put on the rightful throne of France. Cauchon forbade her to leave the prison, threatening to convict her of heresy if she did. But Joan answered that if she could possibly escape she would.

On Thursday, February 22, the interrogation took place in the robing room of the castle. After a few preliminary questions regarding her rituals of faith, such as going to confession, Joan told the court that when

she was thirteen years old she had first heard a voice from God, which badly frightened her. The voice had told her to be good, to go to church often, and to leave Domrémy and go elsewhere in France. There she should free the city of Orléans from the siege by the English and Burgundians. The voice gave her explicit instructions: whom to see and what to do. As to putting on male clothes, she said it was her own idea. She told her judges about the letters she had sent to the English at Orléans telling them to withdraw and give up the siege.

Each day Joan was questioned for several hours, the questions coming at her from all directions, and often several questions at once. For a naïve peasant girl she handled them with what seemed to be the skill of an expert lawyer, but it was more a case of simple honesty and forthrightness. Her judges were amazed. The high point of the third trial session, on Saturday, February 24, came when they asked her if she considered herself blessed with the grace of

"The Trial of Joan of Arc," by Louis Maurice Boutet de Monvel. Presiding over the court on his throne (upper left) is Pierre Cauchon, Bishop of Beauvais. THE CORCORAN GALLERY OF ART, W. A. CLARK COLLECTION

God, to which she answered: "If I am not, may God effect it: and if I am, may God retain me in it; for I should esteem myself the most unfortunate of women, I would rather die than know that I were without the pale of the grace and love of God."

At the fourth session, on Tuesday, February 27, she was closely questioned about her voices. Now she revealed their names; they were the voices of St. Catherine and St. Margaret, and she recognized them "by their salutations and the manner of their performing reverence." But even before these saints had spoken to her, she had been comforted by St. Michael. She refused to elaborate further.

The fifth session was held on Thursday, March 1. It was here that Joan made one of her most famous predictions: within seven years the English would lose everything they had gained in France. (They did.) Further questioning about her saints then took place. When asked if St. Margaret spoke English, she replied incredulously, "How should she speak English, seeing that she is not on their side?" With an unintentional bit of humor she answered their question as to whether St. Michael appeared to her in the nude: "Do you think that the Almighty has not wherewithal to clothe him?"

The sixth questioning period took place on Saturday, March 3, when the judges asked about the male clothes she wore. They urged her to put on female attire, but she refused. Further questioning went into the details of her armor and some of her actions in battle.

There now occurred a week's respite while Cauchon met with "many venerable doctors and masters versed in divine and canon law." Together they went over all of Joan's testimony to date and decided just where she should be questioned further. Cauchon decided that additional questioning would be conducted by only a small number of judges chosen by him for each session and that it would take place in Joan's prison cell. Because Joan was eliciting far too much sympathy, he saw the dangers in further public trials. Thus, the seventh session took place on Saturday, March 10, in the jail. Jean de La Fontaine asked about her actions in and around Compiègne, the armor she and her compatriots wore, and what riches her king had given her. Joan told him, "I require nothing for myself of my king but very good arms, good horses, and money to pay the people of my hôtel." La Fontaine wanted to know what sign confirming her holy mission she gave the king when she first picked him out from the assembly. On this score Joan was adamant in her refusal to answer.

The eighth and ninth sessions took place in the prison on Monday, March 12. In the morning Joan was asked about a breach-of-promise suit she was supposed to have brought against a youth from the town of Toul. This she denied, saying that she had consecrated her virginity to heaven as long as God wished it. In the afternoon she told her judges about her plans to go to England and release her hero, the duke of Orléans, from his captivity there.

At this point in the trial the Inquisition entered the scene. Jean Lemaître, vicar of the Inquisitor, was sent by Paris to try Joan on matters of faith. He joined Cauchon in conducting the court, and together they proceeded to question Joan in prison on Tuesday, March 13. The subject was the coronation of King Charles VII, and dealt with the angel who brought the crown and who had been seen by Joan doing reverence to the king by bowing before him. The angel, she stated, was seen and recognized by the clerics present.

On Wednesday, March 14, there were two sessions of questioning in prison. In the

Pierre Cauchon, with a recorder, continues the trial in Joan's prison cell.

city). Turning on the bishop of Beauvais, she gave him a warning which revealed the strength of her own faith: "You state that you are my judge. I am not aware that you are such; but I charge you take heed and do not judge me wrongfully, as in such case you will place your soul in great jeopardy; and I finally forewarn you that should it please the Almighty God to punish you, I have only fulfilled my duty in thus giving you timely notice." At the afternoon session they inquired if she did not believe she had committed mortal sins when she attacked Paris on a feast day, when she jumped from the tower of Beaurevoir, when she wore men's clothes. She denied these were sins; but, if they were, it was for God and her confessor to decide, not them.

On Thursday, March 15, in prison, a touchy subject full of legal pitfalls was presented to Joan. The judges explained the difference between the Church Militant (meaning the pope, cardinals, prelates, clergy, and so forth) and the Church Triumphant (meaning God, the saints, and the souls). They demanded that she commit herself to the Church Militant. Confused by all this, she declared that she did not understand such questions of doctrine but that she knew of no remarks of hers that were contrary to the faith.

Further questioning on this subject continued during the morning session in prison on Saturday, March 17, to which she answered that she came to put the rightful king of France on the throne in God's name, and to the Church Triumphant she submitted all her deeds and actions, not to the Church Militant. It was a stand that, in the fifteenth century, constituted unforgivable heresy. On this occasion the questioning became so unorganized and malicious, jumping from her angels to her male attire, to her saints, to the love and hatred God might show toward the

morning the judges wanted to know why she had jumped from her prison tower at Beaurevoir. It was, she stated, because she had heard that the people of Compiègne were all to be put to the fire and the sword because of their loyalty to the king, and she had wanted to save them. At this point she predicted that they would be liberated before the festival of St. Martin (a prediction that came true on November 1 when the English and Burgundians were roundly defeated and forced to give up the siege of the

English or the French, that Joan admonished her interrogators, "Good brothers, do pray speak one after the other." In the afternoon questions concerning her virginity were put to her. She maintained that one of the reasons she wore male attire was better to protect herself from the attempted sexual attacks of her guards. In such clothes her chastity was more secure. Asked if her saints would still visit her if she were to lose her virginity, Joan stated that no revelation had been made to her on that score.

Thus ended the weeks of interminable questioning. Had the die for the death sentence not already been cast, Joan, in any other age, might have gone free. Her innocence of the charges made against her was apparent even to many of her judges. Now it was necessary to turn her own testimony against her in such a way as to leave not a shadow of a doubt that the court was acting with irreproachable legality in condemning her to death. To do this, the court ordered that all the proceedings to date be condensed in a number of articles, legally verified. These were then read to Joan for her approval, which she gave with a few minor changes. Their reading took two days, Tuesday and Wednesday, March 27 and 28, at the end of which time Cauchon announced that a judgment would be rendered according to law and reason.

At this point Cauchon began to have grave doubts about the outcome of the trial should the verdict be based on the questions put to Joan and on her answers. He conceived the plan, which he persuaded his colleagues to accept, of suppressing all of Joan's answers by reducing the original seventy articles to twelve. These would be presented objectively as problems of law to eminent authorities who would be asked for their learned opinions. On April 5 the twelve articles were sent by Cauchon to the men selected, with a request to comment on them "in the interests of the Faith." The substance of these articles consisted of a summary of the interrogations she had undergone during the long months in prison: the wearing of men's clothing; the conversations with her saints, Michael, Catherine, and Margaret, all of whom she claimed she saw in person and even touched; the revelations to her that she would lead a French army to victory over the English; her insistence that she had performed nothing but by virtue of the revelations and the direct commands of God; her attempt to escape by trying to jump to her death from a certain high tower rather than delivering herself into the hands of her adversaries; her belief in her own entrance into paradise with the virginity of her body and soul intact (thus bypassing Church guidance); and lastly, her ignoring of the Church Militant and communing directly with God, especially as regards her revelations.

When, on April 10, Cauchon had received virtually no comments on the twelve articles, he was both surprised and worried. Sending his men to find out why the learned were so reluctant to give their opinions, he found that they were suspicious of the whole trial and all its aspects: Cauchon's competence in trying it, his partiality, the number of judges trying the case, the English riding herd on the court for a guilty verdict, Joan's not being allowed to appeal to the pope or to the Council of Basel (a congregation of the whole universal Church), the accused having no one to represent her, and many other irregular procedures.

Cauchon was undaunted. Late as it was in the proceedings, he would call upon the University of Paris (made pliable to his purposes by a few well-placed bribes) to authenticate the findings of the court. On April 14, there being thirty members present, it was agreed to adjourn until the answers were received from the University of Paris concerning the twelve articles.

About this time Joan became seriously ill. For months she had been subjected to ill-treatment by her guards, to constant interrogation, to many sleepless nights, and to lack of any kind of activity. The English were worried. Would natural causes snatch their prey from them before they could have the satisfaction of burning her? The earl of Warwick summoned two physicians, and warned them, "The king of England would not for the world that she should die a natural death; he has paid dearly for her, and her days must end by the hand of justice; he expects to have her burnt. See her, therefore, and adopt every precaution that she may recover."

On April 18 Cauchon visited her in her cell and, counting on her sick condition, tried to extract a complete recantation. He failed. Again, on May 2, in the presence of sixty-three assessors before whom a pale and weak Joan had been brought, he delivered a public admonition. She was warned that not to yield was tantamount to confessing herself a heretic. But she remained steadfast in her conviction that she had said all she was going to say and that she placed herself in the hands of God. Cauchon was at his wits' end. He was failing badly in his purpose to persuade her to place herself in the hands of the Church. On May 9 they threatened her with torture. She was taken to the torture chamber of the castle where insidious instruments were meticulously described to her. But she refused to say more. Reluctantly Cauchon gave up the idea that torture would make her recant.

On May 23 the answers arrived from the University of Paris. They were all that Cauchon could have hoped for. The sanctimonious faculties announced her guilty of lying, blasphemy, consorting with the agents of the devil, heresy, and many other crimes. Unless, after being duly warned, she admitted her errors to the satisfaction of her judges, she should be turned over to the secular arm of the Church for punishment, which, of course, meant the stake.

Pierre Morice, canon of the cathedral at Rouen, was given the task of reading the warning to her. He exhorted her to renounce her ways and give herself up to the Church. But steeled by the presence of her voices, Joan replied, "Even were the sentence put in force, did I behold the fire prepared, the faggots lighted, and the executioner on the point of throwing me into the flames, I would not in death utter a thing that was not pronounced during the process." Cauchon then decided on a mock trial and threat of execution for the next day.

His bluff paid off. Joan was taken in the prisoner's cart to the burial ground of the abbey, where two scaffolds were erected: one for the judges, and one for Joan and Guillaume Erard, doctor of theology, who was to deliver the sermon. He used as his text a passage from the Gospel According to John. "The branch cannot bear fruit of itself except it abide in the vine." A short distance away stood the executioner and nearby the faggots arranged around the stake. Joan was unaware that all this was merely playacting to frighten her into signing an abjuration. At the end of the sermon the articles of abjuration were read to her. They consisted of barely eight lines in which she agreed never again to carry arms, wear male clothes, or have her hair cut short. As Joan remained silent, Cauchon rose and read her the sentence of condemnation. Others threatened her, and some pleaded with her to sign. "Joan, do as you are advised: will you be the cause of your own death?"

By now, thoroughly frightened and in

Joan finally agrees to sign an abjuration of barely eight lines, but Cauchon substitutes a lengthy and incriminating document.

mortal fear at the prospect of being burned to death, Joan was ready to comply. "Let this schedule be inspected by the clerks of the Church in whose hands I am to be placed; and if they advise me to sign it, and to perform the things that are told me, I am willing to do so." Triumphantly they placed the schedule before her to sign, but the crafty Cauchon, unseen, substituted for the short version another and much longer schedule. Thus Joan unwittingly affixed her X to a document of whose contents she knew nothing. Instead of the brief eight lines, she signed a lengthy, illegal statement.

In this statement she confessed sinning against the Church and asked to be returned to it; she renounced her beloved saints and admitted she lied by pretending to have heard revelations from them; she agreed to give up dressing in men's clothing, cropping her hair short, and wearing armor; she pleaded guilty to despising God and his sacraments (through the Church), to raising seditions, and committing idolatry; she swore that she would never return to the errors aforesaid (in the abjuration) and would remain in union with the Holy Mother Church and be obedient to the Holy Father, the Pope of Rome.

As soon as Joan's signature was affixed to the false schedule, Cauchon pulled from his sleeve a new sentence, one of mitigation in place of the death sentence, and read it to her. "As you have sinned against God and Church, we condemn you, as a matter of grace and moderation, to pass the residue of your days in prison, to share the bread of bitterness and the water of agony, to weep for your sins, and to commit no more in the future."

Joan was now relieved, for at last, she thought, she would be out of the hands of the English and in ecclesiastical custody. But her relief was short-lived, as Cauchon sternly commanded the guards, "Take her back whence you brought her." Warwick was stunned, not realizing Cauchon's guile. He was positive the English had lost their precious prisoner. But Cauchon reassured him. "Do not worry; we shall soon have our hands on her again."

Returned to the prison, Joan was ordered to change from her male clothes into female attire. She obeyed. Her jailers, however, did not remove the male garments from her cell but left them there in a sack. Several soldiers remained in her cell with her. They resumed their previous callous behavior and their attempts to attack her virginity. When these were of no avail, they beat her until she bled. Such tortures went on for two days. Then during the night her guards stole her female clothes. When she asked for them the next morning, they taunted her and told her to put on her male attire. This she refused to do, knowing that to do so would be a violation of her abjuration. But by noon she was forced to put on the male attire so that the guards would allow her to rise and relieve herself. Since these were the only garments her guards would allow her, she had no choice but to continue wearing them.

This news was not long in reaching the ears of the bishop of Beauvais and his vice-inquisitor. Now was the moment for which they had been waiting. Along with eight assessors they hastened to the prison, saw that Joan was once again dressed as a man, and accused her on the spot of being a relapsed heretic. Joan was in tears. She explained that the soldiers had taken away her female attire, that the promises made to unshackle her and allow her to go to mass and receive the sacrament had not been kept, that she was being kept in the English jail instead of being turned over to the Church prison. Cauchon did not care about the truth of her assertions. Closing in for the kill, he at once asked about her saints and if she had heard from them recently. Knowing all was now lost, and wishing to die rather than endure further torture at the hands of the English soldiers, Joan admitted that she had talked with them. "Since Thursday they have declared to me that I was guilty of a great fault [signing the abjuration]. In short, everything which I have said or done since Thursday last has been performed under the dread of being burnt." Torn between her fear of the stake and her faith in her saints, she had finally chosen the latter.

On Tuesday, May 29, Beauvais called the judges together, along with doctors of theology and law, members of the clergy, and other important personages. He reviewed the case to date, then read Joan's last confessions of the previous day. In their considered opinion she was a heretic who, although recently abjured, had now obviously relapsed.

The next morning, May 30, 1431, Brother Martin L'Advenu was sent to tell her of her fate and to hear her confession. She was petrified with fear, but he managed to calm her down. Her request for the sacrament of the eucharist was granted. What had Cauchon to lose at this point? He went to her prison for the last time. She accused him reproachfully. "Bishop, it is owing to you that I die."

He answered, "Ah, Joan, you die because you have relapsed into your former errors." Resigned now, she replied, "Alas, had you placed me in the prisons of the ecclesiastical court, this would not have happened. On this account I appeal from you to God."

At nine in the morning Joan was put in the prison cart, which was then drawn to the Rouen marketplace. There she was burned at the stake and her ashes thrown into the Seine.

The impact of the trial of Joan of Arc on the course of history was momentous. Joan's martyrdom had broken the morale of the English soldiers. They believed they had burned a saint and would be punished for it. In a sense they were. Philip of Burgundy, perhaps influenced by the resentful reactions to Joan's death, soon realized he was of French blood, and signed an alliance with Charles VII on December 21, 1435. This at last gave Paris to Charles. From then on, the English were defeated at almost every turn. On June 17, 1453, complete victory came to the French in the Battle of Castillon,

"The Death of Joan of Arc." An engraving by
Florian after a mural by J. E. Lenepveu.

when six thousand attacking Englishmen
were repulsed and most of them annihilated.
Joan had not sacrificed herself in vain. She
had succeeded in laying the foundations for
a united France, which soon became the
reality for which she gave her life.

The iniquities of the Rouen trial were
so self-evident that in 1455 Pope Calixtus
granted permission to Isabelle Romée and
Joan's brothers to bring suit to prove that
the heresy and other charges against Joan
were false. On July 7, 1456, the judges before whom the case was brought invalidated
the proceedings of 1431. On May 9, 1920,
Joan of Arc was canonized as a saint by
Pope Benedict XV in Rome.

In the annals of trials the interrogation,
condemnation, and execution of Joan are
events in a long line which began before
Socrates and did not end with Galileo, in
which ideas were on trial as well as people.
Joan was tried for her heresies, but as long as
there are dogmas, there will be heretics.
When such people are tried and condemned
by their contemporaries, it is often because
their ideas are so vital; but, unfortunately
for them—and for us—the moment for their
ideas had not yet arrived in history.

Catherine of Aragon

1529

ON NOVEMBER 14, 1501, FIFTEEN-YEAR-OLD Prince Arthur, eldest son of Henry VII of England, married fifteen-year-old Catherine of Aragon, daughter of Ferdinand of Aragon and aunt of Emperor Charles V, thus binding together the realms of Spain and England and presenting a formidable foe to Francis I of France for the supremacy of Europe. Arthur was a sickly child and on the following April 2 he died. According to Catherine she slept with him no more than seven nights, and he had left her as he had found her—a virgin.

In order to keep the alliance of Spain and England intact it was deemed advisable that Arthur's brother Henry should then marry the widowed Catherine. To permit this a special dispensation was needed from the pope, then Julius II. This was granted in a papal bull and a brief dated December 26, 1503, and the way was opened for the marriage. On June 3, 1509, Henry married Catherine. The bride wore white, signifying that she was still a virgin. The marriage lasted fifteen years without serious incident.

Court life in those days was sexually promiscuous, and Henry VIII had his affairs along with the rest. Then he fell in love with one of his wife's ladies-in-waiting, Anne Boleyn. But Anne would not submit to his advances and instead asked that Henry divorce Catherine and marry her. Thus, somewhere between 1524 and 1526 Henry began

FAVORING A PLAN FOR OBTAINING A DIVORCE from his wife. The easiest way was to declare false the 1503 bull and brief permitting Henry to marry Catherine. He instructed Cardinal Wolsey to sound the pope on the possibilities of such a separation. He spent fortunes in sending agents to all the major universities in England, France, Italy, and Germany to gather information and opinions to prove he had a legitimate case for divorce against Catherine. He received many favorable opinions, the gist of which was that the pope had no dispensing powers such as he had used in 1503. This Pope Clement III vigorously denied. At the same time, on December 23, 1527, he gave Henry a dispensation for marriage to Anne Boleyn, or anyone else he chose, *provided* his marriage with Catherine was declared void.

Through Cardinal Wolsey Henry tried to persuade Catherine to give up her throne and take up religious vows, thus paving the way for the dissolution of their marriage, leaving Henry free to marry Anne. Catherine refused. Henry's answer was to claim that their marriage was never valid, since she was not a virgin when she married him, and he reiterated that Pope Julius II had no authority to grant them a dispensation to get married in the first place. He insisted the matter be brought to trial.

So great was the pressure put by Henry on Pope Clement that His Holiness finally

Henry VIII and Catherine of Aragon, his first wife. Natioanl Portrait Gallery, London

yielded and issued a bull granting a commission to Cardinals Wolsey and Campeggio to hear and determine all matters concerning the king's marriage and his predecessor's dispensation. Since the pope was now the virtual prisoner of Emperor Charles V, who was Catherine's nephew and loyal supporter, he actually did not want the question settled and delayed Campeggio's trip to London until late in 1528.

Once he had arrived in London Campeggio tried the one approach that would quickly and conveniently solve the whole problem and get the irresolute Clement out of his dilemma as a pawn between King Henry and Emperor Charles. He attempted desperately to convince Catherine she should enter a religious order. The queen obstinately refused. Campeggio relayed this reaction to the pope and suggested the pope himself decide the issue. But Clement was weak and did not want the responsibility.

As a consequence the legatine court finally convened on May 31, 1529, in the parliament chamber of Blackfriars in London. Henry VIII's machinations had finally paid off, and the validity of his marriage to Catherine of Aragon was ready to go on trial. Henry had no doubts about the outcome.

The first business before the court was to read legate Campeggio's commission from Pope Clement. This provided for suitable appointments where the king and queen could stay and conveniently have access to the courtroom at Blackfriars, and for the two papal legates, Cardinals Wolsey and Campeggio, to sit in judgment, before whom the king and queen should appear. Catherine knew it was a farce and that it was illegal and simply a scheme by Henry to break his marriage to her so he could marry Anne. As George Cavendish, gentleman usher to

Cardinal Wolsey, said at the time, "This was the strangest and newest sight and device that ever was read or heard in any history or chronicle in any region; that a king and queen be convented and constrained by process compellatory to appear in any court as common persons, within their own realm or dominion, to abide the judgment and decrees of their own subjects, having the royal diadem and prerogative thereof."

But Henry was not to be denied his way, and on June 21, 1529, the real trial got under way when both Henry and Catherine were summoned to appear before the court. In the courtroom were tables, benches, and bars, and a place for the judges to sit. There was also a cloth of state under which the king sat, with the queen at some distance beneath him. In front of the judges sat the officers of the court: Dr. Stephens, the chief scribe; and Cooke, the apparitor. Directly in front of the king and the judges were the archbishop of Canterbury, Dr. Warham, and the other bishops. On both sides were the counselors. Those for the king included Doctors Sampson and Bell; for the queen, Dr. Fisher, bishop of Rochester; Dr. Standish, bishop of St. Asoph in Wales, and Dr. Ridley. It was Fisher who was to defend the queen to the last.

When they were ready to begin, the crier called, "King Henry of England come into court," to which the king replied, "Here, my lords." Then the crier called out, "Catherine, Queen of England, come into the court." But Catherine, who had long since decided not to recognize the authority of the court and to appeal for a direct verdict from Rome, did not answer. Instead she rose from her chair, made her way directly to the king, and kneeled before him. Then, ignoring the court, she made her impassioned plea directly to Henry.

Sir, I beseech you, for all the loves that hath

Anne Boleyn, the second wife of Henry VIII.

Cardinal Thomas Wolsey.

been between us, and for the love of God, let me have justice and right. Take of me some pity and compassion, for I am a poor woman, and a stranger born out of your dominion. I have here no assured friend, and much less indifferent counsel. I flee to you as to the head of justice within this realm. Alas! Sir, wherein have I offended you, or what occasion of displeasure have I designed against your will and pleasure? Intending (as I perceive) to put me from you, I take God and all the world to witness that I have been to you a true, humble, and obedient wife, ever conformable to your will and pleasure, that never said or did anything to the contrary thereof, being always well pleased and contented with all things wherein ye had any delight or dalliance, whether it were in little or much, I never grudged in word or countenance, or showed a visage or spark of discontentation. I loved all those whom ye loved, only for your sake, whether I had cause or no; and whether they were my friends or my enemies. This twenty years I have been your true wife or more, and by me ye have had divers children; although it hath pleased God to call them out of this world it hath been no default in me. And when ye had me at the first, I take God to be my judge, I was a true maid without touch of man; and whether it be true or no, I put it to your conscience. If there be any just cause by the law that ye can allege against me, either of dishonesty or any other impediment, to banish and put me from you, I am well content to depart, to my great shame and dishonour; and if there be none, then here I most lowly beseech you to let me remain in my former estate, and receive justice at your princely hands. . . . I most humbly require you, in the way of charity, and for the love of God, who is the just judge, to spare the extremity of this new court, until I may be advertised what way and order my friends in Spain will advise me to take. And if ye will not extend to me so much indifferent favour, your pleasure then be fulfilled, and to God I commit my case.

She rose, curtsied to King Henry, and

on the arm of her receiver-general, Griffin Richardes, left the hall. The king ordered the crier to call her back, which he did several times. Her receiver-general advised that she was being summoned back, but she answered, "On, on. It maketh no matter, for it is no indifferent court for me, therefore I will not tarry: go on your ways." Thus she left the court for her first and last appearance.

Although Henry wanted desperately to be rid of Catherine so he could marry Anne, he wanted to have for his subjects a far more valid reason for divorcing Catherine than his own lust; thus his questioning of the validity of his marriage to Catherine. As soon as the queen had left the court, Henry addressed it, praising the virtues of his wife.

Forasmuch as the queen is gone, I will, in her absence, declare unto you all, my lords here presently assembled, she hath been to me as true, as obedient, and as conformable a wife as I could in my fantasy wish or desire.

Wolsey now cleverly gave Henry the opportunity to state his case by asking the king to disclaim that Wolsey had anything to do with the king's bringing action against Catherine, which all rightfully suspected. Henry willingly obliged. "My Lord Cardinal, I can well excuse you herein, Marry, ye have been rather against me in attempting or setting forth thereof." Then Henry launched into a long speech in which he set forth his contrived case.

And to put you all out of doubt, I will declare unto you the special cause that moved me hereunto; it was a certain scrupulosity that pricked my conscience upon divers words that were spoken at a certain time by the bishop of Bayonne, the French king's ambassador, who had been here long upon the debating for the conclusion of a marriage to be concluded between the princess, our daughter

The trial of Queen Catherine.

Mary, and the duke of Orléans, the French king's second son. And upon this resolution and determination thereof, he desired respite to advertise the king, his master thereof, whether our daughter Mary should be legitimate, in respect of the marriage which was some time between the queen here, and my brother, the late Prince Arthur. These words were so conceived within my scrupulous conscience, that it bred a doubtful prick within my breast, which doubt pricked, vexed, and troubled so my mind, and so disquieted me, that I was in great doubt of God's indignation; which (as seemed me), appeared right well; much the rather for he hath not sent me any issue male; for all such issue male as I have received of the queen died incontinent after they were born, so that I doubt the punishment of God in that behalf. Thus being troubled in waves of a scrupulous conscience, and partly in despair of any issue male by her, it drave me at last to consider the estate of this realm,

and the danger it stood in for lack of issue male to succeed me in this imperial dignity. I thought it good, therefore, in relief of the weighty burden of scrupulous conscience, and the quiet estate of this noble realm, to attempt the law therein, and whether I might take another wife in case that my first copulation with this gentlewoman were not lawful, which I intend not for any carnal concupiscence, nor for any displeasure or mislike of the queen's person and age, with whom I could be as well content to continue during my life, if our marriage may stand with God's law, as with any woman alive; in which point consisteth all this doubt that we go now about to try by the learned wisdom and judgment of you our prelates and pastors of this realm here assembled for that purpose; to whose conscience and judgment I have committed the charge according to the which, God willing, we will be right well content to submit ourself to obey the same for my part. Wherein after I

28

once perceived my conscience, wounded with the doubtful case herein, I moved first this matter in confession to you, my lord of Lincoln, my ghostly father. And forasmuch as then yourself were in some doubt to give me counsel, moved me to ask farther counsel of all you my lords, wherein I moved you first my lord of Canterbury, axing [asking] your license, forasmuch as you were our metropolitan, to put this matter in question; and so I did all of you, my lords, to the which ye have all granted by writing under your seals the which I have here to be showed.

The archbishop of Canterbury rose and quickly confirmed Henry's last statement. "That is the truth of it, please Your Highness. I doubt not but all my brethren here present will confirm the same."

But the bishop of Rochester would have none of it and there followed a bitter argument.

ROCHESTER: No, Sir, not I, ye have not my consent thereto.

HENRY: No! ha' the! Look upon this, is not this your hand and seal?

ROCHESTER: No, forsooth, Sire, it is not my hand nor seal!

HENRY: (to Canterbury) Sir, how say ye, is it not his hand and seal?

CANTERBURY: Yes, Sir.

ROCHESTER: That is not so, for indeed you were in hand with me to have both my hand and seal, as other of my lords had already done, but then I said to you, that I would never consent to such an act, for it were much against my conscience; nor my hand and seal should never be seen on such an instrument, with much more matter touching the same communication between us.

CANTERBURY: You say truth, such words ye said unto me, but at the last you were fully persuaded that

I should for you subscribe your name and put a seal myself, and ye would allow the same.

ROCHESTER: All which words and matter under your correction my lord, and supportation of this noble audience, there is no thing more untrue.

HENRY: Well, well, it shall make no matter, we will not stand with you in argument herein, for you are but one man.

With that the court adjourned until the next day of the session.

The court resumed on June 25 with Wolsey and the bishop of Rochester in debate. The king's counsel reiterated the allegation that the marriage was not good from the beginning because of carnal knowledge between Catherine and her first husband, Prince Arthur, the king's brother. At this Rochester took vehement exception, stating he knew the truth of the matter. But Wolsey questioned him as to how he knew the truth. "Forsooth, my lord," answered Rochester, "I know that God is truth itself, nor He never spoke but truth. And forasmuch as this marriage was made and joined by God to good interest, I say that I know the truth the which cannot be broken or loosed by the power of man upon no feigned occasion."

To which Cardinal Wolsey replied, "So much doth all faithful men know as well as you. Yet this reason is not sufficient in this case; for the king's counsel doth allege divers presumptions, to prove the marriage not good at the beginning, ergo, say they, it was not joined by God at the beginning, and therefore it is not lawful; for God ordaineth nor joineth nothing without a just order. . . . To say that the matrimony was joined of God, ye must prove it farther than by that text which ye have alleged for your matter."

The trial went on for days until Henry summoned Wolsey and ordered him to go with Cardinal Campeggio to the queen and again try to persuade her to go into a religious order. They failed.

By this time the vacillating Pope Clement had received Catherine's appeal and was being pressed by Emperor Charles to stop the proceedings. He wrote Cardinal Wolsey saying that he could not deny Queen Catherine her right to appeal her case from the legatine court to Rome. This was what Cardinal Campeggio was waiting for.

July 23 was the day that final judgment was expected to be passed by the two papal legates, and Henry was confident that the outcome would be in his favor. But Campeggio had other thoughts.

On this day the king stationed himself outside the courtroom but in such a position that he could both hear and see what was going on. The court opened with the reading in Latin of all their proceedings thus far, after which the king's counsel called for a fast judgment. But Campeggio confounded the court and the king by adjourning the proceedings until the first of October on the grounds that since Roman courts were on vacation until then, he was bound to follow such procedure in England as well. He said:

I will give no judgment herein until I have made relation unto the pope of all our proceedings, whose counsel and commandment in this high case I will observe. The case is too high and notable, known throughout the world, for us to give any hasty judgment, considering the highness of the persons and the doubtful allegations; and also whose commissioners we be, under whose authority we sit here. It were therefore reason, that we should make our chief head [of] counsel in

the same, before we proceed to judgment definitive. I come not so far to please any man, for fear, meed, or favor, be he king or any other potentate. I have no such respect to the persons that I will offend my conscience. I will not for favor or displeasure of any high estate or mighty prince do that thing that should be against the law of God. I am an old man, both sick and impotent, looking daily for death. What should it then avail me to put my soul in the danger of God's displeasure, to my utter damnation, for the favor of any prince or high estate in this world? My coming and being here is only to see justice ministered according to my conscience, as I thought thereby the matter either good or bad. And forasmuch as I do understand, and having perceivance by the allegations and negations in this matter laid for both the parties, that the truth in this case is very doubtful to be known, and also that the party defendant will make no answer thereunto, [but] doth rather appeal from us, supposing that we be not indifferent, considering the king's high dignity and authority within this his own realm which he hath over his own subjects; and we being his subjects, and having our livings and dignities in the same, she thinketh that we cannot minister true and indifferent justice for fear of his displeasure. Therefore, to avoid all these ambiguities and obscure doubts, I intend not to damn my soul for no prince or potentate alive. I will therefore, God willing, wade no farther in this matter, unless I have the just opinion and judgment, with the assent of the pope, and such other of his counsel as hath more experience and learning in such doubtful laws than I have. Wherefore I will adjourn this court for this time, according to the order of the court in Rome, from whence this court and jurisdiction is derived. And if we should go further than our commission doth warrant us, it were folly and vain, and much to our slander and blame; and [we] might be accounted for the same breakers of the order of the higher court from whence we have (as I said) our original authorities.

With that the court was dismissed. But the duke of Suffolk spoke up bitterly, expressing his own and his king's anger at the outcome. "It was never merry in England whilst we had cardinals among us." His remark portended the end of Catholicism and the acceptance of Protestantism as the official religion of England. It also provoked an answer from Cardinal Wolsey that sealed his own doom, as he concurred with the findings of his fellow legate, Campeggio. "Consider that we be but commissioners for a time, and can, nay may not, by virtue of our commission proceed to judgment without the knowledge and consent of the chief head of our authority, and having his consent to the same; which is the pope."

During the next two years (1530 and 1531), Henry defied the pope's order and sought to gather opinions from all over Europe that were favorable to his cause. The pope had also forbade Henry to marry anyone, and instructed him to treat Catherine as his lawful wife and to get rid of Anne Boleyn under threat of excommunication.

Thus, the battle lines were drawn between the pope and Catholicism, and Henry. The king replied by inducing Parliament in July 1530 to make his cause a national one. On April 5, 1533, he succeeded in getting a convocation to declare against the marriage of Henry and Catherine. That same year the Act of Appeals put an end to papal jurisdiction in England. Finally, Cranmer, who had recently been appointed archbishop of Canterbury, held court along with three bishops at Dunstable, and rendered a verdict declaring the marriage of Henry and Catherine null and void. Henry promptly married Anne Boleyn. Rome reacted. On June 11, 1533, the pope declared the marriage of Henry and Anne null and void and threatened to excommunicate Henry if he didn't take Catherine back. But all this was little consolation to Catherine. She was on her deathbed and died shortly after.

The trial of Catherine of Aragon laid a foundation for the English monarchy's conversion from Catholicism to Protestantism. True, England had had enough of the corrupt Catholic Church and was ripe for the acceptance of Protestantism. But it was not Henry's interest in this religious squabble that furthered the Protestant cause. It was his own passion that dictated his renunciation of Catholicism, since that was the only way he could shed a wife he no longer wanted for a younger beauty of his choice, Anne Boleyn. That beauty, the mother of the future Protestant queen, Elizabeth, soon lost her head on the block because of her infidelity to Henry. And England to this day has remained Protestant.

Galileo Galilei

1633

WHEN IN THE EARLY YEARS OF THE SIX-teenth century the Polish scientist Nicolaus Copernicus made known the theory, based on various findings that preceded him, that the earth revolves around the sun, it caused no repercussions. In spite of the fact that both the Catholics and the newly rebellious Protestants believed in Ptolemy's and Aristotle's theory that the earth was the center of the universe and that the sun and all the planets revolved around it, Copernicus drew no wrath, no outcry, no great denunciations, although he did have many detractors.

How was it, then, that nearly one hundred years later, the world's most eminent scientist, Galileo Galilei, espousing and advancing the Copernican theory, was to incite papal wrath and ecclesiastical condemnation that were to shock both the Catholic and non-Catholic worlds and saddle the Catholic Church with one of its most unwanted, thorny problems?

The answer lies not in the similar scientific theories each man believed in and taught, but in the effort made by Galileo to impose his theories on the Church; to sway the Church away from its accepted dogma that the earth was the center of the universe. As many a martyr before him, Galileo was to learn the fate of the heretic who questions the view of an existing religious hierarchy. Copernicus, on the other hand, had exercised caution, even to the point of being RELUCTANT TO HAVE HIS WORKS PUBLISHED. Although his followers knew of their contents, they were not published until he was on his death-bed.

Galileo, though not the inventor of the telescope, put it to its best use, and was thus the first seriously to turn it on the heavens, searching for scientific facts that would explain the wonders of the universe. By it he increased the number of known planets and satellites from seven to eleven. Indeed, so astute were his scientific findings that he was soon famous in both lay and ecclesiastical circles, probably becoming the best-known man in Europe. His lectures were always crowded with enthusiastic followers. In 1610 the grand duke of Tuscany appointed him his personal philosopher and mathematician, and the Venetian senate appointed him to a professorship for life at a high salary. Lured by this offer from Venice, he left Padua, the only state in Italy that dared stand up against the power of Rome, little realizing that in moving he was putting his head between the jaws of the ecclesiastical lion.

Even more misleading, in March 1611 he was triumphantly received at Rome by the Tuscan ambassador, Pope Paul V, and Cardinal Barberini (later to become Pope Urban VIII). To the latter two he showed his discoveries and was delighted when they fully confirmed his observations.

In 1610 he had published *Sidereus Nuncius*, in which he gave the results of using his telescope to search the heavens: the planet Jupiter had satellites, Saturn had a ring, Venus passed through phases like the moon, the sun had spots. Galileo's triumphs were approaching their zenith. But at the time of his 1611 visit to Rome opponents were already appearing who claimed that Galileo's theories contradicted the Bible. They even denied the existence of satellites of Jupiter that were readily seen through Galileo's telescopes. Now Galileo, instead of keeping strictly to science, entered into the

"Galileo with a Young Scholar," by Cesare Cantagalli. In 1610 the grand duke of Tuscany appointed him his personal philosopher and mathematician. INSTITUTO STATALE D'ARTE DI SIENA

"Galileo Galilei," in an engraving by Pietro Bettellini. THE NEW YORK PUBLIC LIBRARY

Pope Paul V ordered the Congregation of the Inquisition to censor Galileo's theories. BIB-LIOTHÈQUE NATIONALE, PARIS

religious implications of his findings by protesting in an intemperate letter the interpretation of scripture that one Father Cassini, a Dominican, used in attacking the Copernican doctrine as taught by Galileo. For the next several years Galileo, both in published works and personal teachings, argued for his theories.

On December 21, 1613, Galileo wrote an eloquent letter to his friend Father Castelli, professor of mathematics at Pisa, in which he stated:

It appears to me, therefore, that no effect of nature, which experience places before our eyes, or is the necessary conclusion derived from evidence, should be rendered doubtful by passages of Scripture which contain thousands of words admitting of various interpretations, for every sentence of Scripture is not bound by such rigid laws as is every effect of Nature. . . . Since two truths can obviously never contradict each other, it is the part of wise interpreters of Holy Scripture to take the pains to find out the real meaning of its statements in accordance with the conclusions regarding Nature which are quite certain, either from the clear evidence of sense or from necessary demonstration.

Such a radical declaration of independence delighted his friends, enraged his enemies. The controversy came to a head when Pope Paul V became thoroughly displeased with Galileo's brazen demands that the Church reinterpret the Scriptures in relation to the demonstrated laws of nature. On February 19, 1616, the Congregation of the Inquisition received two propositions to censure: first, that the sun was the center of the world and consequently immovable locally; and second, that the earth was not the center of the world, nor immovable, but moved around itself by rotation. On February 23 the gathering declared them both foolish and absurd, the first being heretical since it contradicted numerous texts of Holy Scripture, the second erroneous in point of faith. They ordered Galileo, through Cardinal Bellarmine, to abstain from teaching such a doctrine on pain of imprisonment. Galileo promised to obey them, thinking that this whole matter was merely a question of discipline, not of doctrine.

In 1622 Pope Paul V died and was eventually followed by Galileo's friend Cardinal Barberini as Urban VIII. In April 1624 he received Galileo cordially and pronounced that the Copernican theory had not been condemned by the Church as heretical but was considered "temerarious," or in other words a rash opinion. Galileo, encouraged by the temper of the times, decided to publish a new book which he hoped would influence toward Copernicanism the minds of both ecclesiastics and laymen. So in May 1630 he went to Rome and sought permission of Pope Urban VIII to publish it. The pope turned the matter over to Father Visconti, who reported that some passages would have to be corrected to show that the question was being treated purely as a hypothesis.

Florence, where Galileo lived, was now hit by a plague, and correspondence between that city and Rome was badly disrupted. However, the Inquisitor of Florence received from Rome the power to approve officially of the *Dialogue* under certain conditions indicating that the work dealt only with the mathematical question connected with Copernicanism, that it would not assert Copernicanism to be a positive truth but merely a hypothesis, that there would be no alluding to the interpretation of the Scripture, and that it should be stated that by the decree of 1616 the authorities were aware of the reasons against it, and had enjoined Galileo from teaching it.

Besides the preface (probably written by Father Riccardi and amended by Galileo), *Dialogue* was divided into four parts, each being one day's discussions between three men. The three talkers were Salviati, a Florentine; Sagredo, a Venetian; and Simplicio, a simpleton who would express the doctrine of the day as a foil for the others to tear apart and project the true theories of Galileo. Many of the arguments of Simplicio were similar to those uttered by Pope Urban VIII, whether Galileo realized it or not, and the pope was incensed. The first day's conversations dealt with the dimensions and motion of heavenly bodies, the moon's rough terrain as opposed to the

The Imprimatur of the Catholic Church on the work, withdrawn by Pope Urban VIII. THE NEW YORK PUBLIC LIBRARY

Pope Urban VIII, who was shocked and dismayed by the "Dialogue." FOGG ART MUSEUM, HARVARD UNIVERSITY

contemporary polished-surface belief, and the spots on the sun. The second day dealt with the revolution of the earth on its axis and how improbable it was that the whole celestial sphere should circle the earth in twenty-four hours. The third day took up the matter of certain positions of known stars, followed by a refutation of the Aristotelian idea of the universe (a number of concentric hollow spheres with the earth in the center) and the basic arguments for the Copernican theory. The fourth day was devoted to the subject of tides, about which Galileo knew little and which was full of errors. The entire tenor of the *Dialogue* was to make the opponents of Galileo's theories look ridiculous in their arguments.

The printing of the *Dialogue on the Two Greatest Systems in the World* was completed in 1632, and Galileo sent some bound, gilt copies to Rome. It was dedicated to Ferdinand II, grand duke of Tuscany.

All over Europe the *Dialogue* was hailed as the most important book that had ever been printed. Owing to the plague in Florence, however, copies of the book were weeks late in reaching Rome, where the reaction was quite the opposite.

The followers of the Aristotelian school were incensed. The pope was highly displeased, saying that Galileo had entered upon ground he never should have touched. He was appalled that his ecclesiastics had been deceived into giving the book a license to be published. A special commission a month later reported that Galileo had disobeyed orders by affirming as an absolute truth, instead of as a hypothesis, the movement of the earth, and had further disobeyed by not even mentioning the order of 1616 to abandon the opinion that the earth revolved and that the sun was the center of the universe.

Why was the Inquisition so upset and what was the justification for maintaining that Galileo's theory of the earth and all the satellites revolving around the sun contradicted the Scriptures? The answer to this question is inherent in a literal interpretation of both the Old and New Testaments of the Holy Bible. Did not Moses say that God created the earth in five days and the

Title page drawn by Stefan Della Bella for Galileo's great work "Dialogue on the Two Greatest Systems in the World." The three figures depict Aristotle, Ptolemy, and Galileo in the guise of Copernicus. THE NEW YORK PUBLIC LIBRARY

rest of the universe in one? But Galileo claimed that the earth was but a speck in a vast and unexplained series of universes. How could God have possibly spent so much time on a speck and so little time creating these unending universes? Where were heaven and hell in such a vast complex? And how could God look down on His people on earth from His heaven if the earth were traveling at the speed of one thousand miles a minute around the sun? Did not Moses say that God planted the sun, the moon, and the stars in the firmament and did he not say that the firmament was heaven? And that "God came down from heaven to see the tower which the children of men builded"? Was not Elijah carried upward in a whirlwind, and did not Jesus Christ ascend to heaven? Further, how could the deity keep track of the faithfulness and wickedness of his children with the earth in such an orbit?

If the scientific theories of Galileo were accepted, what would happen to the Church's interpretation of the Scriptures? Even the most faithful of true believers would begin to doubt scriptural infallibility. Thus, the Church had no choice but to strike down Galileo and silence him for the rest of his days. Arrogantly, although perhaps without deliberate intent, Galileo had forced his good friend Pope Urban VIII into a position from which Urban had no alternative. Whatever Urban, the man, thought of the Copernican findings, as pope he could not condone any onslaught on the infallibility of the Holy Scriptures.

Another Church report drawn up at the time listed eight accusations against the philosopher.

1. Having, without leave, placed at the beginning of his work the permission for printing, delivered at Rome.
2. Having, in the body of the work, put the

true doctrine in the mouth of a fool, and having approved it but feebly by the argument of another interlocutor.
3. Having quitted the region of hypothesis by affirming, in an absolute manner, the mobility of the earth and the stability of the sun, etc.
4. Having treated the subject as one that was not already decided, and in the attitude of a person waiting for a definition, and supposing it to have not been yet promulgated.
5. Having despised the authors who were opposed to the above-mentioned opinion, though the Church uses them in preference to others.
6. Having affirmed (untruly) the equality supposed to exist, for understanding geometrical matters, between the divine and human intellect.
7. Having stated, as a truth, that the partisans of Ptolemy ought to range themselves with those of Copernicus, and denied the converse.
8. Having wrongly attributed the tides to the stability of the sun and mobility of the earth, which things do not exist.

An order was issued to the Inquisitor of Florence to ban the book in Italy and all foreign countries. It took effect in July 1632, while the *Dialogue* was at the height of its popularity, and Galileo was at the height of his success.

Galileo was forthwith summoned to Rome. He appealed to Cardinal Barberini and the grand duke of Tuscany that his advanced age (seventy years) and his ill health made it difficult to comply, but the pope threatened to bring him to Rome as a prisoner if he did not come at once. On January 20, 1633, Galileo slowly set out for Rome, arriving on February 13. He was met by representatives of the Tuscan ambassador, Niccolini, and escorted to his palace, a gesture implying freedom and official welcome. However, after a short stay at the

Galileo in prison. THE NEW YORK PUBLIC LIBRARY

palace he was taken to the office of the Inquisition and put in prison. The charges against him were grave. "May God forgive him," said Pope Urban VIII, "for having involved himself in these questions. . . . There is one argument which nobody has been ever able to refute, which is that God is Almighty and may do as He sees fit. If He can do all, why question His works?"

Because of his renowned position and his reputation throughout Europe as the world's leading man of science, Galileo was given every consideration in jail, including the ambassador's servants to bring him special food and a valet who took care of him.

On April 12, 1633, Galileo appeared for the first time before the court. He admitted to the authorship of the *Dialogue*. He admitted that his opinion regarding the movement of the earth around a fixed sun had been formerly condemned in 1616 by the Congregation of the Index as contrary to the Holy Scriptures. But he maintained that Cardinal Bellarmine had told him it was possible to hold the Copernican doctrine as a hypothesis. He did not remember, after all these years, being told that he could not teach it in any manner. He did not mention these matters to the master of the Vatican when asking for the imprimatur for the *Dialogue* because he felt, rather than upholding the theory of a mobile earth, he was proving that the ideas of Copernicus were *not* acceptable. He fooled no one, and only infuriated the Holy See all the more.

How much Galileo was tortured in order to wring from him a confession of heresy and make him repent no one knows. Like all prisoners questioned by the Inquisition, he was forced to take the vow of silence on threat of excommunication. And Galileo was a good Catholic as well as an able scientist.

At the second official inquiry, on April 30, Galileo admitted to his judges, "I freely confess that on rereading my *Dialogue* it seems to me to have been so edited that to the reader unaware of my true intentions, the arguments for the Copernican systems, which I meant to refute, are represented in such a way that they may have been *for* rather than *against*." He went on to say that vain ambition and pure ignorance had caused him to write in a way that could be misinterpreted. After this second session he was allowed to return to the ambassador's house.

On May 10 he was called to the palace of the Holy See where he was told he had eight days in which to prepare his defense. Having already prepared it, he immediately launched into it. He pleaded that he had done his best to avoid all fault in the book, which he had dutifully submitted to the Grand Inquisitor. Referring to the injunction of 1616 Galileo went on:

I say, then, that as at that time reports were spread abroad by evil-disposed persons, to the effect that I had been summoned by the Lord Cardinal Bellarmine to abjure certain of my opinions and doctrines, and that I had consented to abjure them, and also to submit to punishment for them, I was thus constrained to apply to His Eminence, and to solicit him to furnish me with a certificate explaining the cause for which I was summoned before him; which certificate I obtained, in his own handwriting, and it is the same that I now produce with the present document.

From this it clearly appears that it was merely announced to me that the doctrine attributed to Copernicus of the motions of the earth and the stability of the sun must not be held or defended and . . . beyond this general announcement affecting every one, any other injunction in particular was intimated to me, no trace thereof appears there.

But the court again refused to accept his reasonings. The *Dialogue* was turned over to the Index, and it was decided to question Galileo under threat of torture as to his basic meaning, devoid of such ambiguities.

On June 21 he was recalled before the Holy See and asked how long he had held the opinion that the sun, not the earth, was the center of the universe. Galileo replied, "For some time since. That is to say, before the determination of the Sacred Congregation of the Index, I considered the two opinions, that of Ptolemy and that of Copernicus, were subject to discussion, because either of them might be correct according to Nature. But later . . . convinced by the wisdom of my superiors, my doubts

ceased, and I have since held as I still do, that the opinion of Ptolemy is correct and cannot be doubted."

The court then read certain passages from the *Dialogue* which were irreconcilable with what he had just said. He protested that in the book he had stated the pros and cons of the case, but he himself did not agree with the condemned theory. "I do not hold, and have never held, the opinions of Copernicus since the order was given me to abandon them." Then in almost weary resignation he said, "In any case, I am here in your hands. Do as you think best."

After signing his forced confession Galileo was returned to prison. The next day, June 22, he was taken to the monastery of Santa Maria Sopra Minerva, where before the cardinals and the prelates of the congregation he heard his sentence and read his abjuration.

First he was accused of openly violating the order given him not to maintain Copernicanism, of unfairly gaining permission to print his book without informing them of the prohibition of 1616, of still believing in the condemned opinion. Although he left it undecided and perhaps probable, this was still a grave offense, since an opinion contrary to Scripture, of course, could not be probable.

A long sentence was then read, the essence of which was that the *Dialogue* was henceforth prohibited, Galileo was to be condemned to the prison of the Holy Office for as long as the Holy Office decided, and he was to recite seven penitential psalms once a week for three years.

Then, on his knees, Galileo was forced to read his abjuration. In it he agreed in the future always to believe whatever the holy catholic and apostolic Roman Church holds, preaches, and teaches; to relinquish and never again teach the false dogma which

"Galileo Devant Le Saint Office," by Robert-Fleury. Brushing aside his feeble defense, the court demands his abjuration. LOUVRE, PARIS

maintains that the sun is the center of the world and immovable and that the earth is not the center and moves; to abjure, execrate, and detest his own errors and heresies contrary to the holy Church, as well as agreeing to denounce and report such heresies in others; and to fulfill and observe entirely all the penitences imposed upon him by the Holy Office.

The Church's purpose in judging Galileo guilty was to check the spread of Copernican doctrine among the faithful and to discredit the authority of the world's most famous scientist. The abjuration and notice of Galileo's punishment were sent on July 2, 1633, to all the vicars "so that it may come to the knowledge of all professors of philosophy and mathematics . . . that they may understand the gravity of the fault he has committed as well as the punishment they will have to undergo should they (likewise) fall into it."

Pope Urban VIII at once commuted Galileo's sentence to a secluded residence in the palace of the Tuscan ambassador. Shortly thereafter he was allowed to transfer to the palace of the archbishop of Siena, Piccolomini, one of his dearest friends and admirers. However, when word reached Rome that Piccolomini was expressing opinions that Galileo had been unjustly condemned, they gave him permission to retire to his house at Arcetri near Florence, provided he would consider himself virtually under house arrest and receive no one but his family and relatives.

Gradually Galileo lost his sight and became almost totally blind. In 1638, after many pleas to Rome on the part of his friends and relatives, the Church was finally convinced that Galileo was very sick and had little time to live. They allowed him to return to Florence on condition that he speak to no one regarding the movement of the earth. There, on January 8, 1642, Galileo died at the age of seventy-eight, fortified by the last rites of the Church and "the benediction of Urban VIII."

Galileo's contributions to mankind were prodigious: his investigations into mechanics and physics, his discovery of the theory of the pendulum and of the law of falling bodies, his invention of the thermometer, and his advances in the uses of the telescope.

If the trial of Galileo Galilei leaves one dismayed that even so great a mind can bend before the onslaught of his questioners and persecutors, it nevertheless stands as a landmark in the struggle of mankind to establish the right to challenge and reject timeworn dogmas that are accepted on faith, even when the challenger is labeled a heretic.

Charles I of England

1648

WHEN CHARLES STUART WAS BORN IN 1600 the concept of the divine right of kings was not only firmly established but unquestioned in England. With the beheading of Charles I on January 30, 1649, the traditional monarchy in England died, never again to achieve the absolute state known to kings for centuries before that date. What had happened in those few years to change the political destiny of a great world power so abruptly and throw it into a bitter civil war? Many things—temporal, religious, and social.

Under the rule of Charles's father, James I, England had been at peace for many years. This peace brought prosperity and wealth to the Protestant merchants and landed gentry of England. English trade had flourished, and with it a new middle class had begun to emerge. Money breeds independence, so it was quite natural that in the only legislative body in which they could be represented, the knights and burgesses of the House of Commons began to assert themselves. Although the real responsibility for the government was lawfully the king's, he could and occasionally did call together his nobles and a delegation from the people to help him. But only on his own initiative. Otherwise the king, by virtue of tradition, considered himself responsible only to God.

As a safeguard against kingly prerogatives, Parliament had previously been granted by THE CROWN WHAT IS KNOWN AS ITS PRIVILEGES: the exclusive right to impose taxes of every kind and the right to petition the king for redress of grievances. Through successive reigns Parliament continually strove to extend its privileges. From the day of his ascension to the throne in 1625 King Charles, dedicated to the infallibility of the divine right of kings, waged a long and intense contest with his Parliament. It lasted a quarter of a century and ended with his beheading. In fact, at his coronation Charles put an important modification into his oath, swearing to respect the liberties of the people only insofar as they did not clash with the prerogatives of the crown, thus setting the stage for the disastrous years to follow. For the first four years Charles and Parliament battled without openly declaring war. Then suddenly Charles, deciding to rule the empire by himself, dissolved Parliament. For the next ten years he refused to summon the legislative body. Only when he became desperate for money did he finally call the Parliament. It did him little good. Instead of granting him funds, they argued for further extension of the powers of Parliament and a lessening of the king's influence in government. This state of affairs lasted another ten years. Other events tended to alienate Charles from his people.

Shortly after the funeral of James I, Charles married Henrietta Maria, daughter of the king of France, a Catholic. This necessitated a special dispensation from the pope, which was obtained. To the people of England, who were anti-Roman and staunchly Protestant, this was an affront for which they could never forgive him. Infuriated, they petitioned him to forbid any English Catholic to enter the queen's service, "that all Jesuit and Catholic priests, owing allegiance to the See of Rome, should be sent away from the country according to the laws already existing." The king said, "The laws on this subject shall be enforced." It soon became apparent, however, that Charles was something less than sincere. The reason for his apparent acquiescence was that he and the duke of Buckingham (both his father's and now his own closest adviser) were very eager to get funds from the Commons to further their war plans. Buckingham, admiral of the fleet, was engaged in a bitter personal quarrel with Cardinal Richelieu, thus bringing England into war with France. Buckingham's naval ineptitude resulted in the British navy's being disastrously cut down to one-third its original size. Public indignation rose against Buckingham, and the king was blamed. The murder of Buckingham in 1628 came too late to restore the people's confidence in Charles.

Charles dissolved Parliament in March 1629, and personally took over the government. He used his prodigious power of the court of Star Chamber, first to punish his enemies, then to fill up his treasury by imposing enormous fines on them. In this way he raised considerable sums to carry on his government without Parliament. At the same time he abused his legal power of taxing the maritime counties to raise funds for his navy by levying the same taxes on the inland counties. Obviously, the people subjected to this unlawful tax objected.

"Charles I on Horseback," by Anthony Van Dyck. NATIONAL GALLERY, LONDON

Charles made himself equally unpopular with the people on the religious front. The ruling Church of England, presided over by the archbishop of Canterbury, was in those days extremely wealthy, its bishops and clergy being supported by revenues from vast amounts of property. The churchmen were entirely independent of any control by their parishioners. They had their own laws, legislature, courts, judges, and capital. Over this vast realm within a realm Charles appointed a dedicated man named Laud as the archbishop of Canterbury. Unfortunately, Laud applied himself far too vigorously to what he believed was his one great duty in life: supporting and confirming the authority of the king and the power and influence of the English episcopacy. In so doing he clashed with the large and increasing English populace who hated the whole episcopal system. The English people were incensed at what they believed were Laud's popish worship ceremonies. They devotedly cherished Christianity in its pure uncontaminated form, thus earning for themselves the designation of Puritans. Here, then, was another major cause of contention between Charles and a large number of his subjects. Not content with limiting to England this religious struggle, Laud attempted to extend the power of the Church of England into Scotland at the time when Charles went there to be crowned. He ran headlong into the stubborn resistance of the established Presbyterian Church. With typical Stuart arrogance, Charles took his army north to subdue the Scots by force. The army, however, was far more in sympathy with the Scots than with the king. Therefore, upon the more practical advice of his council, he gave up his contest with Scotland. All that he had accomplished was to sow further seeds of discontent among the people of England, who themselves harbored strong fellow feelings with the Scots. And to add to his humiliation, Charles was again forced to call Parliament in November 1640 to pay for sending the Scots home from their invasion of England.

This new Parliament was headed by John Pym, whose chief aim was to make the king dependent on Parliament. To this end he destroyed the king's only efficient advisers, the first of which was the earl of Strafford, whom Charles had appointed virtual king over the people of Ireland and had then put in charge of the campaign against the Scots. Strafford became so arrogant and so oblivious to the people's desires that Pym and the House of Commons finally succeeded in having him tried for treason and put to death. By a series of intrigues and maneuvers

William Laud, Archbishop of Canterbury, who incurred the wrath of the Puritans and Presbyterians.

Charles was forced by Commons and his own House of Lords to agree to Strafford's death. Laud soon followed on the chopping block. By now, their confidence greatly increased by these victories, the members of Commons demanded more and more concessions of Charles. To put an end to the king's authority to dissolve Parliament at will, they passed a bill providing that henceforth both the Houses of Lords and Commons could not be discontinued or dissolved without their own consent. The peers dared not reject it; the king, though violently opposed, was now aware of the dangers besetting him, and was forced to sign the measure. This established a major turning point in English political history. The Commons now became its own master.

As the year 1641 drew to a close, Charles

decided he had made sufficient concessions to Commons. In January 1642 he went to the House of Commons in person and demanded that five parliamentary leaders be handed over to him to be tried for high treason. An indignant Commons refused. The long-coming civil war began in earnest when the king formally raised his standard at Nottingham in August 1642. Sides were quickly aligned: the Episcopalians joined the king, along with the gentry and nobility; the mechanics, artisans, merchants, and common people backed the Parliament. Rural districts under the control of wealthy landlords backed the king; the cities and towns sided with Parliament. England was divided as never before. Charles lost at every turn.

By the spring of 1646 the king was utterly defeated in war. In an evasive action he surrendered to the Scottish army. In return for their protection and backing the Scots demanded that he become a Presbyterian, but Charles would have no part of it. On January 30, 1647, they turned him over to the English Parliament.

Meanwhile a third force, and ultimately the ruling one, entered the picture: the army, headed by Lord General Fairfax, a leading member of the House of Commons, had refused to disband at the orders of Parliament after the end of hostilities. They knew full well that such a course would mean the end of their power. But though Fairfax was nominally head of the army, the real power behind the army command at this time was Oliver Cromwell, a genius at combining long-range plans with daring and immediate actions to achieve his ultimate goal: to send Charles to the block and so put an end to the monarchy in England. But he was determined to do it legally. With Cromwell remaining in the background, the House of Commons would decree the death penalty for Charles I of England.

Charles I strides into the House of Commons and demands that five leading members be given over to his authority. THE FREE LIBRARY OF PHILADELPHIA, CARSON COLLECTION

At the time Charles was taken prisoner, Parliament was radically divided into two factions: a moderate group of Presbyterians and a group known as the Independents, whose leader was Oliver Cromwell. Thus, this latter group was closely linked to the army, which had won the war against the king for Parliament. Because of this serious legislative division the king was hopeful. In May 1648 a second civil war broke out, with Royalist risings in South Wales, Kent, Essex, and the north, followed by another invasion from Scotland. The army under Fairfax and Cromwell had no trouble defeating the

"Oliver Cromwell," by Robert Walker. NATIONAL PORTRAIT GALLERY, LONDON

Royalists. But while they were away, the Presbyterians gained control of the House of Commons and reopened negotiations with the king, an action codified as the Treaty of Newport. It was, however, a vain gesture, for as soon as the war was over, the army at once repudiated the treaty. Meeting on November 16, 1648, the army council resolved to bring the king to justice for making war on the people.

To do this with at least some semblance of legality it was necessary to have a House of Commons composed entirely of those who backed the army. Accordingly, on December 6 and 7 a Colonel Pride and his men were stationed at the approaches to Westminster and refused to admit to Parliament any of those who had supported the pro-

posed treaty with the king. A rump House of Commons, reduced to about seventy members (143 having been ejected), clearly (if not legally) opened the way to setting up a court to try Charles. The army, whose march on London was never effectively opposed, was now in complete charge both in Parliament and outside. Cromwell, who would never have endorsed such a militant seizure of Commons, was away at the time and did not return until the eighth of December. Faced with a fait accompli, he accepted it and said he was glad of it.

The king, who was being held in Hurst Castle, was well aware that he did not have long to live. At midnight on the seventeenth of December he was awakened by the sound of troops in the castle yard. Although he feared assassination, he was not molested. Two days later he began his journey to Windsor Castle under heavy escort.

On December 23, the day that he reached his old castle, the House of Commons voted that he should be brought to trial, and appointed a committee to draw up the impeachment. An ordinance was adopted appointing a high court to try him. It was to be composed of one hundred fifty commissioners, including peers, chief justices, baronets, knights, aldermen, and many other important personages. But when, on the second of January, the ordinance was presented to the House of Lords, the latter would have none of it. "There is no Parliament without the King," declared Lord Manchester, "therefore the King cannot commit treason against Parliament." The Commons then created, by passing another ordinance, the High Court of Justice. They persuaded John Bradshaw, a lawyer but a somewhat ambitious fanatic, to take the chair of lord-presidency of the court. On January 10 he accepted. The following few days were spent in organizing the court and setting up court procedures and functions, during which it was decided to move the king from Windsor Castle to St. James's Palace in London. On Friday, the nineteenth of January, a body of cavalry, headed by a Major Harrison, escorted the king to St. James's Palace, which was completely surrounded by guards. Even his bedroom had two guards outside. The only attendant he was now allowed to have was Sir Thomas Herbert, who slept by his bedside and was to stay with him to the end.

On the morning of January twentieth the high court met privately in the Painted Chamber and settled the final details of the proceedings. Shortly after noon it was announced that the king was arriving, carried on a sedan chair, and was at that moment passing between the two files of soldiers. Cromwell ran to the window and returned pale and excited. "My masters, he is come! He is come! . . . I desire you to let us resolve here what answer we shall give the king when he comes before us; for the first question he will ask us will be, by what authority and commission do we try him." After a pause, Henry Martyn said, "In the name of the Commons and Parliament assembled, and all the good people of England." No objection was raised, and the court proceeded to Westminster Hall in solemn procession, led by Lord-President Bradshaw. The president took his place in a chair of crimson velvet. He had taken the precaution of lining his hat with iron, fearful of an attack by the Royalists, who might have infiltrated the spectators' gallery. To his right and left were members of the court. Cromwell and Martyn seated themselves modestly out of the way in the rows behind the lord-president. Then the spectators were let into the galleries. When all noise and

John Bradshaw, president of the High Court of Justice that was set up to try King Charles.

talk had subsided, the act of the House of Commons setting up and giving authority to the high court was read, along with the names of those appointed to serve. Of the 135 appointed, only sixty-nine were present. Notably absent was Lord Fairfax. When his name was called, a veiled woman (believed later to have been Lady Fairfax) called out from the gallery, "He has more wit than to be here." The roll call having been dispensed with, Bradshaw ordered, "Mr. Sergeant, bring in your prisoner."

The king appeared under the guard of Colonel Hacker and thirty-two officers. He was conducted to a chair of crimson velvet that faced the court and was directly opposite the chair of Lord-President Bradshaw. He looked hard and sternly around at the tribunal; then, without removing his high hat, sat down. But immediately he stood up again and surveyed the spectators and the court with an air of superiority that infuriated his enemies. He sat down again amid silence.

Bradshaw rose immediately and addressed the king.

Charles Stuart, King of England: The Commons of England being deeply sensible of the calamities that have been brought upon this nation, which are fixed upon you as the principal author of them, have resolved to make inquisition for blood; and, according to that debt and duty they owe to justice, to God, the kingdom, and themselves, they have resolved to bring you to trial and judgment, and for that purpose, have constituted this High Court of Justice, before which you are brought.

He then ordered Cooke, the solicitor general, to read the charges.

As Cooke rose the king tapped him on the shoulder with his cane, saying, "Hold! Silence!"—at which point the gold head of the cane dropped off. Having no servant to pick it up, the king retrieved it himself. When he sat back in his chair, his changed expression indicated that he had realized the precarious status of his position.

Cooke then read the long indictment, which began by accusing Charles Stuart "of a wicked design to erect and uphold in himself an unlimited and tyrannical power to rule according to his will, and to overthrow the rights and liberties of the People, yea, to take away and make void the foundations thereof, and of all redress and remedy of misgovernment, which by the fundamental constitutions of this kingdom, were reserved on the People's behalf, in the right and power of frequent and successive Parliaments or national meetings in Council." There then followed a list of specific places and dates where Charles Stuart had "traitor-ously and maliciously levied war against the present Parliament and the people therein represented." During these wars "much innocent blood of the free people of this nation hath been spilt, many families have been undone, the publick treasury wasted and exhausted, trade obstructed and miserably decayed, vast expence and damage to the nation incurred, and many parts of the land spoiled." The indictment then called for Charles Stuart to answer to the charges of said treason and crimes.

During the reading of the indictment the king, as if uninterested, looked sternly around at the galleries, then at the court. He rose and looked around again, then sat down. At the words "Charles Stuart as a tyrant, traytor, murderer, and a publick and implacable enemy to the Commonwealth of England," he smiled, or even, as some chroniclers have it, laughed in the court's face.

BRADSHAW: Sir, you have now heard your charge. The court expects your answer.

THE KING: I would know by what power I am called hither; I was, not long ago, in the Isle of Wight, and there I entered into a treaty with both Houses of Parliament, with as much public faith as it is possible to be had of any people in the world; and we were upon the conclusion of the treaty. Now I would know by what authority, I mean lawful—there are many unlawful authorities in the world, thieves and robbers by the highway—but I would know by what authority I was brought from thence, and carried from place to place, and I know not what; and when I know what lawful authority, I shall answer.

Remember I am your king,

The Trial of Charles I. LIBRARY OF CONGRESS

your lawful king, and what sins you bring upon your heads and the judgment of God upon this land, think well upon it. I say, think well upon it before you go farther from one sin to a greater. Therefore let me know by what lawful authority I am seated here and I shall not be unwilling to answer. In the meantime I shall not betray my trust: I have a trust committed to me by God, by old and lawful descent. I will not betray it to answer to a new and unlawful authority; therefore resolve me that, and you shall hear more of me.

BRADSHAW: If you had been pleased to observe what was hinted to you by the court at your first coming hither, you would have known by what authority; which authority requires you, in the name of the people of England, of which you are elected king, to answer.

THE KING: No, sir, I deny that.

BRADSHAW: If you acknowledge not the authority of the court, they must proceed.

THE KING: I do tell them so; England was never an elective kingdom, but an hereditary kingdom, for near these thousand years: therefore let me know by what authority I am called hither. Here is a gentleman, Lieutenant-Colonel Cobbett, ask him if he did not bring me from the Isle of Wight by force. I will stand as much for the privilege of the House of Commons, rightly understood, as any man whatsoever. I see no House of Lords here, that may constitute a Parliament, and the king, too, should have been in it. Is this the bringing of a king to his Parliament?

BRADSHAW: The court expects you should give them a final answer. If you do not satisfy yourself, though we tell you our authority, we are satisfied with our authority, and it is upon God's authority and the kingdom's.

THE KING: It is not my apprehension, nor yours either, that ought to decide it.

BRADSHAW: The Court hath heard you, and you are to be disposed of as they have commanded.

At this point Bradshaw saw that he was getting into serious trouble. If the king persisted in his refusal to recognize the court and refused to answer to the charge, the trial was stymied. Until the prisoner pleaded one way or the other, the prosecution could not commence. Seeing he was getting nowhere, Bradshaw adjourned the court until Monday, January twenty-second. Amid conflicting shouts of "Justice! Justice!" and "God save the King! God save Your Majesty!", Charles was escorted back to St. James Palace, where he was to ponder on the train of events over the weekend.

When the court resumed on Monday, sixty-two members were present. In spite of a strict order for silence, the king was greeted with loud acclamations from the galleries. As Bradshaw again tried to get Charles to plead on the indictment and recognize the authority of the court, the king remained obstinate.

BRADSHAW: Sir, you may remember at the last court you were told the occasion of your being brought hither and you heard a charge read against you, containing a charge of high treason, and other high crimes against the realm of England, and instead of answering, you interrogated the court's authority and jurisdiction. Sir, the authority is the Commons of England in Parliament assembled, who required your answer to the charge, either by confessing or denying.

THE KING: When I was here last, it is very true I made that question. And truly, if it were only in my particular case I would have satisfied myself with the protestation I made the last time I was here, against the legality of this Court, and that a king cannot be tried by any superior jurisdiction on earth. But it is not my case alone, it is the freedom and liberty of England, and do you pretend what you will, I stand more for their liberties, for if power without law may make laws, may alter the fundamental laws of the kingdom, I do not know what subject he is in England can be sure of his life or anything he calls his own. . . .

BRADSHAW: Sir, you have offered something to the court; I shall speak something to you, the sense of the court. Sir, neither you nor any man are permitted to dispute that point: you are concluded [overruled]; you may not demur to the jurisdiction of the court. They sit here by the authority of the Commons of England, and all your predecessors and you are responsible to them.

THE KING: I deny that, show me one precedent.

BRADSHAW: Sir, we sit not here to answer your questions. Plead to your charge—guilty, or not guilty?

THE KING: You never heard my reasons yet.

BRADSHAW: Sir, your reasons are not to be heard against the highest jurisdiction.

THE KING: Show me that jurisdiction where reason is not to be heard.

BRADSHAW: Sir, we show it you here—the Commons of England. Sergeant, take away the prisoner.

THE KING: Remember that the king of England suffers, being not permitted to give his reasons, for the liberty of the people. God save the King!

On this day the commissioners from Scotland had delivered some papers to the House of Commons expressing a distinct dislike for the current proceedings against the king and declaring their deep interest in his well-being and in peaceful settlements of all disputes. The Commons never looked at them.

On Tuesday, January 23, 1649, the same wrangling went on. Finally Solicitor General Cooke stated that, according to law, if the prisoner refuses to plead guilty or not guilty, and thus opens the way to be fairly tried, it is an implicit confession (*pro confesso*) of guilt, and that he may be speedily judged. Bradshaw called this to the attention of the king, who ignored it and insisted he be allowed to speak on the subject of the liberties of the people of England. Bradshaw at last lost his temper. "Sir, this is the third time that you have publicly disowned this Court, and put an affront upon it. . . . Gentlemen, you that took charge of the prisoner, take him back again."

As the guards led him to Sir Robert Cottor's house, where he was then imprisoned, the crowds outside, now more than ever in sympathy with the king, shouted, "God save the King!"

On Wednesday and Thursday, January twenty-fourth and twenty-fifth, the court examined witnesses in the Painted Chamber, in spite of the fact that the trial could not go into that stage until the king had pleaded. Charles, of course, was not in court. Late in the day of the twenty-fifth the court, sitting in private, passed resolutions that the court would proceed to a sentence of condemnation against the king and that the condemnation would be for being tyrant, traitor, and murderer, and for being a public enemy to the Commonwealth of England. On Friday, January 26, the court again sat in private, and resolved "That the court do agree to the sentence now read" and "That the said sentence shall be engrossed. That the king be brought to Westminster tomorrow to receive his sentence."

The die was cast, and all that remained was to pass sentence. The court had held a two-hour session in the Painted Chamber, and now, at noon on the twenty-seventh, the roll was called in full court. Sixty-seven members were present. Amid cries of "Execution" and "Justice" from the soldiers present and a terrified silence from the civilian spectators, the king entered. Before sitting down, he turned to Bradshaw and said, "Sir, I desire a word to be heard a little, and I hope I shall give no occasion of interruption."

BRADSHAW: You may answer in your turn; hear the court first.

THE KING: If it please you, sir, I desire to be heard. It is only in a word. A sudden judgment—

BRADSHAW: Sir, you shall be heard in due time; but you are to hear the court first.

THE KING: Sir, I desire—it will be in order to what I believe the court will say. A hasty judgment is not so soon recalled.

BRADSHAW: Sir, you shall be heard before the judgment is passed. In the meantime you may forbear. . . . Gentlemen, it is well known to you all that the prisoner at the bar hath been several times convened and brought before this court to make answer to a charge of treason and other high crimes, exhibited against him, in the name of the people of England.

"It's a lie! Not one-half of them!" exclaimed Fairfax. "Where are they or their consent? Oliver Cromwell is a traitor!"

When the resultant clamor had died down, the king said, "I desire that I may be heard by the Lords and Commons in the Painted Chamber; for it is not my person that I look on alone—it is the kingdom's welfare and the kingdom's peace."

This was Charles's last attempt to get a fair and legal trial. It moved not only the spectators but also many members of the court itself. Colonel Downs rose to his feet and exclaimed, "Have we hearts of stone? Are we men?" He was quickly silenced by Cromwell, but he persisted, and addressed the president. "My Lord, I am not satisfied to give my consent to this sentence. I desire the court to adjourn and to hear me, and deliberate." It being parliamentary procedure, the court had no choice. They all went into the adjoining room. It was but a temporary interlude. The doubts of Downs were no match for the determination of Cromwell. The court returned, and Bradshaw told the king his request had been denied. He then launched into his long speech summarizing the faults of which the king had been guilty, at the end of which he instructed the clerk to read the sentence:

CLERK: Whereas the Commons of England in Parliament had appointed them a High Court of Justice for the trial of Charles Stuart, King of England, before whom he had been three times convened; and

at the first time a charge of high treason and other crimes and misdemeanors was read in behalf of the kingdom of England, etc. [Here the charge was repeated and the king required to give an answer, which he refused to do.] For all which treasons and crimes, this court doth adjudge, that he, the said Charles Stuart, as a tyrant, traitor, murderer and public enemy to the good people of this nation, shall be put to death by severing of his head from his body.

BRADSHAW: The sentence now read and published is the act, sentence, judgment, and resolution of the whole court.

THE KING: Sir, will you hear me a word?

BRADSHAW: Sir, you are not to be heard after sentence.

THE KING: No, sir?

BRADSHAW: No, sir; by your favor, sir. Guards, withdraw your prisoner!

THE KING: I may speak after sentence; by your favor, sir, I may speak after my sentence, ever. By your favor—

BRADSHAW: Hold!

THE KING: The sentence, sir—I say, sir, I do —I am not suffered to speak. Expect what justice other people will have!

Charles now spent the rest of that day and the following one by preparing for death. His request for the comfort and prayers of Dr. Juxon, bishop of London, had been granted, and except to bid farewell to those two of his children who were still in England, he refused to see any others.

Shortly after daybreak on the morning of the thirtieth Bishop Juxon arrived and began prayers. At about ten o'clock there was a knock on the door. It was Colonel Hacker come to summon the king to Whitehall, where the scaffold had been erected.

At Whitehall the king spent his last few hours eating a bit of bread and taking a few sips of claret. Soon afterward Colonel Hacker came for the last time. By now Charles was ready, and they walked through a passageway broken through the wall for the occasion, onto the scaffold, where the king was beheaded.

Eleven years later, in 1660, the murder of Charles I was avenged. The regicides were hanged, and drawn and quartered. On May 29, 1660, Charles II, on the occasion of his thirtieth birthday, returned to London and the throne of England amid joyous acclaim. The monarchy had once again been restored. But with one difference: the king was no longer absolute. The doctrine of royal absolutism ended with the death of Charles I on January 30, 1649.

Execution of Charles I.

The Salem Witchcraft Trials

1692

THE YEAR 1692 WAS PERHAPS THE MOST gloomy and despondent period in the entire history of New England. Not many years before, a group of courageous but somewhat bigoted colonists had migrated from Europe to Massachusetts, fleeing from almost inconceivable persecution and suffering in their own country. They settled in the midst of dark and unexplored forests. It is no wonder that their dour dispositions, in no way lightened by the hardships of their crossing and their superstitions, were transmitted to their children. Indeed, owing to peculiar circumstances in the year 1692, their bleak philosophy of life was aggravated all the more, and none were more afflicted with it than the Puritans of Salem township.

The leading Puritan minister of the day, and one who would play an important role in the Salem witchcraft trials and their aftermath, was Dr. Cotton Mather. The following excerpt from one of his sermons will make clear the prevailing belief in and fear of the devil and his disciples. Like most Puritan sermons of that era, it was designed to frighten his parishioners and instill the fear of the devil in them.

No place . . . that I know of, has got such a spell upon it as will always keep the devil out. The meeting-house, wherein we assemble for the worship of God, is filled with many holy people and many holy concerns continually; but, if our eyes were so refined as the servant of the prophet had his of old, I suppose we should now see a throng of devils in this very place. The apostle has intimated that angels come in among us: there are angels, it seems, that hark how I preach, and how you hear, at this hour. And our own sad experience is enough to intimate that the devils are likewise rendezvousing here. It is reported in Job i. 5, "When the sons of God came to present themselves before the Lord, Satan came also among them." When we are in our church assemblies, oh, how many devils, do you imagine, crowd in among us! There is a devil that rocks one to sleep. There is a devil that makes another to be thinking of, he scarcely knows what himself. And there is a devil that makes another to be pleasing himself with wanton and wicked speculations. It is also possible, that we have our closets or our studies gloriously perfumed with devotions every day; but, alas! can we shut the devil out of them? No: let us go where we will, we shall still find a devil nigh unto us. Only when we come to heaven, we shall be out of his reach for ever.

The almost incredible happenings at Salem in 1692 originated with a West Indian by the name of Tituba, servant of a Sam Parris. She and her husband, John Indian, had brought with them many of the superstitions of the native tribes of those islands. During the winters of 1691 and 1692 a group of young girls met at the Parris house for the purpose of learning and practicing Tituba's occult arts: palmistry,

"The Accusation of a Witch," a wood inlay. The arresting officer stands ready to handcuff the victim as one of the girls points an accusing finger at her, and Cotton Mather calls for divine help against the devil inhabiting the suspect. ESSEX INSTITUTE COLLECTION

fortune telling, necromancy, magic, and spiritualism. It began innocently enough, as a game to pass the time. But the members of their group soon became so proficient in these arts that they began to show off before others in the community. They would drop to the floor, writhe in agony, suffer dreadful tortures, and utter loud and piercing outcries. Soon their antics were known to the whole community. As their antics became worse and worse, the village doctor, Dr. Grigg, was called in to minister to the "afflicted" girls. Diagnosis and medical treatment were sadly lacking at this time, so Dr. Grigg resorted to the usual diagnosis of the day and declared the children bewitched.

A handful of "bewitched" girls made up the motley lot: precocious nine-year-old Elizabeth, daughter of Mr. Parris; eleven-year-old Abigail Williams, his niece and member of the household; Ann Putnam, twelve-year-old daughter of the parish clerk, Sergeant Thomas Putnam, and the leading agent in the holocaust to follow; Mary Walcot, seventeen, daughter of Captain Jonathan Walcot, deacon of the parish prior to the formation of the church; Mercy Lewis, also seventeen, and for a time previous in the family of the Reverend George Burroughs and now a servant in the family of Thomas Putnam; Elizabeth Hubbard, seventeen, a niece of the wife of Dr. Grigg, who lived with her; Elizabeth Booth and Susannah Sheldon, both eighteen; Mary Warren,

Tituba, who taught a group of girls some of her West Indian sorcery, asks Mary Wolcott what she sees in the mirror.

twenty, a servant of John Procter; and Sarah Churchill, twenty, a servant of George Jacobs, Sr.

Abetted by three gossips (Mrs. Ann Putnam, mother of Ann Putnam, a Mrs. Pope, and a woman named Bibber), the group soon spread alarm throughout the community. Little else was talked about except the terrible condition of the afflicted girls. They became objects of compassion and wonder, which served only to excite them to more extraordinary manifestations. They interrupted church services with incongruous questions and insolent remarks. Upon being told that there was present in church an old woman against whom a warrant for witchcraft had been issued the day before,

Abigail Williams cried out, "Look where she sits upon the beam, sucking her yellow bird betwixt her fingers." Ann Putnam joined in. "There is a yellow bird sitting on the minister's hat, as it hangs on the pin in the pulpit." At other times the girls became so unruly that they broke up whole meetings. Since they were supposed to be under supernatural impulses, they were never punished, but looked upon with pity, awe, and even terror. Even the minister agreed that the devil himself was working his wrath on these innocent victims. Since established doctrine had it that the devil could not operate upon mortals himself but must do so through his intermediaries, namely witches or wizards, the burning question in all minds was "Who are these agents the devil is using to afflict these girls?" They began to pressure the girls to name names. They were reluctant at first to do so, but when the urgings became insistent, one after another named three women in the community, Good, Osburn, and Tituba. So it followed that on February 29, 1692, warrants charging witchcraft were issued against these three persons. Thus began a massive series of accusations by these afflicted girls against hundreds of innocent persons, which was to culminate in the hanging of twenty persons and the imprisonment of hundreds more.

These first three examinations for witchcraft set the stage for the many that followed. The complainants who procured the warrants in the cases of Sarah Good, Sarah Osburn, and Tituba were Joseph Hutchinson, Edward Putnam, Thomas Putnam, and Thomas Preston, all strong on common sense and unlikely to be carried away by popular enthusiasm—a fact that shows how nearly unanimous was the feeling that the girls actually were suffering as the result of witchcraft practices.

The Salem Witchcraft Trials

The prelude to these initial examinations was deliberately designed to give them maximum publicity and notoriety. On March 1 the two leading magistrates of the neighborhood, members of the highest legislative and judicial body in the colony, assistants John Hathorne and Jonathan Corwin, entered Salem, followed by an imposing retinue of marshals, constables, and aides. The whole population was out to greet them, "excited to the highest pitch of indignation and abhorrence toward the prisoners." Adjourning to the meeting house, the magistrates took seats at a long table in front of the pulpit, facing the assembly. After prayer Constable George Locker produced Sarah Good, and Constable Joseph Herrick brought in Sarah Osburn and Tituba.

In designating Sarah Good as the first to be examined the prosecutors were clever. She and her children were desperately poor, often without a house to shelter them. Her weak and ignorant husband had left her. Truly, she was a welfare case in an age before such was conceived. No one could have more readily evoked popular suspicion. She was examined as follows:

THE EXAMINATION OF SARAH GOOD BEFORE
THE WORSHIPFUL ESQRS. JOHN HATHORNE
AND JONATHAN CORWIN

Sarah Good, what evil spirit have you familiarity with?

None.

Have you made no contracts with the devil?

No.

Why do you hurt these children?

I do not hurt them. I scorn it.

Who do you employ then to do it?

I employ nobody.

What creature do you employ then?

No creature: but I am falsely accused.

Why did you go away muttering from Mr. Parris his house?

I did not mutter, but I thanked him for what he gave my child.

Have you made no contract with the devil?

No. (Hathorne desired the children all of them to look upon her, and see if this were the person that hurt them; and so they all did look upon her, and said this was one of the persons that did torment them. Presently they were all tormented.)

Sarah Good, do you not see now what you have done? Why do you not tell us the truth? Why do you thus torment these poor children?

I do not torment them.

Who do you employ then?

I employ nobody. I scorn it.

How came they thus tormented?

What do I know? You bring others here, and now you charge me with it.

Why, who was it?

I do not know but it was some you brought into the meeting house with you.

Once the girls have named a member of the village a witch, she is very quickly arrested and thrown into jail. ESSEX INSTITUTE COLLECTION

We brought you into the meeting house.

But you brought in two more.

Who was it, then, that tormented the children?

It was Osburn.

What is it you say when you go muttering away from persons' houses?

If I must tell, I will tell.

Do tell us then.

If I must tell, I will tell: it is the Commandments. I may say my Commandments, I hope.

What Commandment is it?

If I must tell you, I will tell: it is a psalm.

What psalm? Who do you serve?

I serve God.

What God do you serve?

The God that made heaven and earth. (Her answers were in a very wicked, spiteful manner, reflecting and retorting against the authority with base and abusive words; and many lies she was taken in. It was here said that her husband had said that he was afraid that she either was a witch or would be one very quickly.)

The questions the judge put to her presumed her guilt and there was no lawyer to speak for her. All parties in the matter were prejudiced against her. Except for the accusations of the bewitched girls, the afflictions of whom even the prisoner never seemed to question as anything but genuine, there was not the slightest bit of evidence on which to convict her. But they did, and eventually hanged her.

Sarah Good was removed and Sarah Osburn brought in. Born Sarah Warren, she was married in 1622 to Robert Prince, a member of one of the leading families and owner of a valuable farm, and by whom she had two children, James and Joseph. Prince died, and Sarah married Alexander Osburn, who had come over from Ireland and, to pay for his passage, became an indentured servant. He put himself under contract to his sponsor for fifteen pounds. Sarah paid

the balance and hired him to manage her farm. Shortly after, she married him, thus incurring the censure and criticism of the townsfolk. The marriage proved to be unhappy, causing an upset in her mental state. She became bedridden, and as a result could not attend church regularly. As a woman of property who had remarried beneath her station she became the object of scandalous remarks and malicious gossip. Envious neighbors were only too happy to find the afflicted girls pointing their accusing fingers at her. She was examined in the same manner as was Sarah Good. She, too, stoutly denied that she had ever been deceived by the devil.

Upon the completion of Sarah Osburn's examination she was taken out of the meeting place and Tituba brought in for her examination, which proceeded as follows:

Tituba, what evil spirit have you familiarity with?

None.

Why do you hurt these children?

I do not hurt them.

Who is it then?

The devil, for aught I know.

Did you never see the devil?

The devil came to me, and bid me serve him.

Who have you seen?

Four women sometimes hurt the children.

Who were they?

Goody Osburn and Sarah Good, and I do not know who the others were. Sarah Good and Osburn would have me hurt the children, but I would not. (She further saith there was a tall man of Boston that she did see.)

When did you see them?

Last night, at Boston.

What did they say to you?

They said, "Hurt the children."

And did you hurt them?

No: there is four women and one man, they hurt the children, and then they lay all upon me; and they tell me, if I will not hurt the children, they will hurt me.

But did you not hurt them?

Yes; but I will hurt them no more.

Are you not sorry that you did hurt them?

Yes.

And why, then, do you hurt them?

They say, "Hurt children, or we will do worse to you."

What have you seen?

A man come to me, and say, "Serve me."

What service?

Hurt the children: and last night there was an appearance that said, "Kill the children"; and, if I would not go on hurting the children, they would do worse to me.

What is this appearance you see?

Sometimes it is like a hog, and sometimes like a great dog.

What did it say to you?

The black dog said, "Serve me"; but I said, "I am afraid." He said, if I did not, he would do worse to me.

What did you say to it?

"I will serve you no longer." Then he said he would hurt me; and then he looks like a man, and threatens to hurt me. And he told me he had more pretty things that he would give me, if I would serve him.

What were these pretty things?

He did not show me them.

What else have you seen?

Two cats; a red cat, and a black cat.

What did they say to you?

They said, "Serve me."

When did you see them?

Last night; and they said "Serve me"; but I said I would not.

What service?

Hurt the children.

Did you not pinch Elizabeth Hubbard this morning?

The man brought her to me, and made me pinch her.

Why did you go to Thomas Putnam's last night, and hurt his child?

They pull and haul me, and make me go.

And what would they have you do?

Kill her with a knife.

How did you go?

We ride upon sticks, and are there presently.

Do you go through the trees or over them?

We see nothing, but are there presently.

Why did you not tell your master?

I was afraid: they said they would cut off my head if I told.

Would you not have hurt others, if you could?

They said they would hurt others, but they could not.

What attendants hath Sarah Good?

A yellow bird, and she would have given me one.

What meat did she give it?

It did suck her between her fingers.

Did you not hurt Mr. Curren's child?

Goody Good and Goody Osburn told that they did hurt Mr. Curren's child, and would have had me hurt him too; but I did not.

What hath Sarah Osburn?

Yesterday she had a thing with a head like a woman, with two legs and wings.

What else have you seen with Osburn?

Another thing, hairy: it goes upright like a man, it hath only two legs.

Did you not see Sarah Good upon Elizabeth Hubbard, last Saturday?

I did see her set a wolf upon her to afflict her.

What clothes doth the man go in?

He goes in black clothes; a tall man, with white hair, I think.

How doth the woman go?

In a white hood, and a black hood with a top-knot.

Do you see who it is that torments these children now?

Yes: it is Goody Good; she hurts them in her own shape.

Who is it that hurts them now?

I am blind now: I cannot see.

Written by Ezekiel Cheever
Salem Village, March the first, 1692

Tituba was well aware of the monstrous fancies of the day and even with her mentality she had an inborn cunning and primitive imagination. Vividly she dressed up and embellished her lies, describing exactly what the witches she saw were wearing. One of them wore "a serge coat with a white hat." The devil himself appeared "in black clothes sometimes, sometimes serge coat of other color." She described her wild witches' ride "upon a stick, or pole, and Good and Osburn behind me: we ride taking hold of one another." It was obvious that she was well schooled in the gossip of the moment and willfully used it as the basis of her answers.

All three prisoners were brought from the jail in Ipswich, which was about ten miles away, for daily questioning. Osburn and Good steadily maintained their innocence;

Tituba reveled in professing her guilt and implicating the other two as having along with herself consorted with the devil. On March 7 they were transferred to the jail in Boston.

In the examination of Tituba a pattern emerged that was to spell the difference between life and death for those pointed out as witches by the afflicted girls. Tituba began her testimony professing innocence. The girls immediately went into their torments and tantrums. As soon as Tituba began to confess, these spells subsided. She herself then became tormented before the very eyes of the magistrates and the awestruck crowd. With much writhing and contorting she broke loose from her compact with the devil,

As the accused professes her innocence, one of the bewitched girls falls screaming to the floor. If the prisoner admitted to being a witch, the girls immediately ceased their convulsions.

thus ridding herself of the power to afflict. In the days to come those who admitted they were witches were never brought to the gallows. Those who stoutheartedly maintained their innocence were hung.

Before the year 1692 was out, twenty persons would be hanged for the crime of witchcraft and hundreds accused and thrown into jail for the same reason. The pattern was set. The "bitch witches," as George Jacobs, Sr., called the afflicted girls, would point their accusing fingers at whomever suited their fancy at the moment, then go into their fits. The unfortunate object of their spite would be arrested and brought before the magistrates for examination. Whether they denied or admitted the charge, they were thrown into jail to await trial.

By now the jails were overflowing with persons accused of witchcraft. It was high time for them to be brought to trial and have their cases disposed of. Politically the colony of Massachusetts had undergone a change. On May 14, 1692, it was transformed into a royal province with the arrival in Boston of a new governor, Sir William Phips. William Stoughton became the deputy governor. The council remained much the same. For the moment the new government refrained from interfering with the witchcraft proceedings. The new governor's chief concern was with the French to the north of him. He did not understand, nor did he wish to concern himself with, witchcraft. He was perfectly satisfied to yield to the views of his council, and accordingly relegated all authority in these matters to William Stoughton, his deputy governor. It was decided to appoint a special court of oyer and terminer for the witchcraft trials. Stoughton was commissioned chief justice. Appointed associate judges were Nathaniel Saltonstall of Haverhill, Major John Richards of Boston, Major Bartholomew Gedney of Salem, Mr. Wait Winthrop, Captain Samuel Sewall, and Mr. Peter Sargent, all three of Boston. Saltonstall withdrew early in the trials, to be succeeded by Jonathan Corwin of Salem.

The court was opened at Salem in the first week of June 1692. As there was no colony or province law against witchcraft in force when the trials began, the court proceeded under an act of James I passed in 1603, stating that convicted persons were to be sentenced to "the pains and penalties of death as felons." It is unfortunate that no records of the activities of this special court are now to be found. Some information, however, is available in writings from that period.

Bridget Bishop was the only one to be tried on the first day of the court. As she was brought from the jail past the meeting house, Cotton Mather writes, "she gave a look toward the house; and immediately a demon, invisibly entering the meeting house, tore down a part of it: so that, though there was no person to be seen there, yet the people, at the noise, running in, found a board, which was strongly fastened with several nails, transported into another quarter of the house."

In all probability some of the spectators were climbing around in the house, and dislodged a board. The court, however, judged it as conclusive proof that Bridget Bishop was guilty. At her trial she was accused of bewitching the son of Samuel Shattuck, the local hatter and dyer. Shattuck also condemned her for bringing in lace clothes too elaborate for an honest woman. Eighteen-year-old John Cook testified that about six years previous he had seen her form walking across their room and at that moment an apple which he had in his hand flew out of it and into his mother's lap. Bishop then disappeared.

One after another the neighbors of Bridget Bishop charged her with all sorts of extraordinary pranks. John Louder, a servant of John Gedney, Sr., had an argument with Bishop because her fowls used to come into their garden, and he now swore that "Some little time after which, I, going well to bed, about the dead of night, felt a great weight upon my breast, and awakening, looked; and, it being bright moonlight, did clearly see said Bridget Bishop, or her likeness, sitting upon my stomach; and putting my arms off the bed to free myself from the great oppression, she presently laid hold of my throat, and almost choked me, and I had no strength or power in my hands to resist, or help myself, and, in this condition, she held me to almost day."

Upon such evidence Bridget Bishop was condemned, and executed the next week. After her condemnation the court took a recess. They consulted with the ministers of Boston and the neighboring towns regarding the prosecutions, who urged that they be vigorously carried out. Before adjourning, the court revived an old colony law making witchcraft a capital offense.

The court met again on Wednesday, June 29, and, after trial, sentenced to death Sarah Good, Sarah Wildes, Elizabeth How, Susanna Martin, and Rebecca Nurse, who were all hanged on July 19. At the time of Good's execution a church elder, Noyes, pleaded with her to confess because she knew she was a witch. "You are a liar," she said. "I am no more a witch than you are a wizard; and, if you take away my life, God will give you blood to drink." In due time her prophecy came true. A very corpulent man, he died of an internal hemorrhage, bleeding profusely at the mouth.

Evidence given at the trials corroborated and added to the accusations previously brought against the accused at the time of their examinations. Witness after witness produced spectral evidence against the prisoners. Unfortunately for them, Chief Justice Stoughton was a firm believer in witches and wizards. Thus, presentation of spectral evidence to the court of oyer and terminer was tantamount to a verdict of guilty.

It should be stated here that the court did not render the verdict. In each trial there was a jury who decided whether the defendant was guilty or not guilty. In the case of Rebecca Nurse, so obvious was the injustice being done that the jury brought in a verdict of not guilty.

Immediately, all the accusers in the court as well as those outside set up a hideous outcry, to the amazement not only of the spectators but also of the court, which seemed strangely surprised. One of the judges expressed himself as not satisfied with the verdict. The chief justice, "while not wishing to impose on the jury," gave reasons why he thought they had reached the wrong verdict. The jury redeliberated, and she was condemned, upon which the governor granted her a reprieve. But so loud was the clamor of certain Salem gentlemen that he recalled the reprieve, and Rebecca Nurse was executed with the others. But not before, on July 3, 1692, the Reverend Parris had seen to it that she was excommunicated from the church.

The court met again on August 5 and tried George Burroughs, John and Elizabeth Procter, George Jacobs, Sr., John Willard, and Martha Carrier. All were condemned, and, except for Elizabeth Procter, who was pregnant at the time, were executed on August 19.

The next meetings of the court took place

"The Trial of George Jacobs," by T. H. Matteson. The "afflicted" girls go into their tantrums when the prisoner they have named as a witch is brought into court. Jacobs was one of the nineteen people condemned and hanged in Salem in 1692. Essex Institute Collection

on September 9 and 17. The following were condemned and executed on September 22, 1692: Martha Corey, Mary Easty, Alice Parker, Ann Pudeator, Margaret Scott, Wilmot Reed, Samuel Wordwell, and Mary Parker. All asserted their innocence on the scaffold.

After the executions of September 22, 1692, the court fully expected to meet from month to month to continue to "supply new cart-loads of victims to the hangman." But they were destined never to meet again. A radical change was taking place. Ministers and men of prominence were beginning to have serious doubts on the validity of spectral evidence. Increase Mather, president of Harvard, was not as convinced of such evidence as was his son Cotton. "It is better that ten suspected witches should escape," he wrote, "than one innocent person should be condemned." The accusations

of the afflicted girls were becoming embarrassing, especially when the wife of Sir William Phips, after sympathizing with those who suffered prosecution, was accused. So, on October 29, the court of oyer and terminer was dismissed by the governor. What is more, he asked for petitions of release for the one hundred fifty accused witches still in jail. Those who had only spectral evidence against them were released on bond. Unfortunately, prisoners had to pay their jail costs before they could be released, so that not all succeeded in getting out of jail. However, new regulations were put into force requiring the well-being of those prisoners who remained.

To complete the witchcraft trials still outstanding, the acts of the General Court of November 13 and December 16 created special sessions of the Supreme Court of Judicature. Stoughton still presided, but spectral evidence was eliminated as a basis of conviction, although confessed witches were condemned. The court traveled around and new juries were selected. On January 3, 1693, fifty-two witches were tried, but the cases against forty-nine of them were dismissed. Stoughton signed death warrants for the other three and for five others who had been condemned previously. Governor Phips then issued reprieves for all eight, and in May 1693 discharged all remaining witches. Thus ended the tragedy of the Salem witch trials of 1692. Never again was a witch to be condemned to death in the American colonies.

To a world that no longer believes in witches, the Salem trial may seem to be one more example of barbarism which twentieth-century man has by now completely outgrown. There are many lessons to be learned from Salem, however; the most significant, perhaps, being the ease with which absurdities and falsehoods and unfounded charges can spread into a lynch spirit, can be believed in by intelligent and educated persons and by the accused themselves. Mass hysteria, fed by rumor, fear, imagination, speculation, and enmity, is still a potent force in the modern world. We have not seen the last of witch hunts.

John Peter Zenger

1735

SHALL A NEWSPAPER BE PERMITTED TO make damaging statements about a person, blackening his reputation, charging him with acts for which the public has contempt—and then have its editors remain free from prosecution on the ground that all the statements are true? Without such a right, without such immunity from prosecution, there is no freedom of the press, some people will say. For how will a man be able to write the truth about public officials if he can be arrested and charged with libel?

The concept of the right to publish damaging statements, particularly about public officials, was not accepted in colonial America until the historic trial of an immigrant printer, John Peter Zenger, established one of the basic rights of the American people.

The year was 1735. The growing city of New York had a population of almost forty thousand. Dissatisfaction with British rulers ran high, but few of the colonists considered themselves other than Loyalists, and sentiment to secede or to declare independence was barely audible, if it existed at all.

In the old city hall in New York, later to become the first capitol of the United States under the Constitution, the trial of John Peter Zenger was held. The judges were appointees of the very forces that Zenger was accused of libeling, but trial by jury had been established in the colonies, and there was a hope

THAT, THE RULING OF THE JUDGES NOTWITH-standing, a jury might find Zenger not guilty.

A native of Germany, Zenger arrived on American shores in the first years of the eighteenth century, a shy and modest lad of thirteen. An indentured servant, he became apprenticed to a printer, and only in his mid-twenties did he become a free man, fulfilling the dream held by thousands of refugees who were leaving their native lands and traveling as pioneers and immigrants to the promise of the New World.

The British crown colony of New York was at this time under the rule of governors appointed directly by the king. In 1731 William S. Cosby was appointed to the post, a greedy, corrupt, and dictatorial figure who, once he assumed control, set out to exploit his position for his own financial gain. From 1725 to 1731 he had been governor of the island of Minorca in the Mediterranean, where he had confiscated property for his own private benefit, appropriated revenues, and had become intensely unpopular. He spent thirteen months carousing in London and on the Continent before he finally reached New York to take up his duties.

Cosby lost no time in turning his new post into financial gain for himself. He inspired no loyalty in his subjects and from the first days his administration was rocked by scandals. When his immediate predecessor, Rip Van Dam, refused to turn over to

A miniature on enamel of Governor Cosby.
COURTESY OF THE NEW-YORK HISTORICAL SOCIETY, NEW YORK CITY

Cosby a portion of the wages that Van Dam had received while he had been acting governor, Cosby took the case to court. There, the chief justice of the New York Supreme Court, Lewis Morris, ruled against Cosby, whereupon the governor, in his anger, removed Morris from the court. Undaunted in his opposition to Cosby, Morris ran for the assembly from the district of Eastchester and won handsomely.

Zenger, working at this time for the New York *Weekly Gazette*, reported every detail of this election, including the story of how thirty-eight Quakers were illegally disqualified from voting because they would, according to their beliefs, only affirm rather than swear. He told of the intimidation of the voters by the king's sheriff and Cosby's attempt to stuff the ballot boxes. William Bradford, to whom Zenger had been apprenticed, refused to print Zenger's unbiased report, and promptly dismissed him.

Morris now saw his chance to put before the people his case, and those of others who had suffered injustices at the hands of Cosby and his henchmen. He would start and finance a rival newspaper to the *Gazette* and hire Zenger to publish it. Accordingly, Morris, Van Dam, and others set up Zenger in business, and on November 1, 1733, the first issue of the New York *Weekly Journal* made its appearance.

From its first issue the paper spoke out forcefully against the Cosby administration.

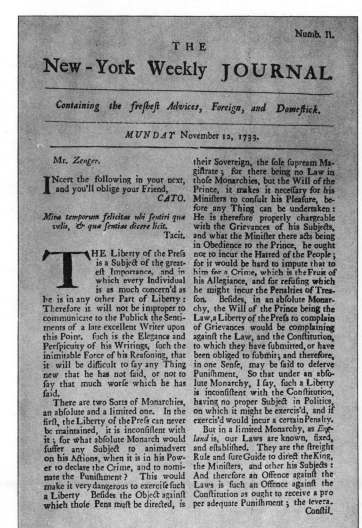

Facsimile of a front page of Zenger's newspaper, "The New-York Weekly Journal."

Diorama of Zenger's printing shop. ZENGER MEMORIAL ROOM, FEDERAL HALL, NEW YORK CITY

Most of the inflammatory articles were written by James Alexander, Lewis Morris, William Smith, Cadwallader Colden, and Lewis Morris, Jr. Despite typographical errors and poor grammar, Zenger's journal grew in popularity. Its only competition was the New York *Weekly Gazette*, Bradford's conservative and government-subsidized paper. Zenger's paper lashed out against the colonial administration, held up to ridicule the governor and his coterie, and indulged in biting satire. Finally, it aroused the open condemnation of the governor's party when it printed two "scandalous" songs that made fun of the office of the governor and other colonial officials.

The governor ordered four issues of the *Journal*, Nos. 7, 47, 48, and 49, condemned and publicly burned by the hangman. The aldermen refused to attend, but the ceremony was carried out, with a black servant stooping down to place into the fire one copy of each of the condemned papers. The lines of battle were thus drawn more tightly, and neither side was prepared to retreat.

On November 17, 1734, John Peter Zenger was arrested. The charge against him was that he printed and published "several Seditious Libels throughout his Journals or News Papers, entitled, *The New-York Weekly Journal*, containing the freshest Advices, foreign and domestick; as having in them many Things, tending to raise Factions and Tumults, among the People of this Province, inflaming their Minds with Contempt of His Majesty's Government." Specifically, the charge named the issues of April 8, 1734, and January 28, 1734.

Upon orders from Governor Cosby, a servant places in the fire one copy each of four issues of Zenger's "The New-York Weekly Journal."

Because an excessive bail of £800 was set for Zenger, he had to remain in jail while awaiting trial. The people of New York were stunned. Zenger's arrest was wholly illegal. If Cosby hoped the *Journal* would cease publication, or would at least be more temperate in its criticism of his administration while its editor and printer was under

arrest, he was disappointed. Support for the *Journal* grew during the nine months Zenger awaited trial. His wife, visiting him frequently in jail, obtained advice and information and hurried back to the printshop to publish the paper.

As the date of his trial approached, Zenger's position became more precarious when the court disbarred the two attorneys who had come forward for the defense, James Alexander and William Smith. But Zenger's friends and supporters were busy in his behalf, and quickly obtained the services of Andrew Hamilton, considered the most outstanding member of the bar in Philadelphia, and perhaps the leading lawyer in the colonies.

The trial was held on August 4, 1735, at city hall on the corner of Nassau and Wall streets. Built in 1700, this was at the time the finest building in the city. The courtroom was crowded to capacity, with every class of people represented, most of whom resented the hardships and injustices that Governor Cosby heaped upon them. They hoped that an acquittal for Zenger would in some way result in their governor being recalled.

The jury of twelve headed by Thomas Hunt, foreman, contained seven of Dutch ancestry who had no sympathy for Cosby's arbitrary English authoritarianism. If a way could be found, they were most likely to vote according to the interests of the popular party.

Fifty-nine-year-old Andrew Hamilton was there to plead the cause of the defense. Hamilton had been carefully briefed on the facts of the case, including the truth of what Zenger had published against Cosby and his government, by Zenger's two previous lawyers, James Alexander and William Smith. Luckily, Hamilton was too famous a personage for the court even to contemplate disbarment action. Although they could not defend Zenger, his two disbarred lawyers were present to assist Hamilton, as was John Chambers, originally designated by the court as counsel for the defense, but whom Hamilton soon overshadowed.

Zenger was being tried under an Information issued by Attorney-General Richard Bradley, charging him with "printing and publishing parts of my [New York Weekly] Journal No. 13 and 23 as being *false, scandalous, malicious, and seditious.*" Zenger, of course, had not written these articles, the supposed authors being James Alexander and Lewis Morris. The presiding judge was James De Lancey, chief justice of the Supreme Court, and an old crony of Governor Cosby. He was assisted by Frederick Philipse, associate justice of the Supreme Court.

Andrew Hamilton heeded the requests of Zenger's friends to act as his chief defense counsel. ZENGER MEMORIAL ROOM, FEDERAL HALL, NEW YORK CITY

City Hall, where the trial of John Peter Zenger opened on August 4, 1735. COURTESY OF THE NEW-YORK HISTORICAL SOCIETY, NEW YORK CITY

The attorney general opened by reading the Information, which quoted from specific articles published in the New York *Weekly Journal* to the effect that many influential men were leaving New York because its governor arbitrarily removed judges, established new courts without the consent of the legislature, took away jury trials as he pleased, denied certain men of influence their right to vote—all contrary to existing law.

Andrew Hamilton then rose and addressed the court. In his opening remarks he confessed, on behalf of his client, that Zenger "both printed and published the two News Papers set forth in the Information," and added that he hoped that in so doing, Zenger had committed no crime.

The chief justice ordered the trial to proceed. Attorney-General Bradley sought to end the trial at that point. "Indeed, Sir, as Mr. Hamilton has confessed the Printing and Publishing these Libels, I think the Jury must find a Verdict for the King; for supposing they were true, the Law says that they are not the less libellous for that; nay indeed the Law says, their being true is an Aggravation of the Crime."

Hamilton at once remonstrated, and immediately stated the grounds on which he would conduct the defense. "Not so neither, Mr. Attorney, there are two Words to that Bargain. I hope it is not our bare Printing and Publishing a Paper, that will make it a Libel: You will have something more to do, before you make my Client a Libeller; for the Words themselves must be libellous, that is, *false, scandalous, and seditious,* or else we are not guilty." According to the law of the times, this was not strictly true, but Hamilton was relying on logic and perhaps the tenor of the people's feelings to argue

Diorama of the trial of John Peter Zenger. ZENGER MEMORIAL ROOM, FEDERAL HALL, NEW YORK CITY

Andrew Hamilton turns to the jury and delivers his plea for freedom of the press to print the truth. Courtesy of The New-York Historical Society, New York City

against the existing common law of libel.

Bradley counteracted by citing numerous precedents and authorities to back his and the court's contention that it made no difference whether the libel was true or false. The government was a sacred body, and it was a crime to libel it. Hamilton rebutted by saying, "May it please Your Honor; I agree with Mr. Attorney, that Government is a sacred Thing, but I differ very widely from him when he would insinuate, that the just Complaints of a Number of Men, who suffer under a bad Administration, is libelling that Administration." He went on to suggest that the attorney general was attempting to set up a Star Chamber proceeding, now outlawed in England; that there was a wide difference between the authority

of judges in Westminster Hall in England and that of provincial judges. He went on to ridicule the attorney general's doctrine "That Truth makes a worse Libel than Falsehood." Then he quoted the rule laid down by Lord Chief Justice Halt in a similar trial. "That he who would take upon him to write Things, it lies upon him to prove them at his Peril." Hamilton dramatically boomed out, "We are ready to prove them to be true, at *our* Peril." The court, however, refused to allow the defense to prove the truth to justify a libel, and admonished Hamilton to have the good manners to accept the ruling of the court.

Hamilton turned to the jury, and in one of courtroom history's most dramatic moments said, "Then, Gentlemen of the Jury, it is to you we must now appeal, for Witness, to the Truth of the Facts we have offered, and are denied the Liberty to prove; and let it not seem strange, that I apply my self to you in this Manner, I am warranted so to do, both by Law and Reason." He then asked Bradley for a standard definition of libel, which Bradley gave according to the rule book.

Hamilton replied by stating that words such as "scandalous," "scoffing," and "ironical" had meaning only as they were understood by the persons judging them. Unwittingly the chief justice agreed. "Then," pursued Hamilton, "it follows that those twelve men [the jury] must understand the Words in the Information to be *scandalous*, that is to say *false*; and when they understand the Words to be so, they will say we are guilty of Publishing a false Libel, *and not otherwise*." Hamilton was asking the jury to judge what Zenger had published not in terms of scandal and irony, but in terms of falsehood and truth.

The chief justice replied, "No, Mr. Hamilton, the jury may find that Zenger printed and published those Papers and leave it to the court to judge whether they are libellous." To Hamilton—who made this eloquently clear to the jury—if this were the case, juries would in effect be rendered useless. Obviously, no jury would accept such a status, and thus a defense of the rights of the jury was added to the defense of John Peter Zenger.

Hamilton launched into a lengthy and often digressive defense, punctuated with repeated interruptions by the court and the attorney general. He concluded:

The Question before the court and you, Gentlemen of the Jury, is not of small nor private concern, it is not the Cause of a poor Printer, nor of New York alone, which you are now trying: No! It may in its Consequence, affect every Free man that lives under a British Government or the main of America. It is the best Cause. It is the Cause of Liberty; and I make no Doubt but your upright Conduct, this Day, will not only entitle you to the Love and Esteem of your Fellow-Citizens; but every Man who prefers Freedom to a Life of Slavery will bless and honour You, as Men who have baffled the Attempt of Tyranny; and by an impartial and uncorrupt Verdict, have laid a noble Foundation for securing to ourselves, our Posterity, and our Neighbours, That, to which Nature and the Laws of our Country have given us a Right—The Liberty—both of exposing and opposing arbitrary Power (in these Parts of the World, at least) by speaking and writing Truth.

Bradley made his closing comments for the prosecution, and the chief justice warned the jury to heed his charge that they were to decide only if the words set forth in the Information made a libel.

The jury withdrew. They were out only ten minutes, and returned with a verdict of not guilty. The courtroom went wild, and demonstrated with many cheers. Their cries were taken up by the mob outside and spread down Broadway. Freedom of the press had once and for all been established in the American colonies—a freedom that was to be reaffirmed in the Constitution of the United States of America; and though often challenged and in danger, it was a freedom that would be vigorously defended, down to the publication of the Pentagon Papers during the war in Vietnam.

John Peter Zenger was never called as a witness and never uttered a word during his entire trial. It was a battle of legal minds, in which he was the defendant; actually an issue, or several of them, was on trial, not a man. For his part, Zenger spent almost ten months in jail, with severe personal hardships to himself and to his family, but emerged a hero in the community, a symbol of the right of subjects to stand up and criticize governmental authorities.

The case of John Peter Zenger illustrates the oppressive nature of excessive bail, under which a man is held for a lengthy period awaiting trial. It provided the drama of two attorneys being disbarred for defending a client who was unpopular with the court; another attorney, of exceptional prestige, ignoring the rulings of the court and then turning, over the heads of the court, directly to the jury; and finally, a jury bringing in a verdict almost in direct contradiction to the instructions given by the court. Furthermore, the Zenger case established, as no previous one had, the concept of truth as a defense against libel.

But, most significantly no previous case made such a contribution to the right of freedom of the press. There could be no free press if government officials could have critics arrested, if criticism were condemned as scandalous, if the truth of the criticism were considered irrelevant, and if the only issue in the libel case was whether the defendant was guilty of being the printer and publisher.

The Common Council of the City of New York honored Andrew Hamilton for his "learned and generous defense of the rights of mankind." Indeed, posterity, which has so often paid homage to Zenger, might give greater recognition to the mastermind of the case, who was not the defendant, but his learned counsel.

As for Zenger, after his trial he continued quietly to publish books and periodicals until August 4, 1746, when he unobtrusively passed away.

The Impeachment Trial of Andrew Johnson

1868

FEW MEN HAVE COME INTO THE LAND'S highest office with as formidable a task facing them as did Andrew Johnson. Born in North Carolina and bred in Tennessee, he was a self-educated youth who had vigorously opposed powerful financial interests in his home state. A Democrat, he was chosen as the running mate for Lincoln in the latter's struggle against George McClellan, with the hope of weaning away Democratic votes, presenting a national unity ticket, splitting some of the pro-Southern sentiment, and adding Johnson's strength to the radical Republican and abolitionist votes that had nowhere to go but to Lincoln.

Their victory was closer in the popular than in the electoral columns (Lincoln received 55 percent of the popular, 91 percent of the electoral votes). Johnson became vice-president. Two matters at the inauguration have been singled out by historians. First there was Lincoln's olive branch, which he held out to the secessionists, to whose early defeat he could now look forward. "With malice toward none, with charity for all . . ." This was the same Lincoln who had earlier preached "the Christian principle of forgiveness on terms of repentance," for which he was denounced by the abolitionist Thaddeus Stevens. And a second matter that is prominent in the details of the inauguration was the behavior of Andrew Johnson,

who is said to have come to the ceremony in a state of intoxication. Johnson's apologists were later to insist that he was ill and had merely taken an extra strong shot of whiskey, but his behavior at the inauguration was to plague him for years.

After the initial shock of Lincoln's assassination, there was a general feeling of optimism in the radical Republican camp in Congress. This dominant group was seeking not only to wipe out slavery but also to establish—if necessary by the same force that had won the Civil War—some steps toward the education of blacks and their preparation for participation in American life. The radicals laid down terms for the return of the former secessionist states to the Union. In the days immediately following his inauguration, Johnson promised full cooperation to the radicals, and pledged that there would be no dealings with those who had committed treason against the Union. To Sumner he stated that they were in agreement on the necessity of bringing about black suffrage; and to Thaddeus Stevens he is reported to have said, "To those who have deceived, to the conscious, influential traitor, who attempted to destroy the life of the nation—I would say, on you be inflicted the severest penalties of your crime."

In terms of statehood, however, Congress and the President began to have divergent views of Reconstruction. Eleven states had

President Andrew Johnson. LIBRARY OF CONGRESS

as a full voter, strengthening the representation of the states that had just gone down to defeat.

During the summer of 1865 Johnson and the radicals drew further apart. Congress was not in session, and the President used the opportunity to implement his own program. He recognized a government in Virginia which the radicals considered a triumph of the old Confederacy. He offered liberal amnesty terms and laid down conditions for the formation of state governments that would lead to the reestablishment of the old South. For the dismayed radicals Johnson had become "His Accidency, the President."

When Congress came back into session the Republicans were in an angry mood. Various measures, some of which were central to the entire Reconstruction program, were passed, vetoed, and then passed again over the President's veto. All the presidents before Johnson, from Washington to Lincoln, had in total vetoed fewer acts of Congress than did President Johnson during his brief period in office. Between the executive and legislative branches of the government an unbending struggle for supremacy was shaping up.

The United States Congress passed the Fourteenth Amendment to the Constitution (which gave American citizenship a broad definition and provided that no citizen could be deprived of his life, liberty, or property without due process of law), and made ratification of the amendment a prerequisite for readmission to the Union. Johnson opposed the amendment and urged the states not to ratify it. The President denounced the Freedmen's Bureau and vetoed an 1866 act of Congress extending its life. He issued wholesale amnesties and pardons to the men whom he had so recently denounced as traitors, vetoed a District of Columbia black

seceded from the Union, and the radicals feared that if the secessionists were not barred from holding office and from having power in their own states, and if these states returned to the Union in the hands of those who had led them out of it, the Republican program in Congress would be lost by the votes of the very people who had just been militarily defeated. But Johnson, following the example set by Lincoln, favored the restoration of the states—they came to be known as the Johnson states—and demanded the seating of their delegations in Congress. More than that, the Thirteenth Amendment had been passed, calling for the abolition of slavery. Under the original Constitution, representation in Congress for slaveholding states was based on a census that counted a slave as three-fifths of a man. Now, under this amendment, the freedman was counted

suffrage bill, denounced blacks as too ignorant to cast a ballot, and vetoed a whole series of Reconstruction bills as well as the historic Civil Rights Act of 1866. In the fall of 1866 the President went on a whistle-stop tour, appearing in numerous Northern cities to attack Congress, the Civil Rights Act, and even the proposed and as yet unratified Fourteenth Amendment. But popular sentiment was not with the President. He was literally driven off the platform at several points, and the November elections marked further victories for his opponents. During the course of his speeches Johnson angrily denounced his congressional opposition in intemperate tones and unrestrained manners.

In an effort to humiliate the President on the one hand, and on the other, to reduce his office to one of impotence so that he could not carry out his program and would be forced to turn to Congress for militant Reconstruction, Congress passed the highly dubious, most controversial Tenure of Office Act. The bill provided that persons appointed to civil office by and with the advice and consent of the Senate shall be entitled "to hold such office until a successor shall have been in like manner appointed and duly qualified." The President could no longer without the consent of the Senate remove from office those whom he had appointed with that body's consent. Originally, in an early version of the bill, cabinet members were excluded; later it was ambiguously stated that cabinet members shall hold their offices "for and during the term of the President by whom they may have been appointed, and for one month thereafter, subject to removal by and with the advice and consent of the Senate." Early in March 1867 the President sent the Congress his veto message, and the bill was passed over his veto.

Convinced that the Tenure of Office Act was unconstitutional, Johnson attempted to remove the secretary of war, Stanton, and replace him first by Grant (who declined to play the President's game), and then by a weak adjutant general, Lorenzo Thomas. Congressional leaders now claimed that Johnson was in violation of the law, that he was guilty of a "high crime and misdemeanor" such as demanded by the Constitution as a prerequisite for removal. The hue and cry for impeachment could be heard in the nation's press, in the streets, and in Congress.

The effort to impeach Johnson, which had failed to gain a sufficient number of adherents in the House on earlier occasions, received great impetus from the Thomas episode. The radicals felt that they had garnered the strength to remove the President, and in the House they debated an impeachment resolution from February 22 to 24, 1868. The resolution was probably as brief as anything so momentous in the history of Congress; it read, in full, "Resolved, That Andrew Johnson, President of the United States, be impeached of high crimes and misdemeanors in office."

With Thaddeus Stevens, a fiery radical, summarizing and closing for the anti-Johnson forces, the vote was overwhelming: 126 for impeachment, 47 against (only a majority was required). A committee of two (Thaddeus Stevens and John A. Bingham) was authorized to communicate the House's action to the Senate, and a few days later the House elected a committee of managers to conduct the prosecution of the impeachment before the Senate. It was a powerful group, containing several of the most popular, eloquent, and capable congressmen.

The impeachment trial of Andrew Johnson, President of the United States, opened before the Senate on March 5, 1868. For

Thaddeus Stevens summarizes and concludes the case of the anti-Johnson forces in the House of Representatives.

successful impeachment a two-thirds majority, or 36 of the 54 members who had been seated in the Senate, was required. If the vote proceeded along party lines, impeachment was to be expected, for there were 42 Republicans, 4 Conservative Republicans (who supported the President), and 8 Democrats.

The managers presented an indictment containing eleven articles, which were largely repetitious, and essentially consisted of one general and three specific accusations against Johnson. The specific ones involved the deliberate violation of law in the attempted removal of Stanton; an alleged issuance of unlawful orders to General W. H. Emory at a time when Congress and the President

each feared military action against itself from the adversary; and statements reputed to have been made by Johnson in the whistlestop tour in which he was charged with having denied the legitimacy of Congress. In a more general sense, the articles accused the President of being "unmindful of the high duties of his office, and the dignities and proprieties thereof, and of the harmony and courtesies which ought to exist between the executive and legislative branches of the government." Johnson was charged with having attempted "to bring into disgrace, ridicule, contempt and reproach the Congress of the United States," activity that would not be likely to endear him to congressmen.

Johnson, through his attorneys, sent an answer to the Senate on March 23, 1868. He defended his action on the Stanton matter, denied that he had said that Congress was not legally empowered to pass the legislation it did, and stated that he exercised his right of freedom of opinion and freedom of speech to state his opinions on such matters.

On March 30, before a packed gallery for which special tickets were issued, General Ben Butler made the initial speech for the managers:

Now, for the first time in the history of the world, has a nation brought before its highest tribunal its chief executive magistrate for trial and possible deposition from office, upon charges of maladministration of the powers and duties of that office. In other times, and in other lands, it has been found that despotisms could only be tempered by assassination, and nations living under constitutional governments even, have found no mode by which to rid themselves of a tyrannical, imbecilic, or faithless ruler, save by overturning the very foundation and frame-work of the government itself. And, but recently, in one of the most civilized and powerful governments of the world, from which our own institutions have been largely modeled, we have seen a nation submit for years to the rule of an insane king, because its constitution contained no method for his removal.

Our fathers, more wisely, founding our government, have provided for such and all similar exigencies a conservative, effectual, and practical remedy by the constitutional provision that the "President, Vice-President, and all civil officers of the United States shall be removed from office on impeachment for and conviction of treason, bribery, or other high

Photograph of the trial managers. Back row: James F. Wilson; George Boutwell; John A. Logan; Front row: Benjamin F. Butler; Thaddeus Stevens; Thomas Williams; John A. Bingham. mall caps>Library of Congress</small>

crimes and misdemeanors." The Constitution leaves nothing to implication, either as to the persons upon whom, or the body by whom, or the tribunal before which, or the offenses for which, or the manner in which this high power should be exercised; each and all are provided for by express words of imperative command.

What is an impeachable high crime or misdemeanor? thundered Butler, and replied. It is

one in its nature or consequences subversive of some fundamental or essential principle of government, or highly prejudicial to the public interest, and this may consist of a violation of the Constitution, of law, of an official oath, or of duty, by an act committed or omitted, or, without violating a positive law, by the abuse of discretionary powers from improper motives, or for any improper purpose.

On the question of freedom of speech, Butler inveighed strongly against Johnson's defense.

Is it, indeed, to be seriously argued here that there is a constitutional right in the President of the United States, who, during his official life, can never lay aside his official character, to denounce, malign, abuse, ridicule, and condemn, openly and publicly, the Congress of the United States—a coordinate branch of the government?

It cannot fail to be observed that the President (shall I dare to say his counsel, or are they compelled by the exigencies of their defense?) has deceived himself as to the gravamen of the charge in this article? It does not raise the question of freedom of speech, but of propriety and decency of speech and conduct in a high officer of the government.

Andrew Johnson, the private citizen, as I may reverently hope and trust he soon will be, has the full constitutional right to think and speak what he pleases, in the manner he pleases, and where he pleases, provided always

he does not bring himself within the purview of the common law offences of being a common railer and brawler, or a common scold, which he may do (if a male person is ever liable to commit that crime;), but the dignity of station, the proprietaries of position, the courtesies of office, all of which are a part of the common law of the land, require the President of the United States to observe that gravity of deportment, that fitness of conduct, that appropriateness of demeanor, and those amenities of behavior which are a part of his high official functions. He stands before the youth of the country the exemplar of all that is of worth in ambition, and all that is to be sought in aspiration; he stands before the men of the country as the grave magistrate who occupies, if he does not fill, the place once honored by Washington; nay, far higher and of greater consequence, he stands before the world as the representative of free institutions, as the type of man whom the suffrages of a free people have chosen as their chief. He should be the living evidence of how much better, higher, nobler, and more in the image of God, is the elected ruler of a free people than a hereditary monarch, coming into power by the accident of birth; and when he disappoints all these hopes and all these expectations, and becomes the ribald, scurrilous blasphemer, bandying epithets and taunts with a jeering mob, shall he be heard to say that such conduct is not a high misdemeanor in office? Nay, disappointing the hopes, causing the cheek to burn with shame, exposing to the taunts and ridicule of every nation the good name and fame of the chosen institutions of thirty million of people, is it not the highest possible crime and misdemeanor in office? and under the circumstances is the gravamen of these charges. The words are not alleged to be either false or defamatory, because it is not within the power of any man, however high his official position, in effect to slander the Congress of the United States, in the ordinary sense of that word, so as to call on Congress to answer as to the truth of the accusation. We do not go in, therefore, to any question of truth or falsity. We rest upon the scandal of the scene. We would as soon think, in the trial of an indictment against a termagant as a common scold, of summoning witnesses to prove that what she said was not true. It is the noise and disturbance in the neighborhood that is the offence, and not a question of the provocation or irritation which causes the outbreak.

Butler's conclusions placed a heavy burden on the senators.

The responsibility is with you; the safeguards of the Constitution against usurpation are in your hands; the interests and hopes of free institutions wait upon your verdict. The House of Representatives has done its duty. We have presented the facts in the constitutional manner; we have brought the criminal to the bar, and demand judgment at your hands for his great crimes.

Never again, if Andrew Johnson go quit and free this day, can the people of this or any other country by constitutional checks or guards stay the usurpation of executive power.

I speak, therefore, not the language of exaggeration but the words of truth and soberness, that the political welfare and liberties of all men hang trembling on the decision of the hour.

Johnson was represented by William Maxwell Evarts, leader of the American bar, and Benjamin R. Curtis, formerly a justice of the Supreme Court. The reply of the defense was more tempered, but to the point. The attorneys argued both that the President had not violated the letter of the law, because Stanton had been appointed by Lincoln, not Johnson, and that cabinet officers were meant to be advisers to the President, and therefore it was not intended that they stay in office when their services were no longer wanted.

Through many long weeks and many witnesses the trial held the attention of the country. Popular sentiment in the North was clearly against Johnson, and toward the end of the trial, on May 11, a Republican from Maine who had broken party lines and was supporting Johnson, took notice of the sentiment in the streets.

To the suggestion that popular opinion demands the conviction of the President on these charges, I reply that he is not now on trial before the people, but before the Senate. In the words of Lord Eldon, upon the trial of the queen, "I take no notice of what is passing out of doors, because I am supposed constitutionally not to be acquainted with it." . . . The people have not heard the evidence as we have heard it. The responsibility is not on them, but upon us. . . . And I should consider myself undeserving the confidence of that just and intelligent people who imposed upon you this great responsibility, an unworthy place among honorable men, if for any fear of public reprobation, and for the sake of securing popular favor, I should disregard the convictions of my judgment and my conscience.

Much of the debate at the trial centered upon what Johnson had said in his speeches, and whether newspaper reports were accurate or garbled. The managers read into the trial record entire versions of these talks, particularly one given in Cleveland, and emphasized the sections dealing with Congress.

We have witnessed [Johnson is reported to have stated] in one department of the government every effort, as it were, to prevent the restoration of peace, harmony, and union; we have seen, as it were, hanging upon the verge of the government, as it were, a body, calling or assuming to be the Congress of the United States, when it was but a Congress of a part of the States; we have seen Congress assuming to be for the Union when every step they took was to perpetuate dissolution, and make disruption permanent. We have seen every step that has been taken, instead of bringing about

A full view of the Senate sitting as a court of impeachment for the trial of Andrew Johnson.
LIBRARY OF CONGRESS

reconciliation and harmony, has been legislation that took the character of penalties, retaliation, and revenge.

Despite their popular backing, the managers were fearful that there would be defections from the Republican ranks sufficient to prevent the two-thirds majority necessary for conviction. On Monday, May 11, a conference was held, to obtain an indication of how the vote would go, and there it was found that the first article in the arraignment was weak and that the greatest strength might be marshaled to support the managers on Article Eleven. On the following Saturday there was a debate on the order of the vote, and the order proposed by the impeachers was upheld by a vote of 34 to 19, with one senator out of the room at the time. The vote on Article Eleven was taken, with 35 voting guilty, 19 not guilty. By one vote, impeachment had been defeated. There

were still ten other articles, but the outlook was gloomy for the radicals; they needed time. There were motions and countermotions for adjournment, and by a vote of 32 to 21, the Senate adjourned until Tuesday, May 26, at noon.

In the ten-day period between their setback and the next scheduled vote the managers worked desperately to obtain a favorable vote. In the House of Representatives they openly charged that members of the Senate were being bribed to vote in favor of the President, with $30,000 having been offered for the purchase of three votes. Butler made a report of the investigation of this charge to the House on the eve of the next scheduled Senate meeting. His committee had subpoenaed witnesses; here is a report of one interrogation: Representative Benjamin Butler is questioning Thurlow Weed, who claimed to have information on the alleged bribery.

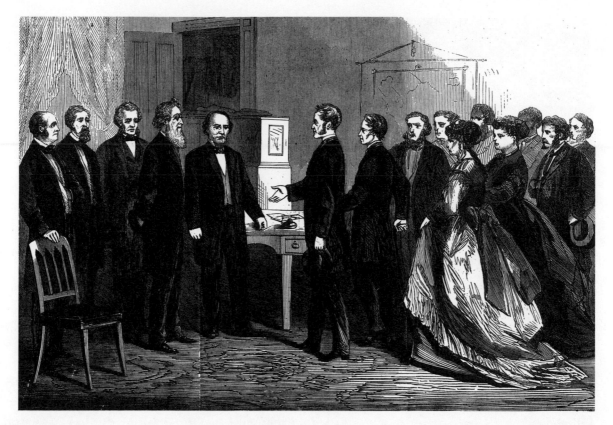

Johnson's supporters rush to congratulate him on the verdict of acquittal by one vote. LIBRARY OF CONGRESS

Q: Who was the man that talked with you about purchasing votes?

A: The subject was often talked about in New York.

Q: By whom to you?

A: I suppose, to answer your question in the spirit it was put, the next conversation I had was with Webster, Woolley, and Shook; they came to my room at the Astor House.

Q: When?

A: I think it was a week after Adams was there.

Q: Shook, Woolley, and Webster?

A: Yes, sir; and my impression is, though I am not very very confident, that that was the first time I ever saw Woolley.

Q: What was there said about it?

A: Substantially what Adams said; it was said that there was a proposition made for votes and for money.

Q: What sum was mentioned?

A: $30,000, I think.

Q: For one vote or more?

A: For three votes. But three names were mentioned that I remember.

But it was to no avail, for even the scandal that hung over the defecting Republicans was not sufficient to save the managers from defeat.

Few have questioned the good fortune of American democracy that seven Republicans deserted their party and voted for the President. Within a year, several of the principal figures were dead: Thaddeus Stevens, perhaps the most dynamic of all the militant Reconstructionists; and two of the seven Republicans who voted with the Democrats. Of the other five dissident Republicans, all went down to defeat at the hands of their voters; they had sacrificed their political futures by voting for acquittal. John

F. Kennedy was later to tell the story of one of these men, Senator Edmund G. Ross, as a "profile in courage."

There remained less than half a year between the failure of impeachment and the elections, and no one seriously considered the President as a candidate for reelection. He was succeeded by Ulysses S. Grant, and this war hero gave the country eight years of inefficiency and corruption often cited by Johnson supporters as evidence of the decline that had set in within the Republican ranks. Andrew Johnson returned to the United States Senate as Senator from Tennessee. The nation was reunited, radical Reconstruction was defeated, and the efforts of the Republicans to impose a Northern rule on the South were liquidated. America had been saved from folly—or had it?

For there is another side to the story. The historians who for decades have been vindicating Johnson were also indicting the Reconstructionists, accusing them of attempting to impose a rule of backwardness and ignorance on the South. The nation went into a period of some eighty or ninety years during which blacks were virtually disenfranchised in the South and shorn of all power in the economic, social, judicial, and political arenas. The gains for which the war had been fought, except for the abolition of chattel slavery, were lost. The South had won the peace, new Black Codes were everywhere triumphant, and the Civil War was clothed in nostalgic glory, while Reconstruction was vilified. For this view of history, Johnson is a hero, Butler a villain.

But a new view of history arose with the resurgence of the civil rights movement in the period following the Second World War. After the historic decision of the Supreme Court of the United States, in the 1954 case of *Brown* v. *Board of Education*, in which separate but equal was banned as social policy, and after the rise of the influence of Dr. Martin Luther King, Jr., the past took on a different hue. Some historians conjectured that the tragic history of the hundred years following Emancipation —the pursuit of democracy abroad while it was virtually unknown for one-tenth of the nation at home—might have been different, had the aims of the 1960s been vigorously pursued in the 1860s. And this might possibly have occurred had the impeachment managers succeeded in obtaining just one more vote. As Kenneth Stampp, an authority on the Civil War, writes, "A program that began with the dream of a new day for the Southern yeomanry terminated with the landlords fashioning a new kind of bondage for their black laborers, and with Johnson their witting or unwitting ally."

Finally, what would have been the effect on the American political structure, and particularly on the office of the presidency if the impeachment attempt had succeeded? Some have contended that the presidency would have been reduced to a puppet office, and the independent executive in the American tripartite checks-and-balances system would have been destroyed. Others have contended that a system closer to the European parliamentary one, in which the head of state who has lost the confidence of his legislators is removed, would have been introduced. American presidents thereafter might have been answerable to Congress, and when the chief executive was no longer carrying out the will of Congress, resignation or removal would have been in order. These issues were being heatedly discussed, and the impeachment trial against Andrew Johnson was being carefully studied, as President Nixon came under increased attack following the revelations of the Watergate scandal in 1973.

Oscar Wilde

1895

In 1895 Oscar Wilde was at the height of a dazzling literary career. His wit had gained him entry into the most restricted literary and political salons of London; his conversation was considered brilliant and without equal, and his comedies were playing to large and enthusiastic audiences. On the Continent as well as in England, Wilde's name was widely known. In fact, Sarah Bernhardt herself was to star in *Salomé*.

But Wilde was not only brilliant; he was ostentatious, conceited, self-centered beyond exaggeration; and if he had many admirers, he was not lacking in enemies. Among the latter was the marquis of Queensberry, eccentric and erratic, who might well have been remembered in history primarily for having his name given to the rules that govern the sport of boxing had he not become even more famous as the adversary and persecutor, though not exactly the prosecutor, of Oscar Wilde.

That a man of Wilde's renown should be the center of a great deal of gossip was not at all unusual. But Wilde seemed to seek the gossip, relish it, and delight in being talked about. Many in Victorian England who heard about Wilde's escapades could not believe their ears. They thought that sexuality between men was extremely rare, something involving the criminal or the demented; little did they realize to what extent such practices were followed by members of all social classes. If rumors concerning Oscar Wilde reached many circles, people were prone to dismiss them more as the pose of an aesthete than as the practice of a playwright.

For the marquis of Queensberry the pose was particularly troubling, for Wilde's companion in his sorties through British society was the marquis's own son, Alfred Douglas, known to Wilde by the affectionate name of Bosie. Between the marquis and his children there was great bitterness that excited London society as it watched denunciations, lawsuits, and even a public fistfight that resulted in an arrest.

Determined to compel Wilde to discontinue the friendship with his son—a determination that may have stemmed as much from anger toward the younger man as toward the older one—the marquis began to harass both of them. He threatened to disown his son completely if the association with the notorious author were not terminated, and when this threat brought no result, he called on Wilde at his home, from which he was thrown out.

On February 14, 1895, Oscar Wilde's greatest success, *The Importance of Being Earnest*, opened at the St. James's Theatre in London. Four days later, the marquis left a card for Wilde at the latter's social club, the Albemarle. The card read, "To Oscar Wilde posing as a somdomite." The

Oscar Wilde. LIBRARY OF CONGRESS

Oscar Wilde and Lord Alfred Douglas.

misspelling has gone down in history, as have the events that followed.

Ten days later, Wilde received the card at his club, and discussed the matter with attorneys and friends. To his attorney he denied any homosexual activity. A few days later, Wilde obtained a warrant for the arrest of the marquis on a charge of criminal libel, and the trial opened at the Old Bailey in London on April 3. After an opening speech had been made on Wilde's behalf, Wilde took the stand and related some facts of his personal and literary life. Cross-examined by Edward Carson, an old schoolmate of his, Wilde held his own on literary matters. He defended the artistry in *The Picture of Dorian Gray*, and was examined on letters he had written to Lord Alfred Douglas.

Q: Is that not an exceptional letter?

Edward Carson, Q.C., M.P., senior counsel for the marquis of Queensberry, who is shown on the right.

A: It is unique, I should say.

Q: Was that the ordinary way in which you carried on your correspondence?

A: No; but I have often written to Lord Alfred Douglas, though I never wrote to another young man in the same way.

Q: Have you often written letters in the same style as this?

A: I don't repeat myself in style.

Q: Here is another letter which I believe you also wrote to Lord Alfred Douglas. Will you read it?

A: No; I decline. I don't see why I should.

Q: Then I will.

Savoy Hotel,
Victoria Embankment, London.

DEAREST OF ALL BOYS,

Your letter was delightful, red and yellow wine to me; but I am sad and out of sorts. Bosie, you must not make scenes with me. They kill me, they wreck the loveliness of life. I cannot see you, so Greek and gracious, distorted with passion. I cannot listen to your curved lips saying hideous things to me. I would sooner—than have you bitter, unjust, hating. . . . I must see you soon. You are the divine thing I want, the thing of grace and beauty; but I don't know how to do it. Shall

I come to Salisbury? My bill here is £49 for a week. I have also got a new sitting-room. . . . Why are you not here, my dear, my wonderful boy? I fear I must leave—no money, no credit, and a heart of lead.

Your own OSCAR

Q: Is that an ordinary letter?
A: Everything I write is extraordinary. I do not pose as being ordinary, great heavens! Ask me any question you like about it.
Q: Is it the kind of letter a man writes to another?
A: It was a tender expression of my great admiration for Lord Alfred Douglas. It was not, like the other, a prose poem.

Wilde's case began to falter, however, when his associations with lower-class youths, and particularly male prostitutes and blackmailers, began to be brought out by the defense. On the stand Wilde seemed more concerned to impress than to win. When the lower-class status of a youth was emphasized to cast suspicion on the relationship he stated, "I recognize no social distinctions at all of any kind, and to me youth, the mere fact of youth, is so wonderful that I would sooner talk to a young man for half-an-hour than be—well, cross-examined in Court."

But his wit served as a trap into which Carson lured him. When asked if he had ever kissed a certain servant of Lord Alfred Douglas, he replied, "Oh, dear, no! He was a peculiarly plain boy. He was, unfortunately, extremely ugly." So that was why he had not kissed him—not because he was a boy, but because he was ugly! Carson hammered away, and Wilde retreated, flustered, in anger. The episode is described by Frank Harris in his well-known biography of Wilde.

"Did you ever kiss him?" he [Carson] asked. Oscar answered carelessly, "Oh, dear, no. He was a peculiarly plain boy. He was, unfortunately, extremely ugly. I pitied him for it."
"Was that the reason why you did not kiss him?"
"Oh, Mr. Carson, you are pertinently insolent."
"Did you say that in support of your statement that you never kissed him?"
"No. It is a childish question."
But Carson was not to be warded off; like a terrier he sprang again and again.
"Why, sir, did you mention that this boy was extremely ugly?"
"For this reason, if I were asked why I did not kiss a door-mat, I should say because I do not like to kiss door-mats."
"Why did you mention his ugliness?"
"It is ridiculous to imagine that any such thing

Sir Edward Clarke, Q.C., M.P., senior counsel for Oscar Wilde at all three trials.

could have occurred under any circumstances."

"Then why did you mention his ugliness, I ask you?"

"Because you insulted me by an insulting question."

"Was that a reason why you should say the boy was ugly?"

(Here the witness began several answers almost inarticulately and finished none of them. His efforts to collect his ideas were not aided by Mr. Carson's sharp staccato repetition: "Why? why? why did you add that?") At last the witness answered:

"You sting me and insult me and at times one says things flippantly."

The case was going poorly for Wilde. His own attorneys were amazed as the evidence accumulated. In reality he had become the defendant, and he sought gracefully to withdraw. Justice Collins called for a directed verdict of not guilty against the marquis, "that it was true in substance and in fact that the prosecutor [Wilde] had 'posed' as a sodomite."

Many of Wilde's friends urged him to flee to France before he was taken into custody, but he refused. There was a delay of several hours before a warrant for his arrest was issued. It seemed as if some authorities wanted to avoid prosecution, but Wilde did not cooperate, and together with a younger man, Alfred Taylor, he was arrested and held without bail. The trial of the two defendants opened on April 26, 1895, and continued until the first of May. There was considerable evidence showing that Wilde had been in hotel rooms with young men. On the witness stand Wilde was strong on literary matters. Asked about a poem by Lord Alfred Douglas entitled "Two Loves," he was particularly examined with regard to the line "I am the Love that dare not speak its name."

Q: Was that poem explained to you?

A: I think that is clear.

Q: Is it not clear that the love described relates to natural love and unnatural love?

A: No.

Q: What is the "Love that dare not speak its name"?

A: "The Love that dare not speak its name" in this century is such a great affection of an elder for a younger man as there was between David and Jonathan, such as Plato made the very basis of his philosophy, and such as you find in the sonnets of Michelangelo and Shakespeare. It is that deep, spiritual affection that is as pure as it is perfect. It dictates and pervades great works of art like those of Shakespeare and Michelangelo, and those two letters of mine, such as they are. It is in this century misunderstood, so much misunderstood that it may be described as the "Love that dare not speak its name," and on account of it I am placed where I am now. It is beautiful, it is fine, it is the noblest form of affection. There is nothing unnatural about it. It is intellectual, and it repeatedly exists between an elder and a younger man, when the elder man has intellect, and the younger man has all the joy, hope and glamour of life before him. That it should be so the world does not understand. The world mocks at it and sometimes puts one in the pillory for it. (Loud applause, mingled with some hisses.)

Mr. Justice Charles: If there is the slightest manifestation of feeling I shall have the Court cleared. There must be complete silence preserved.

The defense made a strong case. They challenged the character of witnesses who were blackmailers, showed inconsistencies in the testimony against Wilde, and called for acquittal. The jury found the defendants not guilty on several counts, but disagreed on a number of others, and Wilde was now to be subjected to still another trial. Bail was applied for and set, and large sums were posted by a Reverend Stewart Headlam, who risked his position in the Church of England, and by Lord Douglas of Hawick, the oldest surviving son of the marquis of Queensberry. Again Wilde was urged to leave the country, but he adamantly refused, and on May 20, 1895, the third trial in the series opened. The trials of Taylor and Wilde were separated, and over the strenuous objection of Wilde's attorneys the Taylor case was heard first. Alfred Taylor was found guilty, and the Wilde verdict was now certain to be guilty.

Again there were the procurers, the blackmailers, the seamy side of London life that the upper classes of England supposedly had little contact with. And again there was cross-examination on Wilde's association with Douglas. After reading a letter written by Wilde to Bosie, the prosecutor examined the defendant.

Q: Why did you choose the words, "My own Boy," as a mode of address?

A: I adopted them because Lord Alfred Douglas is so much younger than myself. The letter was a fantastic, extravagant way of writing to a young man. As I said at the first trial, it does not seem to me to be a question of whether a thing is right or proper, but of literary expression. It was like a little sonnet of Shakespeare.

Q: I did not use the words "proper" or "right." Was it decent?

A: Oh, decent? Of course; there is nothing indecent in it.

Q: Do you think that was a decent way for a man of your age to address a man of his?

A: It was a beautiful way for an artist to address a young man of culture and charm. Decency does not enter into it.

Q: Doesn't it? Do you understand the meaning of the word, sir?

A: Yes.

Q: "It is a marvel that those red rose-leaf lips

Solicitor General Sir Frank Lockwood, Q.C., M.P., who prosecuted the third trial for the crown.

of yours should have been made no less for music of song than for madness of kisses." And do you consider that decent?

A: It was an attempt to write a prose poem in beautiful phraseology.

Q: Did you consider it decent phraseology?

A: Oh, yes, yes.

Q: Then do you consider that a decent mode of addressing a young man?

A: I can only give you the same answer, that it is a literary mode of writing what is intended to be a prose poem.

Q: "Your slim gilt soul walks between passion and poetry . . . Hyacinthus, whom Apollo loved so madly, was you in Greek days." You were speaking of love between men?

A: What I meant by the phrase was that he

was a poet, and Hyacinthus was a poet.

Q: "Always, with undying love"?

A: It was not a sensual love.

On his associations with young men Wilde was less poetic in defense of his actions.

Q: How long had you known Taylor?

A: I met him first in September 1892.

Q: Did you visit him?

A: Yes, I paid visits to his rooms, but I have not been there more than five or six times in my life.

Q: Was there any but male society there?

A: Oh, no; entirely male.

Q: What were their names?

A: I met Mavor and Schwabe there. I only went there to tea parties lasting half an hour or so, and I cannot after a lapse of three years remember whom I met. You ask me to remember whom I met at a tea party three years ago. It is childish. How can I?

Q: Did you meet Charles Hason there?

A: No, I met him at a dinner.

Q: The boys Wood, Mavor, and Parker, what was their occupation?

A: One doesn't ask people such questions at a tea party.

Q: Did Taylor strike you as being a pleasant companion?

A: Yes, I thought him very bright.

Q: Did you know what his occupation was?

A: No; I understood that he had none.

Q: Had any of these young men any occupation?

A: Oh, they were young men—singers—I did not ask.

Q: Did you see anything remarkable in the furnishing of Taylor's rooms?

A: No, nothing.

Q: The windows were curtained?

A: Yes, but not obscured.

Q: Did you know that Taylor's male friends stayed with him and shared his bed?

A: No, I know it now.

Q: Does that alter your opinion of Taylor?

A: No, I don't think so. I don't think it is necessary to conclude that there was anything criminal. It was unusual. I don't believe anything criminal took place between Taylor and these boys; and if they were poor and he shared his bed with them it may have been charity.

Q: Did it shock you that he should have done it?

A: No, I saw no necessity for being shocked.

Q: I must press you. Do you approve of his conduct?

A: I don't think I am called upon to express approval or disapproval of any person's conduct.

Q: Would the knowledge that they habitually shared his bed alter your opinion of Taylor?

A: No.

Q: Did you ever sup alone with any young man at the Savoy Hotel about that time?

A: I could not remember. You are asking me of three years ago. Lord Alfred Douglas may have been with me.

Q: But he would be perfectly well known to the waiters at the Savoy?

A: Oh, yes.

Q: Wherever you are well known, he would be?

A: Oh, I don't know that.

Q: You have stayed together at the Savoy, at the Albemarle, at the Avondale, at St. James's Place, at the Metropole at Brighton, at Cromer, at Goring, at the Albion, at Worthing, and at Torquay?

A: Yes. He has not stayed with me at St. James's Place, but I have lent him my rooms there.

Q: Did Charles Parker ever visit you?

A: He might have visited me seven or eight times at St. James's Place, and on one occasion he dined with me at Kettner's, and we afterwards went to the Pavilion.

Q: When did you last see him?

A: In December last, in the street.

Q: Do you remember a young man named Scarfe?

A: Yes. Taylor brought him to see me. Scarfe

represented himself as a young man who had made money in Australia.

Q: Why was he brought to you?

A: Because many people at that time had great pleasure and interest in seeing me.

Q: Did he call you Oscar?

A: Yes.

Q: At once?

A: I had to ask him to. I have a passion for being called by my Christian name. It pleases me.

Q: Did you give him a cigarette case?

A: Yes.

Q: Has he dined alone with you?

A: Yes.

Q: Do you remember Alphonse Conway?

A: Yes. I met him on the beach at Worthing last year in August. He had an ambition to go to sea.

Q: Of what station in life is he?

A: Of no particular station.

Q: Did he not sell papers on the pier?

A: Oh, never while I was there.

Q: What was his mother?

A: She was a widow, and let lodgings.

Q: Did you buy him a suit?

A: Yes, of blue serge.

Q: And a stick?

A: Yes.

Q: And took him to Brighton?

A: Yes, we had twenty-four hours' trip to Brighton. That was a month afterwards.

Q: What rooms had you at Brighton?

A: Two bedrooms and a sitting room. We slept in adjoining rooms.

The jury was out about three hours. They came in to ask one question, and then retired and brought in their judgment a few minutes later. The verdict was guilty, and the judge pronounced sentence:

Oscar Wilde and Alfred Taylor, the crime of which you have been convicted is so bad that one has to put stern restraint upon one's self to prevent one's self from describing, in language which I would rather not use, the sentiments which must rise to the breast of every man of honor who has heard the details of these two terrible trials. That the jury have arrived at a correct verdict in this case I cannot persuade myself to entertain the shadow of a doubt; and I hope, at all events, that those who sometimes imagine that a judge is half-hearted in the cause of decency and morality because he takes care no prejudice shall enter into the case, may see that that is consistent at least with the utmost sense of indignation at the horrible charges brought home to both of you.

It is no use for me to address you. People who can do these things must be dead to all sense of shame, and one cannot hope to produce any effect upon them. It is the worst case I have ever tried. That you, Taylor, kept a kind of male brothel it is impossible to doubt. And that you, Wilde, have been the centre of a circle of extensive corruption of the most hideous kind among young men, it is equally impossible to doubt.

I shall, under such circumstances, be expected to pass the severest sentence that the law allows. In my judgment it is totally inadequate for such a case as this. The sentence of the Court is that each of you be imprisoned and kept to hard labor for two years.

Oscar Wilde spent two years in jail for acts that had been legally declared criminal only a few years before his arrest. His imprisonment may have made a martyr of him and may have contributed to the clamor that arose some years later for a change in the legal codes with regard to what is termed unnatural sexual relations between consenting adults.

The Wilde case left bitterness among his friends, many of whom felt that he had been abandoned and betrayed by Alfred Douglas. That Wilde held this opinion himself is revealed in many passages in the long letter he wrote in prison, *De Profundis*. Many have contended that, had he not sought to protect Douglas, Wilde would not have been found guilty himself.

Out of his harsh imprisonment there came demands for penal reform. Soon after his release he published *The Ballad of Reading Gaol.* Although it was not published under his name, the authorship was almost public knowledge. In this work, Wilde expressed the sufferings of all prisoners:

I know not whether Laws be right,
  Or whether Laws be wrong;

All that we know who lie in gaol
  Is that the wall is strong:
And that each day is like a year,
  A year whose days are long.

This too I know—and wise it were
  If each could know the same—
That every prison that men build
  Is built with bricks of shame,
And bound with bars lest Christ should see
  How men their brothers maim.

Captain Alfred Dreyfus

1894 and 1899

To the English-speaking world the 1890s are remembered by many as the years of dilettantism and decadence. For France it was an era of turbulence and turmoil, when resentment and hatred of man against man rose to new heights, and when each Frenchman found it necessary to stand up and be counted. To be counted meant to be on one side or the other in a great internal battle that turned lifelong friends into lasting enemies. It was the era of Dreyfus, a man around whom a bitter struggle was raging, for whom trials were held and duels took place. Worldwide demonstrations bespoke the outrage of humanity; some persons were killed and others committed suicide. Through much of this Dreyfus, incarcerated on Devil's Island in the Atlantic, sought to hold on to a semblance of hope and sanity, not even aware of the clamor surrounding his name and exile.

On July 20, 1894, a French army officer by the name of Marie Charles Ferdinand Walsin-Esterhazy (or just Esterhazy, as he came to be known) offered to sell documents and military secrets to the German military attaché in Paris, Lieutenant Colonel Max von Schwartzkoppen. At first repulsed by the German officer, Esterhazy was insistent, and in Germany, Schwartzkoppen's superiors displayed interest. Some time later in the summer, Esterhazy left a note for Schwartzkoppen in the latter's mailbox. This note

never reached its expected destination because a French agent stole it and delivered it to counterespionage officials of the French military. Written in ink, and unsigned, it mentioned a list of items of varying interest that the writer would be delivering to Schwartzkoppen during the coming months. The note (which has gone down in history as the *bordereau*, usually translated as the memorandum, schedule, or list) received considerable attention when examined by the French, for it meant that there was a traitor in the ranks. The writer promised an artillery manual and spoke of going off to maneuvers. Obviously, this was a soldier who was writing; an officer, possibly a high one.

Thus the bordereau arrived in the hands of the French. To conceal that it had been stolen from a mailbox, it was torn into bits and then was put together again. Ordinarily, an intercepted letter of this nature might have gone to Lieutenant Colonel Hubert Henry, a friend of Esterhazy and a man who, some historians conjecture, might have been a German agent as well, or perhaps a double agent. But Henry was on leave. Had he been in Paris and seen the bordereau, he might have recognized the handwriting, and history would have been different. In Henry's absence, Colonel Sandherr received the item.

It was not the first indication that the French had had of treason in the army. A message to Schwartzkoppen from his Italian counterpart, the military attaché to Paris, Lieutenant Colonel Panizzardi, had been intercepted. It spoke of maps and referred to a scoundrel by the initial D.

French officers ran to their files and examined the names of personnel starting with the letter D. At last they came to Dreyfus, and there they felt they had their man. The haughty, cold, pretentious Dreyfus, the Jew whose people recognized no national boundaries and loyalties and who, motivated only by an avaricious struggle for wealth, so these officers felt, knew neither patriotism nor ethics.

Now there was the question of verifying the identity of the culprit by comparing the handwriting. The task was assigned to a major, Marquis Du Paty de Clam, who was equivocal. He called in an expert from the Banque de France who was equally unsure. The famed Bertillon was consulted and in all likelihood forewarned that identification was desirable. Bertillon saw what he was asked to see: that the bordereau and the specimens from the Dreyfus file were in the same handwriting. During the investigation, Lieutenant Colonel Henry returned from his leave and, apprised of the situation, immediately ordered that Dreyfus be arrested, but without any publicity.

Summoned to appear at headquarters on Monday, October 15, 1894, in civilian clothes, Alfred Dreyfus came and was greeted by Du Paty, who showed him a bandaged thumb, and asked him to write a letter that would be dictated. He started to dictate from the bordereau, and Dreyfus wrote. At one point Du Paty demanded to know why Dreyfus was trembling, and as Dreyfus calmly explained that he was cold, Du Paty became enraged. It was easy to see the similarities between the present writing of Dreyfus and the bordereau, and it was

Colonel Du Paty de Clam dictates a test letter to Captain Alfred Dreyfus in which he intersperses parts of the bordereau.

apparent that the calm was but a façade that not only concealed the guilt, but even demonstrated it. Finally, Du Paty shouted to Dreyfus that he was under arrest for treason. Dreyfus looked bewildered and protested his innocence. At this point Du Paty offered Dreyfus a gun, but the accused declined to commit suicide, and said that he would live to prove his innocence and vindicate his honor.

At the War Department, General Auguste Mercier, the minister of war, recognized that the case against Dreyfus was shaky. Some of the information in the bordereau would not normally come into the hands of an officer like Dreyfus, and he was not at the time scheduled to go off on maneuvers. The case must rest on two matters: a confession or unassailable handwriting identification. But, with all the pressure and threats, a confession was not forthcoming. And the handwriting experts were confused, divided among themselves, and quite unconvincing. It looked as if the wrong man was in jail, and it was best to rectify the error before the matter became public and the army became the recipient of unfavorable press.

It was a period of widespread and virulent anti-Semitism in France, with no newspaper more violently anti-Jewish than *La Libre Parole*. So it was natural that Lieutenant Colonel Henry, fearful that his friend Esterhazy might be apprehended as the true author of the bordereau, leaked the information to *La Libre Parole* that the Jew Dreyfus was being held as a traitor and that some people in the War Department, probably paid off by a syndicate of international Jewry, were preparing to let the traitor go free. General Mercier read *La Libre Parole* of November 1, and immediately realized that if Dreyfus were freed his position as minister of war would be in jeopardy. Worse, the government itself might topple.

Mathieu Dreyfus, brother of the accused, apprised of the fate of Alfred, had at once rushed to his aid. He begged Charles Demange, venerable and prestigious attorney, to become Dreyfus's counsel. Demange consented—provided that after interviewing the prisoner he was convinced of his innocence. The interview took place in prison, and Demange, convinced that the evidence was so paltry that no court could convict, readily agreed to become Dreyfus's attorney. Demange, as much as Dreyfus, had confidence in the integrity of the military, and neither could believe that prejudice would overcome reason.

The court-martial of Captain Alfred Drey-fus opened in a great hall near the prison in Paris, on Wednesday, December 19, 1894.

It could be said that the Dreyfus case was lost in the first round, when the court voted to hold its session *in camera*. The public and press were barred. Only the seven military judges, the attorneys for the prosecution, attorneys for the defense, and the accused were present, together with any witness who happened to be testifying at a particular time. Such Star Chamber proceedings, so long held in disrepute in France as well as in other Western countries, could now be revived because of the military nature of the trial and the claims, entirely unfounded, that top-secret questions of national interest were involved.

At first Demange and Mathieu Dreyfus saw in the trial nothing more than errors of experts in conflict. True, Demange stated that, if Dreyfus were not a Jew, he would not have been arrested. By the second day of the trial the utter emptiness of the case against Dreyfus was becoming apparent. Henry testified with vehemence for the prosecution. He stated that as far back as the month of March an honorable person—absolutely honorable—had notified the service that an officer was committing treason. Then in June the same person named the officer. "And this traitor," he shouted, "there he is!" Dreyfus jumped to his feet and demanded to know the name of the anonymous accuser. With a theatrical gesture Henry tapped his cap and said, "There are secrets in an officer's head that even his cap must not know." He would not have to name the officer, but merely swear on his honor that he had told the truth. With dignity he assured the court, "I so swear!"

Then came the handwriting experts. Bertillon came on the third day of the trial and spoke for three hours. He drew figures and made gestures, baffling everyone in the court.

Found guilty, Dreyfus suffers a humiliating degradation following conviction.

He even repudiated the burgeoning science of handwriting analysis and compared it with astrology.

Within the court the sentiment seemed to favor the accused, and at the War Department there was fear that the government would fall with acquittal. Some suggested that a compromise be reached, that the guilt be declared as not proven, but others were not to be deterred from their objective. During the trial, Du Paty approached the presiding judge, Colonel Maurel, and handed him a sealed envelope. Du Paty claimed to have no knowledge of the contents; he simply said that there was another envelope inside, that

he had been given this by a cabinet member and that the contents should be made known to the judge of the court. There is a dispute as to whether this was the only such secret envelope given to Maurel during the trial. In this envelope, which came to be known as the secret file or *dossier secret*, were forgeries, irrelevancies, and hearsay, all implicating Dreyfus in this and other acts of treason. These, of course, were not unsealed and read in open court.

For three hours Demange summed up. There was nothing to the trial, he declared, but the bordereau, which Dreyfus could not have written because it contained information unknown to him. The prosecution denied that it was its responsibility to offer a motive, contending that the similarity of handwriting was enough to condemn Dreyfus. The prisoner emphatically protested his innocence, and the judges retired to their chambers. There, unknown to the defense and in violation of French law, they opened the secret envelope and read the contents. The deliberations lasted one hour; the verdict was unanimous. Guilty. The judgment was read in open court. Only the defendant, in accordance with French military law, was absent. Demange sobbed.

Two weeks later the dreaded degradation took place. Alfred Dreyfus was publicly stripped of his uniform and compelled to walk the gauntlet of his former comrades, as they spat their condemnation on him. Shortly thereafter he was placed on a ship that took him to years of imprisonment on Devil's Island.

In the summer of 1895, some months after the exiling of Dreyfus, a new head of the intelligence bureau of the General Staff was named, Lieutenant Colonel George Picquart. By the following summer Picquart became convinced that an innocent man

Dreyfus was imprisoned at Devil's Island. His hut, surrounded by a barricade, is on the top of the center island.

had been condemned, and brought the matter to the attention of his superiors, only to be told that the case was closed. Although Picquart vowed that he would not carry to his grave the message of Dreyfus's innocence, it did appear that the prisoner on Devil's Island was on the road to becoming a forgotten man.

Mathieu Dreyfus was desperately trying to reopen the case and to discover new evidence that would definitely establish his brother's innocence. Mathieu despaired lest the matter be shrouded in silence. The break Mathieu was hoping for came when *Le Matin*, a liberal Parisian newspaper, obtained a copy of the bordereau and on November 10, 1896, printed it for the first time. The entire case had rested on a supposed similarity of handwriting, and now it was clear for all to see that Alfred Dreyfus, in spite of the so-called expert handwriting analyst, could not have written the incriminating note. Who, then, was the author?

While almost one year was to pass before Mathieu learned the identity of Esterhazy and the part he played in the case, neither did he realize that Picquart was becoming the center of attention in the affair. Just a few days before the publication of the bordereau, Picquart was sent on a mission far from Paris, so that he would be out of the way. With Picquart removed, Colonel Henry was free to continue to rearrange papers, make forgeries, and cover the trial that might lead to Esterhazy, Du Paty, and himself, and even to attempt to prepare a case against Picquart.

Why Picquart, after one year of struggle with his conscience, finally decided to reveal his evidence is not clear. It is said that he fell from a horse and had a foreboding of death. In April 1897 he prepared a memorandum to be handed to the President of France upon his death, in which all that he knew about Dreyfus was revealed. In June he confided his information to an attorney and friend, Louis Leblois, particularly citing a picture postcard in Esterhazy's handwriting, known as the *petit bleu*, which he had obtained and which resembled the bordereau. Leblois in turn revealed the information to the vice-president of the French Senate and one of the most influential men in the nation's political life, Auguste Scheurer-Kestner. With the espousal of the cause of Dreyfus by Scheurer-Kestner, the Revisionists (as the Dreyfusards came to be known) won their most influential ally thus far.

In November 1897 Mathieu learned the name of the author of the bordereau. With evidence in hand, he went with Demange to the War Department, but to no avail. Rebuffed everywhere, Mathieu made public statements accusing Esterhazy of writing the bordereau, in an effort to goad him into a libel suit. When this failed, he printed and distributed two thousand copies of a pamphlet in which he named Esterhazy as the traitor. A new wave of agitation over the case began to rise. The anti-Semitic press eagerly awaited Esterhazy's answer. Faced with increasing evidence that Esterhazy was the author of the bordereau, the War Department was finally forced to order his arrest. The War Department, however, insisted that the arrest had nothing to do with the Dreyfus case, that Esterhazy was being tried on an entirely different charge of passing on secrets. Dreyfus's guilt had long ago been established, not only on the basis of the handwriting in the bordereau, but also on a great deal of other information: a mysterious confession that could neither be confirmed nor discounted, and other data so secret that national security was involved and hence disclosure was impossible.

The trial of Major Esterhazy on January 29, 1889.

In this confused atmosphere, Esterhazy was given a two-day trial in January 1898. Amid wild charges from the Anti-Semitic League to the effect that the Jewish syndicate was spending millions to bribe the judges, the latter brought in a verdict of not guilty. Esterhazy was exonerated.

By now, however, many Frenchmen began to have serious doubts as to the guilt of Dreyfus. Elsewhere in the world the name of Dreyfus was becoming increasingly known, particularly among intellectuals, professors, writers, musicians, and others. Friendships were broken over the affair, never to be mended. Oscar Wilde, himself just out of prison and living in Paris under an assumed name, befriended Esterhazy. The youthful André Gide became a Dreyfusard, as did Marcel Proust. Wherever the intellectuals went, and particularly in the literary salons, the subject of Dreyfus dominated, and the debates became acrimonious until camps were so clearly divided that paths seldom crossed. Those who had not yet been drawn into the struggle were not long in taking sides. Among such people were France's leading Socialist, Jean Jaurès; a journalist and politician already known as The Tiger, Georges Clemenceau; and the acknowledged dean of French writers, prolific novelist, and world-famous member of the Academy, Émile Zola. On the morning of January 13, 1898, only two days after the acquittal of Esterhazy, there appeared in *L'Aurore*, in blazing black letters across the front page, what has probably become the most famous headline in the history of journalism: J'ACCUSE. Within minutes the entire edition had been sold out. The most damning indictment of French injustice had appeared in print.

The trap that the Revisionists had set for their enemies was obvious, and *La Libre Parole* urged the War Department not to become the victim by abetting Zola's wish to be arrested in order to cause the Dreyfus case to be reopened. After all, who was Zola? He was not even a Frenchman, they asserted, but a man born of an Italian father who still carried the foreign name; he was not a fine writer, this member of the Academy, but a cheap pornographer who portrayed all that was lowly in human life. But the clamor for a reply to Zola was too loud, his friends and enemies too numerous,

On January 13, 1898, "L'Aurore" prints Zola's indictment of all those involved in convicting Dreyfus.

and the eyes of the world now too clearly focused on the next episode in the Dreyfus drama for this to be ignored.

The problem was how Zola could be arrested and charged with libel, without the entire Dreyfus case being reopened in court. The answer found by the government was that the libel charge would be based on the few words in *J'Accuse* where Zola charged the ministry of war with ordering the judges to acquit Esterhazy. All the rest would be ignored in the case. Consequently, Zola and the editor of *L'Aurore*, A. Perrenx, were arrested.

The Zola trial lasted for little more than two weeks. For all the effort to exclude any mention of Dreyfus, for all the interruptions by the judge whenever the leading character's name was even whispered, the man on Devil's Island dominated the proceedings. At the height of the proceedings Zola himself addressed the jury, and none could silence him as he thundered the name of Alfred Dreyfus.

By my forty years of work, by the respect earned by the work of my life, I swear that Dreyfus is innocent. By all I have gained, by the name I have made, and my contribution to the growth of French literature, I swear that Dreyfus is innocent. May all of this perish, my work fail, if Dreyfus is not innocent. He is innocent!

Anatole France came to testify for Zola, and army generals came to testify against him. When a general swore to the existence of documentary proof against Dreyfus, the defense demanded that the documents be produced in court, but instead of producing the documents, the prosecution brought another general to confirm the words of the previous one.

The trial resulted in an eight-to-four verdict (a French jury can convict by a major-

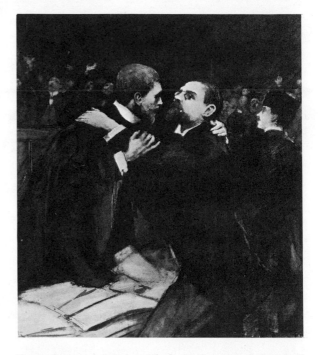

Brought to trial for libel, Zola was defended by Maître Labori.

ity) against Zola, who was thus found guilty of libel. Sentenced to jail and fined as well, he decided to go to England, from where he would direct his appeal. In such voluntary exile, he continued to arouse his countrymen to the wrong they had committed against an innocent man. His efforts were not in vain. It was now widely surmised that Esterhazy had written the bordereau.

In June 1899 a new minister of war, Eugène Cavaignac, took office. He made a careful study of the entire matter, and early in July, feeling he had conclusive proof of the guilt of Dreyfus, presented his conclusions to the deputies. For the first time he disclosed the details of the correspondence between Schwartzkoppen and Panizzardi, including a document that actually named Dreyfus. His case against Dreyfus was forceful and convincing, and to the documentation Cavaignac added the alleged fact that Dreyfus had confessed. When a vote was taken, the chamber was unanimous in support of Cavaignac, with fifteen Socialist members abstaining. The Dreyfus supporters were crushed. Not since the first days of the movement was the outlook so bleak for Revision. So elated was the government with the Cavaignac statement that it was ordered to be posted on bulletin boards in every city, town, and hamlet of France.

As Zola had risen to the occasion a year earlier, now rose Col. Picquart. He addressed an open letter to the premier in which he referred to the three documents mentioned by the minister of war; two were dated 1894, and had no bearing on the Dreyfus case; and the third was a forgery! Before the posters arrived in the French towns, Cavaignac felt humiliated and betrayed, and Esterhazy and Picquart were both ordered arrested, the former for treason, the latter for revelation of secret army documents. Cavaignac assigned a subordinate, one Cuignet, to re-examine the documents, and Cuignet revealed that the Panizzardi document consisted of two sheets of paper glued together to appear as if they were one. It was clear that the shabby forger was Colonel Hubert Henry, who in turn was immediately arrested.

On the night of Henry's arrest, Joseph Reinach, one of the most indefatigable Dreyfusards and the man who was later to produce a remarkable seven-volume account of the case, predicted to Demange that on the next day they would read of Henry's suicide. The prophecy was fulfilled. All that remained now was for a new trial of Dreyfus to be ordered, and this was not long in coming. The trial was scheduled for the little-known town of Rennes.

Dreyfus, in overcoat and hat, lands at Port Haliguen in July 1889 for a second trial.

In the Chamber of Deputies the followers of Dreyfus were furious. If the judges at the first Dreyfus trial had illegally received evidence, and if there had been forgeries, then the man responsible for this should be arrested. He was General Mercier, who had been minister of war in 1894.

Now it was Mercier versus Dreyfus, the honor of the army against the life of the Jew. Mercier let it be known that he would be present at Rennes, and there he would make available incontrovertible evidence against Dreyfus.

At six o'clock on the morning of August 7, 1899, just five weeks after Dreyfus's arrival from Devil's Island, the trial opened, and a sergeant led the accused into court. Alfred Dreyfus entered in the uniform to which he had been restored. As he entered there was a gasp from his family, his friends, and those who remembered him. Five terrible years had taken their toll. Barely forty years old, Dreyfus was gray, emaciated, aged. Only with the greatest effort could he stand erect in the military style in which he had been trained. Yet he walked in with hardly a show of emotion, saluted, and took the seat to which he was led.

For many of the great figures—Republicans, Socialists, Revisionists, writers, scientists, poets—the man who walked into the court was not only a pitiable figure, but a great disappointment. Despite himself, he had become their hero, not for any heroic qualities, but because of the events surrounding him. He was hardly aware of the furor over his name, and certainly had no grasp of the great social forces that revolved around it.

Appointed public prosecutor for the Rennes trial was one Carrière, but behind him stood General Mercier, who at times conducted the case as if he were in Carrière's role. Whereas both Carrière and Mercier were treated with courtesy by the judge, not only Dreyfus but Demange and Labori, his counsel, were handled curtly and rudely. The battle lines were drawn. Only two major figures were absent: Henry, who was dead, and Esterhazy, safe in England.

Zola came from exile across the Channel, confident that France was safe for him; and Picquart, who had spent almost eleven months in jail, was released (never to be tried, in fact) and came to the trial first as observer, then later as witness.

Again, as in 1894, Mercier demanded that the trial be held behind closed doors; again, the defense objected, but not with the strenuous protest that might have proved successful. Mercier hinted that documents so secret and explosive would be revealed that, if they were to be seen in open court, the country would be endangered. So again the public was excluded.

Inside the courtroom, one Colonel Chamoin, who had been selected to represent two cabinet members (the ministers of foreign affairs and of war), was caught by Labori as he sought to slip some new sheets into the secret file that was being presented to the judges. The colonel apologized, and explained that that morning, on the way to court, he had by chance met General Mercier, and the latter had asked him to kindly take along the extra papers so that the files would be more complete! There was a demand made on the premier that Chamoin be arrested; but the premier was at that point anxious to keep his coalition government intact.

There were almost a hundred witnesses at the Rennes trial, of whom about a score came for the defense. There were handwriting experts and army colleagues of the accused, but all were overshadowed by a single figure: Mercier. Arrogantly, he unraveled a case against Dreyfus, repeating some old material,

Dreyfus dramatically reasserts, "I am innocent!" at his second court-martial.

creating some new, offering opinion, hearsay, and crafty hints that there was more. Now Labori hammered away at the role of Mercier in the first trial and particularly at the secret documents, and the deliberate violation of the law by the general. The position of Mercier became more uncomfortable and untenable under cross-examination. The general again insisted that Dreyfus had written the bordereau; as for Esterhazy's confession, well, Esterhazy had lied. Mercier wiggled out of every corner.

Thus the trial continued for the first week. On August 14, Labori and Picquart were walking toward the court when the attorney was shot. While the would-be assassin escaped, another man, presumably an accomplice, grabbed the fallen attorney's briefcase. One can only conjecture that someone believed that the briefcase contained material that would incriminate Labori or Dreyfus, or at least that the Dreyfus defense would collapse with the disappearance of Labori and his briefcase. Rumor had it that the attorney had been killed; but the wound was not a grave one, and the enemies of Dreyfus were soon charging that the attempted assassination was all a frame-up, that the syndicate had shot Labori to arouse sympathy for the Jewish defendant, and to solve the problem of dissension within the ranks of the defense.

The trial lasted for more than a month. The world expected a verdict of not guilty, perhaps worded in such a way as to save face for the military; the verdict might read, for example, not proven. The defense expected exoneration, of Dreyfus and Demange because they had not lost faith in the integrity of the army; of Labori because of worldwide pressures. But verdicts are often dictated by political considerations rather than evidence. Again Dreyfus was found guilty of treason, this time by a vote of five to two.

Dreyfus is reunited with his wife and children at Carpentras.

The verdict, however, stated that there were extenuating circumstances, and the accused was sentenced to ten years.

France and her military became the object of a campaign of ridicule. Who had ever heard of extenuating circumstances for treason by a high military officer? Meanwhile, the defendant faced the terrible prospect of five more years of imprisonment.

The French government had one paramount wish at this time in the Dreyfus case: to put it to an end and bury it quietly. Ten days after the conclusion of the trial at Rennes, Dreyfus was pardoned. That day the elderly Dreyfusard, Senator Scheurer-Kestner, died. The following year, after bitter debate within the ranks of the Dreyfusards, the government issued a general amnesty covering all pending cases relating to the affair. Some urged that the central figure reject the amnesty, and insist on another trial and exoneration. Others said that he had already suffered sufficiently. Picquart was especially embittered by the amnesty, and the relationship between the former convict from Devil's Island and the one man in the army who had stood by him deteriorated.

In 1903, amid a greater calm, the ministry of justice unanimously accepted the request for an appeal of the Rennes verdict, but it was not until the summer of 1906 that the judgment of Rennes was set aside and the innocence of Dreyfus officially proclaimed. History was being replayed, but with a different script; and the degradation of 1895 became the restoration of 1906. On July 13 of that year, Dreyfus and Picquart were restored to the French army and elevated to the ranks of major and brigadier general, respectively. One week later, to a wildly cheering crowd estimated at two hundred thousand, Dreyfus was made a Chevalier of the French Legion of Honor. Even greater honor awaited Picquart, who was soon to become minister of war in the cabinet of that old Dreyfusard, Georges Clemenceau.

When war broke out between Germany and France in 1914, Alfred Dreyfus went on active duty. And among the many children of France who died in that war were the son and the son-in-law of Mathieu Dreyfus, and the son of Hubert Henry.

History has many lessons, and one that stands out in this tragedy is the danger that arises when a court, a nation, a military, a leader of a country, cannot admit an error but proceeds to compound it. When the question was posed—Dreyfus or the military? —and when many stated that even if the former were innocent, he must be condemned because the honor of the army and of France was at stake, then all ethical considerations were lost.

Edith Cavell

1915

LONDON IS FILLED WITH MONUMENTS TO many British heroes, but few figures emerge in stone as dignified as the sculpture of Edith Cavell. There she stands, near Trafalgar Square, a majestic woman, with her long flowing robes accentuating the erect and dignified body, inspiring awe in the viewer. Above her head is chiseled one word: Humanity. Below her name the inscription reads "Brussels," followed by the date, "Dawn October 12th, 1915," and a brief statement. "Patriotism is not enough. I must have no hatred or bitterness for anyone." If the spirit of Edith Cavell is captured in these words, the same cannot be said for those who tried and executed her and for those who used her execution to arouse the hatred and bitterness that she denounced.

Born in England in 1865, Edith Cavell was trained in nursing and became dedicated to the alleviation of human suffering. In the early years of the twentieth century she settled in Brussels, where she became director of an institution that has been described as a hospital, a home for invalids, and an institute for surgery. In August 1914, with the outbreak of the First World War, she remained in Brussels, which soon fell to the advancing German army. Orders were posted by the occupying authorities demanding that all French and British soldiers be reported to the Germans. False identification cards and passports, however, were easily obtain-

ABLE, MAKING IT SIMPLE FOR AN UNDER-ground system to be established to help those who wished to escape. Edith Cavell took an active part in setting up such a system, and her nursing home at 149 rue de la Culture became a beehive of activity.

On August 5, 1915, occupation authorities, having been tipped off, raided the nursing home. A letter incriminating the American consul in Brussels was found, and Miss Cavell and her chief assistant, Miss Wilkins, were arrested. After interrogation Miss Wilkins was released, but Edith Cavell was taken to prison.

Held for several weeks in her cell, during which time she was reported to have made a full statement of her activities, Miss Cavell was finally brought to trial on Thursday, October 7, 1915. There were thirty-four other defendants accused of various activities declared illegal under the Occupation. Thirty-one were Belgian, three French, one, Edith Cavell, English. All were to be tried by a German military court headed by a lieutenant colonel and containing two captains and two lower officers. Five members of the Belgian bar appeared for the prisoners.

Miss Cavell sat through the entire proceedings stoically and impassively. There could be no defense for her, for her confession spelled out her guilt in unmistakable terms.

I acknowledge that between November 1914,

and July 1915, I have received into my house, cared for, and provided with funds to help them to reach the front and join the Allied army:

1. French and English soldiers in civilian clothes, separated from the ranks, amongst whom was an English colonel.
2. The barrister, Libiez, of Mons.
3. Prince Reginald of Croy, and one Mlle. Martin, who is one and the same person as the accused Thuliez, with whom I have just been confronted.

A lieutenant in the German army testified that "the woman Cavell managed the headquarters in Brussels" of an organized effort to assist prisoners to reach Holland. A schoolboy was brought in to give evidence against his own mother. And then the trial adjourned until the following day.

On October 8 the recommendations of the prosecutor were made. "All this activity," he stated, "is akin to high treason and the law punishes it with the death sentence." Thus, he asked for death for the British nurse and four others, and for varying prison sentences for the remaining defendants. Of the British nurse, he charged that

Miss Cavell acknowledges that she received into her house between November 1914 and July 1915, French and English derelict soldiers in civilian clothes, amongst whom was an English colonel, and in addition Belgian and French men of military age wishing to reach the front, that she had cared for them and provided them with funds in order to facilitate their journey to the front and their entrance into the ranks of the Allies. She admits in addition, that she escorted most of the men who were brought to her at Brussels to certain spots previously arranged, to hand them over to guides known to her, who were waiting for her. She confesses also that she received news of the safe arrival in Holland of several of these men whom she had in this way conveyed into

Miss Edith Cavell. WIDE WORLD PHOTOS

Holland. She is to be included amongst the chief organisers.

The lawyers for Edith Cavell made a last-minute plea, stating that she was dedicated to but one purpose in life: to help others. She thought that the soldiers would have been killed had they been apprehended in Brussels, and she wished only to save their lives. Was this not the culmination of her entire life-work? In fact, she had helped

German soldiers in her lifetime, just as she had helped others. And now there was no proof that those she had aided had ever borne arms against Germany.

Asked by the court if she had anything to say, Miss Cavell answered, "Nothing."

Held over the weekend awaiting the sentencing, the prisoners were informed of the verdict on Monday, October 11. In late afternoon of that day the prisoners were brought before the court, and there they heard that "the tribunal is of the opinion, partly on the strength of their own statements, and partly on the strength of the assertions of their fellow prisoners, that the following are the chief organizers" . . . and here were read the names of those sentenced to death, among them Edith Cavell. Eight of the accused were acquitted; the rest drew sentences up to fifteen years.

That night there was feverish, if somewhat inept, activity on the part of the American ambassador, Brand Whitlock, to gain reprieve or clemency for Miss Cavell, but without success. Her fellow prisoners urged her to ask for mercy, but she refused. Before dawn the next morning, two of the prisoners, Philippe Baucq, a Belgian architect, and Edith Cavell, were executed by a firing squad.

When news of the execution reached her homeland, anger against the Germans rose to new levels, and enlistments of volunteers increased considerably. The bishop of London called her death "the greatest crime in history," and American newspapers used it to fan the flames of the war spirit.

Following the end of the war, her body was brought to London, where she was given the burial of a war hero. Her courage and bravery, her refusal to ask for mercy, and her indomitable spirit became part of the myth that grew up around the name of Edith Cavell in the years that followed. Her name was put to many uses; often her followers recall her alleged last words (as reprinted in an eight-column headline by the *New York Herald*), "Happy to die for my country," and they forget the words chiseled on her memorial, "Patriotism is not enough."

Nicola Sacco and Bartolomeo Vanzetti

1921

On April 15, 1920, in the little township of South Braintree, Massachusetts, two employees of a shoe factory were murdered and a payroll of slightly more than $15,000 seized by the escaping bandits. It was a perfectly planned crime, having all the earmarks of professional gangsters. It left in its wake two dead men, Frederick A. Parmenter and Alessandro Berardelli. Seven years later, Nicola Sacco and Bartolomeo Vanzetti were legally put to death by the Commonwealth of Massachusetts, having been found guilty of the double murder. Aside from these few facts, however, the partisans of the accused and their opponents agree on few points in a case that aroused millions of people to a pitch of anger that no criminal trial—not even that of Dreyfus—has before or since.

Nicola Sacco and Bartolomeo Vanzetti were Italian-born anarchists who had come to the United States where they had continued their radical agitation, particularly among the Italian colony in eastern Massachusetts. In 1917, faced with universal conscription in a war they opposed, they went to Mexico, an act that was to stigmatize them later as slackers and draft dodgers.

On May 3, 1920, a close friend of both Sacco and Vanzetti, a compatriot named Andrea Salsedo, who was being held for deportation, met his death. In the language of the coroners, he "jumped or fell" from the fourteenth floor of his place of detention in New York City, plunging to death on the concrete pavement below. To the minds of many of his grieving comrades, he "jumped, fell, or was hurled." The death of Salsedo added to the fear surrounding the Italian community, particularly its radical wing.

On May 5 Sacco and Vanzetti, together with two friends, went to pick up a car in a repair shop and were arrested on a streetcar returning to their homes. At the time of their arrest they were both carrying guns, and there is disputed testimony as to whether Vanzetti made an effort to reach for his. Taken into a police station and questioned, they behaved suspiciously, and told many lies concerning their own and their friends' whereabouts on various occasions. Their behavior under arrest became a major point of controversy. It added up, the prosecution contended, to a consciousness of guilt, and thus provided circumstantial evidence against them. To the defense, it emphasized that they had not been notified of the nature of the charges, that they thought they were being held as part of the anti-radical campaign, and that they were merely trying to protect themselves and their friends from deportation or worse.

Soon they were charged with two crimes: an unsuccessful holdup in Bridgewater, Massachusetts, on Christmas Eve, 1919, and the murder of Parmenter and Berardelli on April 15 in South Braintree. However, Sacco

"Vanzetti and Sacco and Their Guards," by Ben Shahn (gouache, 1932). Downtown Gallery, Collection of Patricia M. Healy

produced such an incontrovertible alibi for the Bridgewater occasion that the charge against him was dropped. At this point the entire Bridgewater case might have faded into insignificance were it not that Vanzetti was being tried on this charge before the murder case was tried. On the matter of which of two charges a man is to be tried on first, the laws and customs are contradictory. Unless there are matters of availability of witnesses, competing venues, and the like, a defendant usually has the right to be tried on the more serious charge first, so that he does not come before the court in a murder case, for example, already stigmatized as a convicted criminal in a robbery case. The defenders of Sacco and Vanzetti charged that the prosecution reversed this procedure because the evidence against Vanzetti in the

murder case was weaker than that against Sacco (this is conceded almost universally), and in this way Sacco would be burdened by association with a convicted criminal, and Vanzetti by association with Sacco (who would be identified by numerous witnesses).

The first trial opened at Plymouth before Judge Webster Thayer and lasted little more than a week, during which time Vanzetti did not take the stand in his own defense. Although juries are repeatedly warned that this is not to be interpreted as a sign of guilt, it is felt by many that such warnings are of little avail. The most important single fact about the trial, with its guilty verdict and a sentence of twelve to fifteen years, is that almost immediately after its conclusion Vanzetti charged that he had been double-crossed by his own lawyer. He claimed that John P. Vahey had sold him out to the prosecutor, Frederick Katzmann, and that it was on Vahey's insistence and advice that he had failed to take the stand to deny any connection with the crime. This is a serious charge of a defendant against an attorney, and against Vahey there is one important piece of circumstantial evidence: soon after the trial he went into law practice as a partner of his opponent, Katzmann.

On September 11, Sacco and Vanzetti were indicted for the South Braintree killings, and on May 31, 1921, their trial opened in Dedham, before the same Judge Webster Thayer who had presided over the Plymouth trial and had already given Vanzetti, a first offender, the unheard-of sentence of twelve to fifteen years for the attempted holdup in Bridgewater.

The murder trial itself took more than six weeks. The transcript runs to thousands of pages, supplemented by more thousands of pages of hearings, reports, and documents. At Dedham the prosecution's case rested on several points.

1. Eyewitnesses who claimed to have seen Sacco in South Braintree on the morning before the crime, at the scene of the crime, and leaving it.
2. A gun found in Sacco's possession which was said to have been Berardelli's gun, and which he presumably picked up at the time of the murder.
3. At least one shell taken from the body of Parmenter, which was said by ballistics experts to have been fired from the gun in Sacco's possession.
4. Sacco's absence from work on the day of the crime.
5. The resemblance between the automobile belonging to Sacco's friends, which he occasionally borrowed, and the murder car, found abandoned in the woods near the scene of the crime.
6. The behavior of the defendants at the time of their arrest and interrogation.

Against this, the defendants offered

1. Evidence that many of the eyewitnesses could not have seen the crime, that they had given contradictory information at various times in the investigation, and that their identification of Sacco took place in a prison, without a lineup, and with no one else there.
2. Testimony from people who had seen Vanzetti at various times of the day on April 15, far from the scene of the murder.
3. Testimony from many people who had seen Sacco in Boston at the time of the crime.
4. Explanation of the behavior of the defendants in terms of their fear of deportation and their memory of the Salsedo affair.

Courthouse at Dedham, Massachusetts. DEDHAM HISTORICAL SOCIETY

5. The vehement denials on the stand of the defendants themselves.

It is difficult to read the testimony without being convinced that both sides were trying to sway witnesses, and to use various inducements to have these witnesses change their stories. Both sides were deliberately suppressing information damaging to their case (such suppression is in American law a much more serious charge against a prosecutor than against a defense attorney); and seldom has there been such an array of unreliable men and women who not only contradicted one another but also, in innumerable instances, contradicted themselves and told unbelievable stories. A few highlights will give some idea of what went on in the courtroom.

Lola Andrews was a woman with a doubtful reputation. She changed her story many times during the course of the trial, retracted her entire testimony, then retracted her retraction. She was confronted with pictures that the defense attorneys had shown her during pretrial examination, and she simply denied that she had seen them. Confronted with the stenographic record, she denied that she had said what the transcript stated.

CROSS-EXAMINATION OF LOLA ANDREWS

Q: Did I show you any photograph that night that you thought looked at all like the man you saw?

A: You showed me a lot of photographs that night, and amongst them was one that I told you resembled the man that I saw.

Q: You remember that, don't you?

A: Yes, sir.

Bartolomeo Vanzetti (left) and Nicola Sacco in court during their trial for murder. UNITED PRESS INTERNATIONAL

Q: Do you remember being asked this question: I called your attention to the group of photographs marked "22-36-C," and asked you if you have ever seen any of those men. Answer: "I have never seen any of those men at all. The color of that man's hair and the face and the complexion looks like him." Do you remember so stating?

A: I don't remember so stating that answer to you in that way.

Q: Question: "But a larger man?" Answer: "Yes." Did you so state?

A: I did not, no, sir.

Q: Question: "An older man than he is?" Answer: "I don't know whether this man is 28 or 38." Did you so state?

A: Yes, sir, I did say that.

Q: Question: "But you would not by any means pretend to say that this is the man?" Answer: "No." Did you so state?

A: I did not make that answer.

Q: Question: "Would you say positively that it is not the man?" Answer: "That man there is not the man." Did you so state?

A: I said the man—

Q: Answer my question, please. Did you so state?

A: I don't remember.

Q: Will you say you did not?

A: I will say that I don't remember.

Q: Question: "You are positive?" Answer: "Yes." Did you so state?

A: I don't remember.

THE COURT: What is she speaking about? I don't know as the jury knows.

MR. MOORE: I am reading this, Your Honor, in order to get to the picture, to which this is preliminary evidence. I have already asked with reference to a group of pictures.

THE COURT: That she says she has never seen.

MR. MOORE: Yes.

Q: Question: "Positive that is not the man?" Answer: "Yes." Did you so state?

A: I did not.

Q: Question: "You mean the man with the soft collar, standing, holding in his hand a derby hat is not the man you saw on April 15, 1920, in South Braintree?" Answer: "No, indeed." Did you so state?

A: I did not.

Q: Now, directing your attention to this list of pictures that I have just been referring to, "23-36-C." Now, running those over you find that there is only one man in that picture with a derby hat in his hand, don't you?

A: Yes, sir.

Q: Who is that the picture of now, do you know?

A: It is the same picture that I pointed out to you at that time.

Q: Absolutely, isn't it?

A: Yes, sir.

Q: And at that time you answered me in this wise: Question: "You mean the man with the soft collar, standing, and holding in his hand a derby hat is not the man you saw on April 15, 1920, in South Braintree?" Answer: "No, indeed." Didn't you so answer?

A: I didn't answer you that way.

Q: My question was as I read it, wasn't it? I asked you that question, did I not?

A: Yes, sir.

Q: You answered me in that wise, did you not?

A: I did not answer you the way—

Q: How did you answer me?

A: I told you that he resembled the man I saw at South Braintree.

Q: Question: "Why are you positive that he is not the man?" Answer: "The only way is that man does not look to me that his shoulders would hang down like." Did you so state?

A: I don't remember.

Q: Question: "He hasn't got that slouch?" Answer: "No, and the man I am speaking of even though dressed up would not be a man that looked like this man." Did you so state?

A: I did not.

Later, one witness after another im-

Judge Webster Thayer, who presided at the Sacco-Vanzetti trial. UNITED PRESS INTERNATIONAL

Frederick G. Katzmann, the unrelenting prosecutor in the Sacco-Vanzetti trial. WIDE WORLD PHOTOS

peached Lola Andrews; she was so shaken that at one point, as the official transcript reveals, she simply fainted. But this did not prevent the prosecutor, Katzmann, from stating to the jury that, in his eleven years in the service of the Commonwealth, he had never before "laid eye or given ear to so convincing a witness as Lola Andrews."

Some of the prosecution witnesses simply reversed their story on the stand and denied that they had ever identified the prisoners; others affirmed their identification, although they had denied this to defense representatives.

An important prosecution witness was William Proctor, captain in the Department of Public Safety of the Massachusetts State Police, in charge of the Division of State Police. He had been in the department for

twenty-three years, a captain for sixteen. Proctor had received cartridge shells found at the scene of the shooting. After going through considerable testimony establishing his expert knowledge of ballistics, identifying bullets and Sacco's gun, Proctor was asked a series of questions, and gave answers which are among the most famous in the history of criminal jurisprudence.

Q: Have you an opinion as to whether bullet 3 was fired from the Colt Automatic which is in evidence?

A: I have.

Q: And what is your opinion?

A: My opinion is that it is consistent with being fired by that pistol.

Q: Is there anything different in the appearance of the other five bullets—

A: Yes.

Q: Just a minute, I had not completed. —the other five bullets to which I have just referred which would indicate to you that they were fired from more than one weapon?

A: There is not.

Q: Are the appearances of those bullets consistent with being fired with the same weapon?

A: As far as I can see.

Q: Captain, did you understand my question when I asked you if you had an opinion as to whether the five bullets which you say were fired from an automatic type of pistol were fired from the same gun?

A: I would not say positively.

Q: Well, have you an opinion?

A: I have.

Q: Well, that is what I asked you before. I thought possibly you didn't understand. What is your opinion as to the gun from which those four were fired?

A: My opinion is, all five were fired from the same pistol.

Q: What is the basis of your opinion?

A: By looking the marks over on the bullets that were caused by the rifling of the gun. It didn't seem to cut a clear groove; they seemed to jump the lands, and seemed to to make a different mark than the lands would make.

Later, after the trial was over, Proctor was to swear that he had repeatedly told Katzmann that it was his opinion that the bullets had not been fired from this gun and that Katzmann had elicited from him the information that, although in his opinion they were not fired, it was consistent that they could have been. If this retraction was Proctor's genuine story, if he had informed Katzmann and Katzmann permitted him to testify to a partial truth which was in fact misleading, then the prosecution was guilty of obstructing the law. Katzmann, in his answer to the Proctor affidavit, merely denied

that the information Proctor had given to him had been told to him "repeatedly"! But soon afterward Proctor died, while the case was still under appeal, and the defense was deprived of a valuable ally.

When the defense opened, it brought an array of witnesses who placed both Sacco and Vanzetti at points far removed from the scene of the murder. Sacco's whereabouts in Boston were traced for several hours; Vanzetti was at the home of close friends, where he delivered fish, and then was seen by a man who had been painting his boat. The difficulty in verifying an alibi is that the witness must be able to establish why he can recall that particular day. For the Boston incident, many of Sacco's friends were attending a luncheon in honor of a journalist. There was good documentary evidence that the luncheon did take place, and these people clearly recalled seeing Sacco just before and after. Their stories were consistent. Sacco was in Boston on the fifteenth to go to the Italian consulate, a matter that was sworn to by deposition from a clerk who had since returned to Italy.

One of the upholders of the Vanzetti alibi knew the exact date because she connected it with her mother's going to the hospital; another, with his wife's birthday.

Katzmann, however, was merciless on cross-examination, and he held the witnesses up to ridicule in a manner that has been widely criticized by almost every commentator on the case and that indicates not only his interest in conviction rather than in truth but also betrays the partiality of the court and its judge, a matter that was to become an international scandal.

Of the defendants, Bartolomeo Vanzetti came to the stand first, starting on the morning of Tuesday, July 5. He traced his doings on the day of the crime, told how he had been treated upon arrest and how he did not know the nature of the charge, and related his reasons for leaving the United States in 1917—because he opposed the war and wanted to avoid registration for the draft. In cross-examination there was one point at which the prosecution hammered: that Vanzetti had told dozens of lies at the pretrial examination and at the time of his arrest, all purportedly to protect his friends and because he did not know the nature of the charges against him. Again the alibi was questioned. How could he know so much about what he had done on April fifteenth, if he knew so little about so many other days?

Q: Mr. Vanzetti, do you remember this question and this answer at the Brockton police station that I made of you, which you gave in reply: "Q: Well, do you remember the holiday we had in April, the nineteenth of April, they call it Patriots' Day, the middle of April? A: Yes. I heard that before, but I did not remember that was in April." Do you remember saying that to me at Brockton?

A: What holiday?

Q: The nineteenth of April?

A: What holiday it is?

Q: Patriots' Day.

A: Patriot?

Q. Patriots' Day.

A: Oh, patriotics day.

Q: Yes, do you remember my asking you that question and your making that reply?

A: No, I don't; I don't remember.

Q: Will you say you did not make that reply to that question?

A: No, I don't say that I didn't.

Q: Do you remember the next question: "Q: This year it came on a Monday." You remember the answer: "A: I don't remember." Did you make that reply?

A: No, I don't remember.

Q: Will you say you did not make it?

A: Well, maybe I did. I might have, yes.

Q: Do you remember this question and this answer: "Q: You don't know where you were the Thursday before that Monday, do you? A: No." Do you remember that answer to that question?

A: Oh, yes, I answered some other thing no, that I don't remember in that time, but I remember it now, not only this.

Q: On May sixth, 1920?

A: Yes.

Q: You did not remember where you were on the fifteenth of April, did you?

A: More probable, yes.

Q: But after waiting months and months and months you then remembered, did you?

A: Not months and months and months, but three or four weeks after I see that I have to be careful and to remember well if I want to save my life.

History makes Sacco out to be a less majestic figure than his codefendant. Certainly he was less articulate, less familiar with the English language. On the witness stand, however, he held his own. He followed Vanzetti on the stand (except for a brief interruption when a former witness was recalled). In addition to denying participation in the crime, and explaining his own background and why he had lied upon arrest, Sacco described the manner in which he had been identified by witnesses in the jail, such as the lack of lineup, and the forced posing before the witnesses.

On cross-examination, the prosecution immediately took up the question of patriotism; the following is the opening of the cross-examination of Nicola Sacco:

Mr. Katzmann: Did you say yesterday you love a free country?

A: Yes, sir.

Q: Did you love this country in the month of May 1917?

A: I did not say—I don't want to say I did not love this country.

Q: Did you love this country in the month of

May, 1917?

A: If you can, Mr. Katzmann, if you give me that—I could explain—

Q: Do you understand that question?

A: Yes.

Q: Then will you please answer it?

A: I can't answer in one word.

Q: You can't say whether you loved the United States of America one week before the day you enlisted for the first draft?

A: I can't say in one word, Mr. Katzmann.

Q: You can't tell this jury whether you loved the country or not?

Mr. Moore: I object to that.

A: I could explain that, yes, if I loved—

Q: What?

A: I could explain that, yes, if I loved, if you give me a chance.

Q: I ask you first to answer that question. Did you love this United States of America in May 1917?

A: I can't answer in one word.

Q: Don't you know whether you did or not?

Mr. Moore: I object, your Honor.

The Court: What say?

Mr. Moore: I object to the repetition of this question without giving the young man an opportunity to explain his attitude.

The Court: That is not the usual method that prevails. Where the question can be categorically answered by yes or no, it should be answered. The explanation comes later. Then you can make any inquiry to the effect of giving the witness an opportunity of making whatever explanation at that time he sees fit to make, but under cross-examination counsel is entitled to get an answer, either yes or no, when the question can be so answered. You may proceed, please.

Q: Did you love this country in the last week of May 1917?

A: That is pretty hard for me to say in one word, Mr. Katzmann.

Q: There are two words you can use, Mr. Sacco, yes or no. Which one is it?

A: Yes.

Q: And in order to show your love for this United States of America when she was about to call upon you to become a soldier you ran away to Mexico?

Mr. Jeremiah McAnarney: Wait.

The Court: Did you?

Q: Did you run away to Mexico?

The Court: He has not said he ran away to Mexico. Did you go?

Q: Did you go to Mexico to avoid being a soldier for this country that you loved?

A: Yes.

Q: You went under an assumed name?

A: No.

Q: Didn't you take the name of Mosmacotelli?

A: Yes.

Q: That is not your name, is it?

A: No.

Q: How long did you remain under the name of Mosmacotelli?

A: Until I got a job over to Mr. Kelley's.

Q: When was that?

A: The armistice.

Q: After the war was practically over?

A: Yes, sir.

Q: Then, for the first time after May 1917, did you become known as Sacco again?

A: Yes, sir.

Q: Was it for the reason that you desired to avoid service that when you came back in four months you went to Cambridge instead of to Milford?

A: For the reason for not to get in the army.

Q: So as to avoid getting in the army.

A: Another reason why, I did not want no chance to get arrested and one year in prison.

Q: Did you want to get arrested and spend one year in prison for dodging the draft. Is that it?

A: Yes.

Q: Did you love your country when you came back from Mexico?

A: The first time?

The Court: Which country did you say? You said—

Q: United States of America, your adopted country?

A: I did not say already.

Q: When you came back, I asked you. That was before you went.

A: I don't think I could change my opinion in three months.

Q: You still loved America, did you?

A: I should say yes.

Q: And is that your idea of showing your love for this country?

A: (Witness hesitates.)

Q: Is that your idea of showing your love for America?

A: Yes.

Q: And would it be your idea of showing your love for your wife that when she needed you you ran away from her?

A: I did not run away from her.

MR. MOORE: I object.

THE WITNESS: I was going to come after if I need her.

THE COURT: He may answer. Simply on the question of credibility, that is all.

Q: Would it be your idea of love for your wife that you were to run away from her when she needed you?

MR. JEREMIAH MCANARNEY: Pardon me. I ask for an exception on that.

THE COURT: Excluded. One may not run away. He has not admitted he ran away.

Q: Then I will ask you, didn't you run away from Milford so as to avoid being a soldier for the United States?

A: I did not run away.

Q: You mean you walked away?

A: Yes.

Q: You don't understand me when I say "run away," do you?

A: That is vulgar.

A great deal was made of the question of the cap picked up near the body of the murdered men. Sacco denied it was his, and Katzmann hammered away at the fact that there was a little hole in it, which the DA insisted was made when Sacco hung his cap on a nail in the shop, thus definitely establishing that Sacco was the owner of the cap and hence must have been at the scene of the murder.

Q: I call your attention to Exhibit 27 for identification, to that in the lining. What is it?

A: I never saw that before.

Q: What is it?

A: I don't know.

Q: Don't know what that is?

A: It is a hole.

Q: It is a hole?

A: Yes.

Q: And you never saw that before?

A: No.

Q: Still you say that is your hat?

A: Sure. Never saw that before.

Q: Never saw that before. Was there any hole in your hat when you last saw it?

A: Hole, no.

Q: Sure of that?

A: Pretty sure.

Q: Where did you hang your hats up? If this is your hat, did you ever wear it to work?

A: Yes.

Q: What do you hang it up on?

A: On a wall.

Q: On what on the wall?

A: On the stake, on two stakes.

Q: Two stakes?

A: Yes, sticks.

Q: Sticks of wood?

A: One go across and put my jacket, my pants.

Q: Is there a hook here?

A: What do you mean, a hook?

Q: A hat hook, or clothes hook?

A: Yes, I made myself, for the purpose.

Q: What is it made of?

A: Sticks.

Q: That is wood?

A: Yes. Then there is a nail through.

Q: Is it on the nail you hang your hat?

A: Yes.

Q: That is something you put up for yourself in the Kelley shop, wasn't it?

A: Yes.

Later, a police officer was to state that he had made the hole in this cap when he was scratching it to see what was beneath the label.

It did not take the jury long to bring in verdicts of guilty, and reporters have stated that even Katzmann's assistant, Williams, wept when the verdict included Vanzetti, for he had grave doubts as to Vanzetti's relationship with the affair. Sacco shouted out, "They kill innocent men. They kill two innocent men."

On April 9, 1927, after many appeals and countless protests, the men were again brought before Judge Webster Thayer in his Dedham courthouse and were sentenced. Each was given an opportunity to speak.

Nicola Sacco did more than assert his innocence; he accused Judge Thayer of full awareness of that fact, and expressed his appreciation for the support given to him by intellectuals and his comrades of the working class.

Vanzetti's statement was long and eloquent. It opened on a simple note.

Yes. What I say is that I am innocent, not only of the Braintree crime, but also of the Bridgewater crime. That I am not only innocent of these two crimes, but in all my life I have never stolen and I have never killed and I have never spilled blood.

And it closed on a fiery one.

Well, I have already say that I not only am not guilty of these two crimes, but I never committed a crime in my life—I have never stolen and I have never killed and I have never spilt blood, and I have fought against crime, and I have fought and I have sacrificed myself even to eliminate the crimes that the law and the church legitimate and sanctify.

This is what I say: I would not wish to a dog or to a snake, to the most low and misfortunate creature of the earth—I would not wish to any of them what I have had to suffer for things that I am not guilty of. I am suffering because I am a radical and indeed I am a radical; I have suffered because I was an Italian, and indeed I am an Italian; I have suffered more for my family and for my beloved than for myself; but I am so convinced to be right that you can only kill me once but if you could execute me two times, and if I could be reborn two other times, I would live again to do what I have done already.

I have finished. Thank you.

The court proceeded to sentence the men to death.

Much of the tragedy and most of the drama in the case took place outside the courtroom. The bias of the trial judge, Webster Thayer, was widely attacked. It was rumored that, in many places outside the courtroom, he had made derogatory statements about the accused; he was accused by a professor of unimpeachable integrity of having referred to Sacco and Vanzetti, in the professor's presence, as "anarchist bastards." Thayer never specifically denied this accusation; the few apologists for him have claimed that he conducted the trial with fairness despite this apparent prejudice, and one commentator insisted that he was referring, not to the defendants, but to their lawyers!

As new evidence turned up, and errors in the case became more and more glaring, appeals were made. But under Massachusetts law then in effect, appeals for a new trial had to be heard by the original trial judge, and in one instance after another he rejected the appeals. There were Lola Andrews' retraction, Proctor's accusation that the prosecution deliberately worded a question so as to receive what was known to be a seriously misleading answer, an affidavit from a friend of the foreman of the jury (who died shortly

Vanzetti, with moustache, and Sacco, handcuffed together, arrive at Boston Superior Court to be sentenced to die in the electric chair the week of July 10, 1927. WIDE WORLD PHOTOS

after the end of the trial) that before the trial began, the foreman had stated that the men should get what's coming to them, whether they had committed the crime or not; and there were confessions and mounting evidence that the crime was the work of other men.

Among the unanswered questions raised by the defense were: Who were the other three bandits in the automobile? What happened to the $15,000, and why was none of it ever traced to the accused or their families? How and when were Sacco and Vanzetti able to plan such a carefully timed and perfectly executed robbery?

Radicals and labor leaders, poets, novel-

ists, artists, members of the intellectual community the world over, members of the most aristocratic families in Massachusetts, and some of the most prestigious lawyers in the country took up the cudgels for the defendants in the death house. Among those who joined the protest were Sherwood Anderson, Romain Rolland, H. G. Wells, Alfred Dreyfus, Edna St. Vincent Millay, John Dos Passos, Upton Sinclair, Sinclair Lewis, Maxwell Anderson, Albert Einstein, Thomas Mann, and John Galsworthy.

It was only, however, when Felix Frankfurter, professor of law at Harvard and one of the most astute legal minds in America, decided to enter the controversy, that many neutral parties became involved. In an article in *Atlantic Monthly* Frankfurter gave a cool appraisal of the case. Behind the legalisms, it was an indictment of American justice such as had never before appeared from the pen of a legal mind in this country. He showed the prejudices and errors of Thayer, the absurdities and contradictions of the prosecution's case, and the impossibility of the prosecution's story of the crime.

Among his many other accusations against Thayer, Frankfurter pointed out that, in turning down the appeals, Thayer had referred to testimony that was not in the record!

In the last months of the long period of appeals, there were general strikes for Sacco and Vanzetti in South America; demonstrations in Milan, Turin, London, Berlin, and elsewhere; mass meetings in Asia and Africa. United States embassies were stoned, and American prestige fell to a new low. The State Department sent a memorandum to its ambassadors on the case, but this did little to repair damage, since the memo was itself replete with errors.

As protests mounted in intensity, attention focused on Judge Thayer, Governor Alvan T. Fuller, a three-man advisory committee appointed by Fuller to review the case, the Supreme Court of the United States, and on the FBI. Two former employees of the Department of Justice stated that there was information in the FBI files on the case that had not been revealed, but all efforts to have these files opened were in vain. To this day, no one is certain of whether the files are still in existence, whether they ever existed, and if so, what they would have revealed. But there was at the time, and there remains to this day, a suspicion that the government was suppressing information that would have aided the defendants.

The three-man commission, headed by A. Lawrence Lowell, president of Harvard, seemed determined to bring in a verdict vindicating the trial judge and the integrity of Massachusetts justice. For example, when the alibi witnesses for Sacco insisted that they could place the time of their seeing Sacco because of the luncheon meeting in Boston that afternoon, Lowell shocked and frightened the defense with an announcement that he had information that the event had not taken place at the stipulated time. The very next day, the witnesses came back with copies of their Italian-language newspaper, in which the luncheon was announced. Lowell apologized to the witnesses for the defense, but the episode did not end there. So mortified was the Harvard president by this evidence of his error that he ordered the stenographer to expunge this entire section from the record. Later, when this was called to his attention, he avoided the question studiously; however, to a Harvard student who insisted on an answer, he wrote, "The charge of suppressing evidence in presence of counsel for the accused is an absurdity on its face to anyone who thinks about it." But the charge was not suppression of evidence; it was tampering with the official record of the hearings.

In the end, it was not Sacco and Vanzetti who were on trial; it was American justice, and particularly the justice of the Commonwealth of Massachusetts. With Massachusetts on trial, the sentiment began to rise that, even if the men were innocent, the Commonwealth could not back down. And so the final pleas were rejected by the governor in the face of greater and greater evidence of the miscarriage of justice, and Sacco and Vanzetti went to their deaths.

Katzmann, Lowell, Thayer, and Fuller sank into ignominy and oblivion. For all practical purposes, their public careers were

Following electrocutions of Sacco and Vanzetti at Charleston Prison, thousands of persons form a funeral procession for the eight-mile journey across Boston, while thousands of others look on. WIDE WORLD PHOTOS

over; they were no longer useful to the society they had served. Whatever political and intellectual acumen they had was to be forgotten, as they carried with them forever into their graves the stigma of the role they had played in what came to be known as the judicial murder of Sacco and Vanzetti. Fuller's name was mentioned as a vice-presidential candidate for 1928, but was quickly dropped. There was a report that he would be named ambassador to France, but this too was denied, for in France he would be persona non grata. In November 1927, when he traveled to France, the governor of Massachusetts chose to use a pseudonym. Thayer

and Katzmann were thwarted in their political ambitions; they remained minor figures and fell into obscurity. No political party wanted to be associated with either of them. Lowell retired and to the end vigorously defended his actions, but was bitter and evasive when the facts of the case were called to his attention.

Among the legacies of Sacco and Vanzetti are twenty-three gouaches by Ben Shahn, two anthologies of poetry, plays, novels, short stories, and many works of art. The latter include a large bronze bas-relief by the world-famous sculptor Gutzon Borglum, which a group of prominent citizens (Eleanor Roosevelt, Albert Einstein, Herbert Lehman, and others) sought to present to the Commonwealth of Massachusetts, with the request that it be placed on Boston Common, a recognition by the Commonwealth of the injustices of yesteryear. This offer was refused by Governor Hurley, who contended that there was still a division of public opinion on the matter.

But no one could ever equal in grandeur the words of Bartolomeo Vanzetti:

If it had not been for these thing, I might have live out my life talking at street corners to scorning men. I might have die, unmarked, unknown, a failure. Now we are not a failure. This is our career and our triumph. Never in our full life could we hope to do such work for tolerance, for joostice, for man's onderstanding of man as now we do by accident. Our words—our lives—our pains—nothing! The taking of our lives—lives of a good shoemaker and a poor fish-peddler—all! That last moment belongs to us—that agony is our triumph.

John Thomas Scopes

1925

LAWS RESTRICTING THE TEACHING OF EVOLU-
tionary theory, or for that matter any other
theory that might conflict with a literal interpretation of the Bible, had been introduced into various state legislatures in the
years following World War I. The fundamentalists scoffed at those who admitted the
possibility that men were descended from
some kind of monkey. They defended the
literalness of the Bible as the revealed truth
of God against the onslaught of the Darwin-
ian theory of evolution.

Laws forbidding the teaching of evolution
in publicly supported schools had been
passed in Florida and just missed passage in
Kentucky and North Carolina. Even university professors were intimidated by their
directors from speaking out against the legislation. In Tennessee an obscure legislator
named John Washington Butler introduced
such a bill in the spring of 1925. The lower
house passed the bill, expecting it to be defeated by the more courageous senators.
The Senate passed it, confident that it would
be vetoed by the governor. The governor,
hardly one to risk alienating voters, signed
the bill, but was certain that it would not be
enforced. In fact, in his message to the legislature he said so.

The Tennessee Anti-Evolution Act might
have remained peacefully quiescent had not
a secretary in the national office of the
American Civil Liberties Union in New York

CLIPPED A NEWSPAPER ITEM ANNOUNCING
the passage of the Butler bill. She brought
the item to the attention of the director of
the ACLU, Roger Baldwin, and soon the
organization issued press releases, stating
that it would be willing to undertake to
finance a test case challenging the constitutionality of the law.

In Tennessee the ACLU offer came to
the attention of George Rappelyea, a young
businessman who had been born in New
York. Rappelyea talked with John Scopes,
biology teacher. When he learned that
Scopes taught evolution, he pointed out
that Scopes had been violating the law. He
then asked if Scopes would voluntarily subject himself to arrest and consent to be the
defendant in a test case. Scopes hesitated.
Such an arrest for challenging a law could
seriously jeopardize his record as a teacher.
But, anticipating a quiet legal battle, a few
legal briefs, arguments by counsel, and an
obscure court decision, Scopes consented.

The trial began to assume gigantic pro-
portions when the World Fundamentalist
Association asked William Jennings Bryan
to assist the prosecution. A three-time candidate for President on the Democratic ticket
(and thrice defeated), a former secretary of
state under Wilson, silver-tongued orator
who had lectured against sinners and atheists
from pulpits all over America, Bryan was in
many ways a logical choice. Here was a man

Clarence Darrow (left) and William Jennings Bryan. WIDE WORLD PHOTOS

who would defend the right of the majority of the populace to restrict their teachers to teaching only their own beliefs. Furthermore, Bryan agreed with legislative control of all educators.

Bryan's entrance into the struggle was a challenge that his opponents could not overlook. America's most famous criminal lawyer, Clarence Darrow, long an opponent not only of fundamentalism but of all organized religion, offered his services to the defense without charge—the first and only time in his career that he would serve without a fee. Strangely enough, the enthusiasm at the ACLU was less than unanimous. Many of the most eminent civil libertarians were opposed to the case becoming a forum for a clash between science and religion. It was,

for them, a more basic issue, freedom to teach. Legislatures, they contended, could not be permitted to restrict teachers in the subject matter of their courses and how they were taught. They must not become censors of textbooks, overseers of curricula, and watchdogs of lecture halls.

While the ACLU discussed, debated, and argued the question of whether Darrow should head the defense team, the decision was made by Scopes himself. Assisting Darrow were Dudley Field Malone, a liberal Catholic and a divorced man, and Arthur Garfield Hays, veteran lawyer of many civil liberties battles. On Bryan's side were his son, William Jennings Bryan, Jr., and several local attorneys.

A jury was chosen (including one self-confessed illiterate), and the trial opened. There was only one issue, the prosecution claimed: did John Thomas Scopes violate the Butler Act or did he not? To prove that he did, a few youngsters were rounded up—with the aid of Scopes himself, who convinced them that they were not doing any harm to their teacher—who proceeded to testify to what he had said in the classroom regarding evolution. This was sufficient to establish the case.

The defense, however, had no intention of limiting the scope of the trial to such an accusation. They brought in many of America's most prestigious scientists to defend the theory of evolution. The prosecution, however, blocked all scientific testimony, claiming that the validity of evolution was not the issue. Only the violation of the law could be tried before the court. The judge ruled accordingly.

At the end of a week of dull arguments, Arthur Garfield Hays startled the court, the spectators, and the radio listening audience by announcing that he was calling William Jennings Bryan as witness for the defense. The prosecutor, A. T. Stewart, the local attorney general, objected vigorously. Bryan dramatically silenced him and announced that he was ready to take the stand to defend the true faith against all agnostics and infidels.

Darrow could not have been more delighted. For several hours he cross-examined Bryan, who attempted to defend the Bible as literal history, a task made all the more difficult under the relentless interrogation of Darrow. Stewart attempted to put an end to the examination, but Bryan allowed the questioning to continue. At times he even admitted that the language of the Bible was not necessarily literal, but symbolic.

Darrow finally launched into his most devastating examination of Bryan.

DARROW: Mr. Bryan, do you believe that the first woman was Eve?

BRYAN: Yes.

D: Do you believe she was literally made out of Adam's rib?

B: I do.

D: Did you ever discover where Cain got his wife?

B: No, sir; I leave the agnostics to hunt for her.

D: You have never found out?

B: I have never tried to find out.

D: You have never tried to find out?

B: No.

D: The Bible says he got one, doesn't it? Were there other people on the earth at that time?

B: I cannot say.

D: You cannot say. Did that ever enter your consideration?

B: Never bothered me.

D: There were no others recorded, but Cain got a wife.

B: That is what the Bible says.

D: Where she came from you do not know. All right. Does the statement, "The morning and the evening were the first day," and "The morning and the evening were the second day," mean anything to you?

B: I do not think it necessarily means a twenty-four-hour day.

D: You do not?

B: No.

D: What do you consider it to be?

B: I have not attempted to explain it. If you will take the second chapter—let me have the book. (Examines the Bible.) The fourth verse of the second chapter says: "These are the generations of the heavens and of the earth, when they were created in the day that the Lord God made the earth and the heavens." The word "day" there in the very next chapter is used to describe a period. I do not see that there is any necessity for construing the words, "the evening and the morning," as meaning necessarily a twenty-four-hour day, "in the day when the Lord made the heaven and the earth."

D: Then, when the Bible said, for instance, "and God called the firmament heaven. And the evening and the morning were the second day," that does not necessarily mean twenty-four hours?

B: I do not think it necessarily does.

D: Do you think it does or does not?

B: I know a great many think so.

D: What do you think?

B: I do not think it does.

D: You think those were not literal days?

B: I do not think they were twenty-four-hour days.

D: What do you think about it?

B: That is my opinion—I do not know that my opinion is better on that subject than those who think it does.

D: You do not think that?

B: No. But I think it would be just as easy for the kind of God we believe in to make the earth in six days as in six years or in 6,000,000 years or in 600,000,000 years. I do not think it important whether we believe one or the other.

D: Do you think those were literal days?

B: My impression is they were periods, but I would not attempt to argue as against anybody who wanted to believe it literal days.

D: Have you any idea of the length of the periods?

B: No; I don't.

D: Do you think the sun was made on the fourth day?

B: Yes.

D: And they had evening and morning without the sun?

B: I am simply saying it is a period.

D: They had evening and morning for four periods without the sun, do you think?

B: I believe in creation as there told, and if I am not able to explain it I will accept it. Then you can explain it to suit yourself.

D: Mr. Bryan, what I want to know is, do you believe the sun was made on the fourth day?

B: I believe just as it says there.

D: Do you believe the sun was made on the fourth day?

B: Read it.

D: I am very sorry; you have read it so many times you would know, but I will read it again:

"And God said, let there be lights in the firmament of the heaven, to divide the day from the night; and let them be for signs, and for seasons, and for days, and years. And let them be for lights in the firmament of the heaven, to give light upon the earth; and it was so. And God made two great lights; the greater light to rule the day, and the lesser light to rule the night; He made the stars also. And God set them in the firmament of the heaven, to give light upon the earth, and to rule over the day and over the night, and to divide the light from the darkness; and God saw that it was good. And the evening and the morning were the fourth day."

Do you believe, whether it was a literal day or a period, the sun and the moon were not made until the fourth day?

B: I believe they were made in the order in which they were given there, and I think in the dispute with Gladstone and Huxley on that point—

D: Cannot you answer my question?

B: I prefer to agree with Gladstone.

D: I do not care about Gladstone.

B: Then prefer to agree with whomever you please.

D: Cannot you answer my question?

B: I have answered it. I believe that it was made on the fourth day, in the fourth day.

D: And they had the evening and the morning before that time for three days or three periods. All right, that settles it. Now, if you call those periods, they may have been a very long time.

B: They might have been.

D: The creation might have been going on for a very long time.

B: It might have continued for millions of years.

D: Yes. All right. Do you believe the story of the temptation of Eve by the serpent?

B: I do.

D: Do you believe that after Eve ate the apple, or gave it to Adam, whichever way it was, that God cursed Eve, and at that time decreed that all womankind thenceforth and forever should suffer the pains of childbirth in the reproduction of the earth?

B: I believe what it says, and I believe the fact as fully—

D: That is what it says, doesn't it?

B: Yes.

D: And for that reason, every woman born of woman, who has to carry on the race, has childbirth pains because Eve tempted Adam in the Garden of Eden?

B: I will believe just what the Bible says. I ask to put that in the language of the Bible, for I prefer that to your language. Read the Bible and I will answer.

D: All right, I will do that. "And I will put enmity between thee and the woman"— that is referring to the serpent?

B: The serpent.

D: (reading) ". . . and between thy seed and her seed; it shall bruise thy head, and thou shalt bruise his heel. Unto the woman he said, I will greatly multiply thy sorrow and thy conception; in sorrow thou shalt bring forth children; and thy desire shall be to thy husband, and he shall rule over thee." That is right, is it?

B: I accept it as it is.

D: And you believe that came about because Eve tempted Adam to eat the fruit?

B: Just as it says.

D: And you believe that is the reason that God made the serpent to go on his belly after he tempted Eve?

B: I believe the Bible as it is, and I do not permit you to put your language in the place of the language of the Almighty. You read that Bible and ask me questions, and I will answer them. I will not answer your questions in your language.

D: I will read it to you from the Bible—in your language. "And the Lord God said unto the serpent, because thou hast done this, thou art cursed above all cattle, and above every beast of the field; upon thy belly shalt thou go and dust shalt thou eat all the days of thy life." Do you think that is why the serpent is compelled to crawl upon his belly?

B: I believe that.

D: Have you any idea how the snake went before that time?

B: No, sir.

D: Do you know whether he walked on his tail or not?

B: No, sir. I have no way to know. (Laughter)

D: Now, you refer to the cloud that was put in the heaven after the flood as the rainbow. Do you believe in that?

B: Read it.

D: All right, Mr. Bryan, I will read it for you.

B: Your Honor, I think I can shorten this testimony. The only purpose Mr. Darrow has is to slur at the Bible, but I will answer his question. I will answer it all at once, and I have no objection in the world, I want the world to know that this man, who does not believe in a God, is trying to use a court in Tennessee—

D: I object to that.

B: (continuing)—to slur at it, and while it will require time, I am willing to take it.

D: I object to your statement. I am examining you on your fool ideas that no intelligent Christian on earth believes.

THE COURT: Court is adjourned until tomorrow morning.

The trial was all over but for the formality of a verdict. After nine minutes of deliberation, Scopes was found guilty, and the court fined him $100. Four days later, William Jennings Bryan lay down for a nap after a hearty meal and never awoke.

During the trial, Darrow had practically supplicated the judge to demand of the jury a directed verdict of guilty, so that the entire

Defendant John T. Scopes stands before Judge Raulston after being found guilty by the jury. UNITED PRESS INTERNATIONAL

matter could be taken to a higher court, preferably the United States Supreme Court, where the constitutionality of the law could be argued. Following the verdict, dissension again arose in the ranks of the ACLU. Darrow had fulfilled his role; he had drawn the attention of the world to the bigotry of the fundamentalists and to its effects on education. Now an attorney with greater respectability, some argued, would be more successful in the appellate courts. The name

of Charles Evans Hughes was mentioned by some, and the unsuccessful 1924 Democratic candidate for President, John W. Davis, by others. As for Scopes, he was at first too busy with his graduate studies to be concerned about the choice of an attorney for his appeal; later, he reaffirmed his confidence in Darrow.

Briefs were finally filed, and Darrow appeared. He did nothing to make allies or to soft-pedal delicate issues; he was merciless in his handling of organized religion and scoffed at many dearly held beliefs. Many in the ACLU decided that, if the case were to go to the Supreme Court of the United States, Darrow must be removed. They appealed to Scopes. Again, as before, he expressed confidence in his controversial attorney.

But there was no need to be concerned over who would carry the appeal to Washington, for the case was neither won nor lost. On a technicality involving the error made by the judge in imposing a fine that could legally be set only by the jury—some commentators believe the error was deliberately made, with the connivance of the prosecution—the decision was reversed. No purpose would be served by a new trial, the higher court stated. As for the constitutionality of the Butler Act, four justices out of five (one was a new member of the court) issued their rulings. Two justices ruled that the act was constitutional; one declared it completely invalid; a fourth found it constitutional, but declared that it banned not the teaching of evolution as such, but only of materialistic and atheistic evolution.

There was no road to appeal, and thus the case of *The State of Tennessee* v. *John Thomas Scopes* came to an end. Academic freedom in America is still not a clear-cut achievement, but the trial of Scopes went a long way to help make it a reality.

General Billy Mitchell

1925

IN 1925 CHILDREN STILL POINTED UPWARD when they saw an airplane in the sky, with its upper and lower wings looking more like a kite than the powerful machine it would become. Less than a quarter of a century had passed since the first successful flights of the Wright brothers at Kitty Hawk, North Carolina. People were saying, "Wake up, the war's over!" Many innovations had been tried out during World War I; among others, machines that fought in the air. One of the most daring flyers of the war was Colonel Billy Mitchell.

Although technically only a colonel, many thought of William Mitchell as a general. He had returned from the war convinced of the overwhelming significance of aviation in any future wars. America, he insisted, needed an air force independent of its army and navy, one that would be recognized for its importance as were other branches of the military. Vehemently he called for research, for industry, and for building.

Billy Mitchell's unshakable belief in air power and his unswerving fight to establish an independent United States Air Department alongside the War and Navy departments often brought him into the limelight, but none of his bitter clashes with military authority was more dramatic and portentous than when he set out to prove that air power could indeed defeat sea power. In 1921, appearing before an appropriations committee in Congress, Mitchell insisted that his AIRBORNE BOMBS COULD SINK ANY SEAGOING vessels. When asked how much money he wanted in order to make such a demonstration, he scorned any funds and said all he needed were the targets. "You would recommend that a vessel be turned over to you to make such experiments?" the investigator inquired. He answered, "Yes, sir. Both armored and unarmored vessels."

The secretary of the navy, Josephus Daniels, scoffed and announced that he was prepared "to stand bareheaded on the deck of a battleship and let Brigadier General Mitchell take a crack at me with a bombing airplane."

Early in the spring of 1921, former German warships were allocated to the United States to be used as targets for bombing experiments. Billy Mitchell had the targets he wanted. Mitchell, however, came close to being removed from his post, ostensibly because scrawled on the bombs he and his flyers were about to drop were the words "Regards to the Navy."

Public and congressional pressures were high when the tests took place on June 20, 1921. For this test Mitchell and his colleagues had come up with a revolutionary hypothesis: a direct hit would be unnecessary; a near hit would create a series of powerful movements of thousands of tons of water with such force that a big ship would be devastated.

One by one, day after day, the flyers

attacked the abandoned vessels that lay quiet and lonely in the ocean. And one by one the vessels were sunk by the bombers: first an old submarine, then an obsolete American battleship, followed by a destroyer and a cruiser. The finale was left for the most unsinkable of all ships, the German battleship *Ostfriesland*.

A shocked public opened *The New York Times* on the morning of September 4, 1925, to read of a disaster that had befallen a great dirigible.

SHENANDOAH WRECKED IN OHIO STORM
Breaks In Three And Falls 7,000 Feet
14 Dead, Including Commander, 2 Hurt

The Navy dirigible *Shenandoah*, whose silver beauty had been seen over many American cities, was ripped apart by a thunder squall . . .

General William Mitchell. U.S. AIR FORCE PHOTO

On September 3, 1925, while in a storm over Ohio, the "Shenandoah" broke into three pieces and crashed to the ground. UNITED PRESS INTERNATIONAL

On the day that newspapers announced the tragedy, three items appeared together with the main story. The widow of the commander, Lieutenant Commander Zachary Lansdowne, immediately charged "politics," and claimed that for a year her husband had tried to avoid the fatal flight. Secretary of the navy Curtis D. Wilbur declared that, whereas the loss of the *Shenandoah* did not mean that such craft must be abandoned, it did show their limits. And on an inside page there was a small item; one Colonel William Mitchell paid tribute to the fallen commander and his ship. "He was a man whose loss would be irreparable," and added, "America now lacks a dirigible for war."

Immediately a board of inquiry was appointed to investigate the tragedy and draw lessons from it, but Mitchell did not wait for the findings. This was his opportunity to change the prevailing American attitude toward air power. On Sunday, September 6, another front-page story, datelined San Antonio, Texas, hit the headlines in *The New York Times*.

MITCHELL CHARGES "GROSS NEGLIGENCE" IN SHENANDOAH LOSS

Colonel William Mitchell, Eighth Corps Air Officer, today launched a scathing denunciation of the practices and circumstances pertaining to the administration of national defense.

Referring to the *Shenandoah* and other tragedies, Mitchell accused his superiors. "These accidents are the direct result of incompetency, criminal negligence, and almost treasonable administration by the War and Navy Departments." Then, bitterly commenting on the conduct of these departments during the last few years, he angrily called it "so disgusting as to make any self-respecting person ashamed of the clothes he wears." It is no wonder that the subhead of this *Times* article read, "Expects Arrest Monday."

The trial of Billy Mitchell opened on October 28, 1925, in the damp and dusty room of the outmoded building chosen for the court-martial by the War Department.

On October 28, 1925, crowds line up around the courthouse where the trial is being held. LIBRARY OF CONGRESS

The military tribunal to try Mitchell includes Major General Douglas MacArthur, fourth from the left. LIBRARY OF CONGRESS

A few days previous, President Coolidge had made known the names of the judges—all officers of the army, as the rules of the situation called for. Many of these men were known for their outspoken opposition to Mitchell's campaign. A Congressman who was later to become mayor of New York, Fiorello La Guardia, was sufficiently upset by the personnel of the court to state, "Billy Mitchell is not being tried by a board of his peers but by a pack of beribboned dog robbers of the General Staff."

The first day opened with a surprise move by Colonel Mitchell that succeeded in ousting three members of the court, including its president, on the grounds of bias. Then the formal trial began with reading eight charges for which Mitchell was being tried. He immediately denounced the proceedings. He pointed out that the charges avoided the questions raised by his public statements and reduced the entire matter to whether or not he had said certain things that might hold the War and Navy departments in disrepute.

Mitchell's defense attorney, Representative Frank R. Reid of Illinois, granted that libel was a punishable offense, but argued that it was impossible to libel the War Department because it was an intangible body and Mitchell's statements had attacked a system only. He pointed out that President Coolidge at Annapolis on the previous June 3 had endorsed this right of expression when he said, "The officers of the Navy are given the fullest latitude in expressing their views before their fellow citizens, subject, of course, to the requirements of not betraying those confidential affairs which would be detrimental to the service." The day ended with the defense scoring heavily with this line of argument.

On the second day of the trial Reid nearly brought the court to dissolution. He claimed that while Mitchell was being tried on a charge, contrary to court-martial rules, no accuser had been named. Mitchell's commanding officer would have to bring the charge and appoint a disinterested officer to investigate the situation. The court admitted

Mitchell is defended by the able Representative Frank R. Reid of Illinois, seated at his right.
NATIONAL ARCHIVES

the failure but ingeniously maintained that such proceedings could be waived by simply holding that the President of the United States was the commanding officer and thus the sole accuser and prosecutor. The trial then continued, with the defense reading each of the eight specifications and Colonel Mitchell pleading not guilty to each one as it was read.

On the third day Reid threw another bombshell into the trial by threatening to call President Coolidge himself or, failing that, to put Secretary of War Davis on the stand to confront Mitchell as his accuser. The trial was adjourned until November 2.

The court reconvened on the appointed date and a newspaperman from Texas testified that Colonel Mitchell had actually made the statements for which he stood accused. Since nobody denied his having

made them, and since the defense had pointed out that on the basis of just these statements the President had called together a special aircraft board of investigation, this entire portion of the trial seemed pointless.

Having proved the already accepted fact that these statements had actually been made by Mitchell, the court proceeded to pull off the biggest surprise of the trial. They moved to permit the defense to present evidence of the proof of these statements and establish the truth of the defendant's accusations against the War and Navy departments' air administrations. In effect this put the defense in the unusual position of becoming the prosecution, if not literally in regard to the trial itself, at least as a forum from which to present Mitchell's arguments to the country. Reid at once proposed to subpoena seventy-three witnesses and numerous official documents. The court adjourned to allow time for the subpoenas to be served.

When the court reassembled on November 9, the defense announced that it would prove the truth and validity of Colonel Mitchell's accusations, and proceeded to read into the record a list of sixty-six, among them:

That the *Shenandoah* was designed for the use of hydrogen as a lifting gas and that when helium was substituted without changing the structure her safety factor was reduced.

That the authorities ordering and directing the fatal flight of the *Shenandoah* and the almost fatal flight of the *PN9-1* were wholly unacquainted with the subject of aviation and incompetent for their duties.

That the great bulk of airplanes in the possession of the army were designed and constructed at the time of the war and are antiquated, out of date and unsuited to perform the military mission for which they are used.

That Colonel Mitchell was demoted and transferred because he told the truth before the Aircraft Committee of the House of Representatives.

That the War Department was guilty of almost treasonable administration, due to the fact that up to 1923 there were in Hawaii no plans for the employment of the air service in the aeronautical protection of the islands.

That the War Department has spent a great deal of effort to lead the public to believe that antiaircraft cannon and machine guns constitute a defense against aircraft, lulling the public into a false sense of security against foreign invasion by enemy aircraft.

That no adequate meteorological arrangements are available in the United States for operation of aircraft.

In the days that followed, witness after witness was called by both the prosecution and the defense to answer involved military and technical questions. Interrogating his defense witnesses, Reid hammered away at the deficiencies of the air service's men and equipment. Captain Robert Oldys testified that "personnel and equipment on hand in Hawaii, the Philippines, and the Panama Canal departments bear the ratio of one to five between how many there are and how many there should be there."

The defense called Major Carl Spaatz, later to become the famous general "Touhy" Spaatz, who declared that the bulk of the air service equipment "is either obsolescent or obsolete," and pointed out that only 22 percent of the total aircraft in the army were fit for service. Major H. H. Arnold, later the renowned general "Hap" Arnold, bitterly attacked the use of obsolete planes, and produced a long list of figures showing casualties.

When Major General Frank W. Coe, chief of the coast artillery, testified for the prosecution, Reid questioned him about a statement made to a committee of Congress by Brigadier General H. A. Drum that "with twelve antiaircraft guns of 3-inch calibre" he could keep any bomber that came within range from doing much harm. Could twelve antiaircraft 3-inch guns protect the city of Washington, Coe was asked. "I didn't say they could," he replied.

"Oh, didn't you," Mr. Reid asked. The congressman looked around for a copy of the report of the hearings, but before he could find one, General Coe continued, "Ten thousand antiaircraft guns can't protect the city of Washington." "That is all," said Mr. Reid, and with a smile he dismissed the witness.

A sensational witness appeared at the trial on November 12. The widow of the commander of the *Shenandoah*, Mrs. Zachary Lansdowne, came into court and declared under oath that on the evening before her appearance she had been handed by Mrs. George W. Steele, Jr., wife of Captain

Steele, commander of the Lakehurst Air Station, a false story to narrate on the witness stand. Who had sent it? Captain Paul Foley of the Naval board of inquiry investigating the *Shenandoah* disaster! In a heated discussion, the prosecution attempted to have Mrs. Lansdowne's testimony stricken from the record, but the defense won and it was left in.

The highlight of the defense came when it called to the stand the grand old man of the navy, Admiral Sims (Retired). He bluntly stated that any invading fleet could be destroyed by a properly organized land-based air force. With every word he spoke, he shattered reactionary naval tradition. He charged that most admirals were uneducated; that the battleship was no longer a capital ship, having been replaced by the aircraft carrier. Coming from the most respected naval officer in the country, this was powerful ammunition for the cause of the defense.

Billy Mitchell was being tried under a catch-all clause in the Articles of War, the ninety-sixth, which read in part, "Though not mentioned in these articles, all disorders and neglects to the prejudice of good order and military discipline, all conduct of a nature to bring discredit upon the military service . . . shall be taken cognizance of by a . . . court-martial and punished at the discretion of such court." Thus, the prosecution was basing its case on *what* Mitchell had said, whereas the defense was basing its case on the *truth* of what Mitchell had said.

It is difficult to fight a war when no battle is joined. Here was the Peter Zenger struggle all over again, with the defendant demanding the right to establish the truth of his "libel," and the prosecution contending that since truth was irrelevant, it was no defense. But this was a military court and not a civilian one. The attorney for the defense could not turn away from the judges and appeal to a jury—except, one might say, to the jury of public opinion.

The issue was not the substance of the charges; it was that Mitchell was a lawless person. In the words of Secretary of War Weeks, in a letter to President Coolidge that was read at the trial, "General Mitchell's whole course has been so lawless, so contrary to the building up of an efficient organization, so lacking in responsible team work, so indicative of a personal desire for publicity at the expense of everyone with whom he is associated, that his actions tender him unfit for a high administration position such as he now occupies."

The prosecution, in summing up, called Mitchell a loose talking, imaginative megalomaniac, a charlatan seeking promotion, a demagogue seeking self-aggrandizement. For the defense there would be no summing up. Instead, on December 17, Mitchell spoke for himself for only a few minutes. He defended everything he had said as being the truth, and charged that inaccurate and untruthful information had been passed on to the President with regard to aviation and national defense. Under these circumstances, there was no point in continuing the trial. Mitchell concluded:

This court has refrained from ruling whether the truth in this case constitutes an absolute defense or not. To proceed further with the case would serve no useful purpose. I have therefore directed my counsel to entirely close our part of the proceeding without argument.

Three hours later the judges brought in their verdict. It was read by Major General Robert L. Howze.

The court, upon secret written ballot, two-thirds of the members present at the time the vote was taken, concurring in each finding of guilty, finds the accused guilty of all specifications and of the charge.

Upon secret written ballot the court sentences the accused to be suspended from rank, command, and duty, with forfeiture of all pay and allowances for five years.

The court is thus lenient because of the military record of the accused during the World War, two-thirds of the members present at the time the vote was taken, concurring.

There is a folklore that grows up after an important trial, especially when the stenographic record has mysteriously disappeared. Myths and rumors grow, lies mingle with half-truths, historical facts are conveniently forgotten. When the course of history makes a patriotic hero out of the accused, the story of the trial is likely to be rewritten.

One of the minor myths that developed in later years was that the verdict handed down to Mitchell was roundly denounced by the general public. However, the most influential newspaper in America, *The New York Times*, commented editorially the day following the trial that the verdict could not have been other than it was. "An army exists and functions by the enforcement of discipline. Colonel Mitchell broke the bonds of discipline defiantly. The effect upon the morale of the army would have been disastrous if he had not been convicted."

History, however, would deliver a different verdict. Perhaps, in a sense, Mitchell was gratified at both. For, as a good military man, he might well have believed and understood that military discipline cannot be flouted, that an army cannot exist if an officer goes unpunished for calling his superiors incompetent, criminally negligent, almost treacherous. But he might also have believed that America could not go forward if someone did not make a dramatic appeal to the country on the question of air power. The

trial, even the verdict, may have been his victory. He was both found guilty and vindicated. Even the verdict of guilt might have fitted into his master plan of vindication. He might indeed have been disappointed that the punishment had been so lenient; a stronger sentence would surely have awakened America to his message more rapidly, more dramatically.

Colonel William Mitchell, stripped of his command and rank for five years, resigned from the service. He abandoned a plan for a hunting trip to Africa, and instead organized a tour of the United States. He lectured, wrote, and continued to campaign for his cause.

Mitchell warned about what was then being termed the shrinking world. He continued to call for a unified department of national defense in which the air force would be a separate entity. Viewed often as a prophet as well as a hero, not all his prophecies were accurate. For one, he downplayed Russia as a potential world or even European power. But finally, in 1928, he had his moment of triumph; he obtained from the American Legion the vote he had long sought, favoring a unified air force. Even *The New York Times*, hardly his most consistent supporter, commented editorially that General Mitchell's "triumph is complete."

Now he retreated to Virginia, where he hunted, fished, gave press conferences, issued broadsides, and wrote articles. He found an ever-widening group of supporters, from the Hearst press to Fiorello La Guardia. Although many urged that he be appointed assistant secretary of war for aviation, he was bypassed. Even his rank was not restored. And he continued to make enemies. In a speech before the Foreign Policy Association he attacked the American aviation industry with such vehemence that one of the companies brought a $200,000 libel suit against him. He was accused of jingoism because he warned of growing Japanese air power and the possibility of a surprise attack. By December, 1935, then only fifty-six years of age, he had given up any hope of reentering government service. However, his friends continued to fight for his reinstatement, and on January 16, 1936, the United States Senate voted in favor of it. Unfortunately, the bill was defeated in the House. On February 19, 1936, he died.

Almost every commentator on the Mitchell case writing in the 1950s and 1960s calls attention to the accuracy of his prophecies, as exemplified by World War II, with its blitzkriegs and air wars over England and Germany, and with the destruction of a large part of the American fleet at Pearl Harbor. But, in an even greater long-range sense, Mitchell and his much-vaunted air power may prove to be overrated in modern warfare. Intercontinental ballistic missiles, on the one hand, and guerrilla war, on the other, may combine to reduce air power to the secondary, or even tertiary, position it held when Mitchell was court-martialed.

The Scottsboro Boys

1931-1950

In 1931, IN THE MIDST OF THE DEPRESSION, tens of thousands of Americans traveled from place to place, searching for an odd job, seeking to keep themselves alive.

In Alabama on March 25, 1931, on a freight train crowded with such wanderers, a group of black boys got into a fistfight with some white boys. Because the black boys outnumbered the whites, the whites were defeated and thrown bodily off the train. When they were seen on the railroad track, they anticipated being arrested on a charge of vagrancy, and told the authorities that black kids had fought with them and thrown them off the train. The authorities telephoned ahead, and at Paint Rock, Alabama, a sheriff's posse arrested nine black boys who had been on the train. The oldest of the nine was nineteen, the youngest, thirteen. One was almost blind, and others were suffering from many infirmities.

Two white girls, Ruby Bates and Victoria Price, were found at the railroad tracks. Allegedly, both were prostitutes. It was a fine setting for a lynching; all that was needed was a statement from the girls that they had been raped, and Southern womanhood would be protected. Each girl, it was claimed, had been raped in the freight car by six black boys; in all, nine were covered by the accusation.

Later a Supreme Court justice was to describe the arrest. "Both girls and the Negroes were taken to Scottsboro, the county seat. Word of their coming and of the alleged assaults had preceded them, and they were met in Scottsboro by a large crowd. . . . The attitude of the community was one of great hostility."

Indeed, the judicial words are a remarkable understatement. In a city of fifteen hundred people, a crowd estimated at ten thousand gathered. A brass band played "There'll Be a Hot Time in the Old Town Tonight." The boys were quickly tried, and all but the youngest were sentenced to death. The official transcript of the trial carries the final statement of the prosecutor to the white jury. "Guilty or not guilty, let's get rid of these niggers."

But Scottsboro did not reckon on the possibility that people—white people—might take an interest in the boys. The Communists discovered the case, and soon socialists, liberals, churchmen, civil liberties defenders and just plain people were deeply involved. "They shall not die" became the rallying cry. All over the North and in many parts of the South, Alabama justice was on trial. In Rome, Moscow, Berlin, on every continent and in hundreds of languages, demonstrators demanded that the lives of these boys be saved.

In the Supreme Court of the United States a new trial was granted, and more forcibly than ever before, fundamental issues

Haywood Patterson, one of the nine Scottsboro boys to go on trial in Decatur, Alabama, on April 1, 1933, brings a good-luck sign into court. WIDE WORLD PHOTOS

were raised, such as the exclusion of blacks from juries in the South and the right to adequate counsel. In overturning the verdict, the Supreme Court stated that

in the light of the facts outlined in the fore-part of this opinion—the ignorance and illiteracy of the defendants and their youth, the system of public hostility, the imprisonment and the close surveillance of the defendants by the military forces, the fact that their friends and families were all in other states and communication with them necessarily difficult, and above all that they stood in deadly peril of their lives—we think the failure of the trial court to give them reasonable time and opportunity to secure counsel was a clear denial of due process.

The new trial, with the entire world watching, took place in the sleepy little town of Decatur, Alabama. Einstein had spoken up

in defense of the Scottsboro nine, as had Thomas Mann and other leaders of the intellectual world from every corner of the globe. In Alabama the white Southerners could not understand why people were making such a fuss.

Samuel Leibowitz, the defense counsel, went to Alabama with powerful weapons at his disposal; above all, the repudiation by Ruby Bates of the rape story, and corroboration of the complete rape denial by her boyfriend, Lester Carter, who accompanied her. But the prosecutor, speaking to his all-white jury, had a new weapon. "Show them," he shouted, "that Alabama justice can't be bought and sold with Jew money from New York!"

Again there was a verdict of guilty; again the cries against Southern justice arose throughout America and the world. But this time the trial judge, James Horton, astonished his fellow Alabamians by overturning the verdict, stating that he could find no evidence in the trial record that would point to the guilt of the defendants. For this courageous act Judge Horton was resoundingly defeated in the next election.

Now came the third trial, before a new judge, William Callahan, and again the boys were found guilty. A recent writer quotes this colloquy from that trial:

PROSECUTOR: If we let this nigger go, it won't be safe for your mother, wife, or sweetheart to walk the streets of the South!

LEIBOWITZ: Your Honor, must we continue to try this case in a welter of such inflammatory appeals?

PROSECUTOR: (hurt) I ain't done nothin' wrong. Your Honor knows I always make the same speech in every nigger rape case.

JUDGE: Objection overruled.

The case again traveled to the Supreme Court, and again demonstrations were held, protests were loud, and pressure was unrelenting. In the Supreme Court decision, which is frequently cited to this day, the court ruled for the first time that systematic exclusion of black people from juries was grounds for reversal.

Then came the fourth trial, and a behind-

Samuel Leibowitz (second from left), on May 1, 1935, confers with the defendants just after he has asked the governor of Alabama to pardon them. The Scottsboro boys (from left to right) are Roy Wright, Olen Montgomery, Ozie Powell, Willie Roberson, Eugene Williams, Charlie Weems, and Andy Wright. WIDE WORLD PHOTOS

the-scenes deal was made. Four boys were freed, five were found guilty. The Northerners agreed to stop the protests and the white Southern officials agreed to have all the boys freed quietly within one year. The protests died down, but the Southerners broke their part of the deal, and several of the boys remained in jail. Haywood Patterson escaped and, trailed by bloodhounds, plunged into a river. He allowed the dogs to come after him, and then, with his bare hands, grabbed each dog around the neck and submerged it, choking and drowning the animal.

Not until 1950, nineteen years after the arrest, did the last of the Scottsboro boys, Andy Wright, emerge from jail. Only one has been heard from in recent years, and even he must live under another name, as his parole was based on the stipulation that he must not leave Alabama. Several of the boys have died and others have dropped from sight. It is believed that the two girls have died, as well as many of the other principals in the case.

In the great transformations that have occurred in American courtrooms since 1931, few can compare in significance with the rights of blacks before the bar of justice. In this changing scene, the influence of Scottsboro should not be overlooked.

The Nuremberg Trials
1945

HITLER AND HIS HENCHMEN WERE WARNED not to abrogate the terms of the Treaty of Versailles that ended World War I and limited the German army to a police force of one hundred thousand; not to scuttle the Weimar constitution that had brought democracy to Germany; not to collaborate with the German industrial moguls to set in motion the mechanical wheels of rearmament; not to violate international treaties and agreements. But as early as 1923 the groundwork of Hitler's grandiose plan for German world conquest was exposed to the readers of *Mein Kampf*. And hadn't the world laughed it off as the hallucinations of an insignificant Austrian house painter writing from a prison cell?

Hitler and his National Socialists came to power in January 1933. Prior to that, German army ordnance had secretly collaborated with Germany's leading industrialists to begin a program of rearmament. So effective were they over the years that they were able to place at Hitler's disposal a ready-made military machine, disregarding the international law they were breaking.

On April 4, 1933, thirty days after he had himself proclaimed the führer, Hitler stepped up Germany's preparations for war by creating a reich defense council to prepare plans for mobilization. War plans proceeded at an accelerated pace. At a meeting on November 5, 1937, with his top political

AND MILITARY LEADERS, INCLUDING HERmann Göring, Erich Raeder, and Konstantin von Neurath, he announced his intention to use force to gain his ends.

Hitler's first step toward territorial aggrandizement was to take over Austria. On March 13, 1938, Artur von Seyss-Inquart, both chancellor and president of Austria, approved *Anschluss*—the incorporation of Austria into the German Reich. Czechoslovakia was next. Hitler forced the aging President, Emil Hácha, to sign away his country on March 15, 1939.

On June 22 Hitler ordered a secret mobilization for an attack on Poland. Two months later, on August twenty-fifth, England and Poland signed a mutual agreement pact. Thus, when Hitler's troops crossed the Polish border on September 1, Britain fulfilled her pledge to Poland and on September 3 declared that a state of war existed between England and Germany. France followed England almost immediately with a declaration of war. Warsaw fell on September 23.

There now followed a few months of inactivity, but in May 1940 Hitler's troops, violating all treaties and assurances, overran Luxembourg, Holland, and Belgium. A few weeks earlier, on April 9, ships of the German navy, disguised as British warships and merchantmen, sailed across the North Sea and attacked Norway. At the same time, Hitler brought Denmark within his grip.

The Hitler war machine now had Western Europe under its control. In May the Low Countries were invaded, and the Maginot Line, the much-vaunted defense of France, collapsed. On June 21 the French signed an armistice, and Hitler danced his famous jig. There now remained only England and Russia. Hitler postponed his plans for invading England, and instead, against the advice of Raeder and his other military leaders, turned to a blitz campaign against Russia.

Meanwhile, Joachim Ribbentrop, working for Hitler, kept urging Japan to join Germany against Great Britain and establish herself in the Far East by seizing British territory and destroying British naval forces there.

Adolf Hitler. U.S. Army Photo

These three photographs showing the destruction of the Warsaw ghetto were presented as evidence against the Nazi defendants at Nuremberg. U.S. Army Photos

Japan was reluctant to bring the United States into the war, which she felt would happen if she declared war on the British. But when Germany invaded Russia and tied down this age-old enemy of Japan in that sector of the world, Japan saw her golden opportunity to realize her ambition of a Greater East Asia Co-Prosperity Sphere. Ribbentrop, in a conversation with the Japanese ambassador in Berlin on November 28, 1941, urged that no time be lost, that now was the moment (with America virtually unprepared for war) to strike, and that Germany would enter the war against the United States immediately upon Japan's engaging in war with United States. On December 1 the negotiations between Japan and Washington to settle differences of opinion peacefully had broken down. On December 3 the Japanese ambassador to Rome asked Mussolini if he would honor the Tripartite Pact (September 27, 1940, between Germany, Italy, and Japan) in the event of Japan's declaring war on the United States. Il Duce gave his full assurances. Germany already had.

On Sunday, December 7, 1941—Pearl Harbor.

On October 25, 1941, even before the United States entered the war, President Roosevelt, commenting on Nazi murders of hostages in France, warned the Nazis that they would bring on a "fearful retribution." On January 13, 1942, nine governments-in-exile declared in London that by means of judicial procedures they would punish the Nazi war criminals when the war was over. On October 7, 1942, England and the United States promised that a United Nations war crimes commission would be set up to ferret out such criminals and bring them to justice. On December 17, 1942, the Allied powers notified the Nazis that they would punish all those responsible for persecuting and exterminating the Jews. The Moscow Conference in October 1943, subscribed to by Roosevelt, Churchill, and Stalin, stated that the Allies would hold responsible all individuals who committed war crimes. Regarding the Nazi slaughter of the Jews, President Roosevelt said to the world on March 24, 1944, "None who participate in these acts of savagery shall go unpunished."

True to their word, within a few months after the defeat of Germany the Allies set up judicial machinery to try the major war criminals who had been apprehended and put behind bars.

On August 8, 1945, in a document called the London Agreement, the governments of the United States, the United Kingdom, the Union of Soviet Socialist Republics, and the Provisional Government of the French Republic pledged to prosecute and punish the major war criminals of the European Axis. The Moscow Declaration of October 30, 1943, in regard to German atrocities in Occupied Europe, stated that those German officers, enlisted men, and members of the Nazi party who were responsible for such atrocities should be returned to stand trial in the countries in which they had committed them. Now, in order to try war criminals whose offenses had no particular geographic location, the London Agreement established the International Military Tribunal. The authority for such a court was contained in a charter to the Agreement.

This charter set up a constitution designating as judges four members (one from each of the signatory powers) and four alternate judges. It specified the following acts to be considered crimes coming under the jurisdiction of the International Military Tribunal.

A. CRIMES AGAINST PEACE: namely, planning, preparing, initiating, or waging a war of

Twenty-one top Nazi defendants are in the prisoners' rows at the first Nuremberg trial that began on November 20, 1945. U.S. Army Photo

aggression, or a war in violation of international treaties, agreements, or assurances, or participating in a conspiracy to accomplish the foregoing.

B. WAR CRIMES: namely, violation of the laws or customs of war, including (but not limited to) murder, ill-treatment or deportation to slave labor, ill-treatment of prisoners of war, killing hostages, plundering public or private property, wanton destruction of cities, towns, or villages, or any other devastation not justified by military necessity.

C. CRIMES AGAINST HUMANITY: namely, murder, extermination, enslavement, deportation, and other inhumane acts committed against any urban population, before or during the war, or persecutions on political,

racial, or religious grounds, whether or not such violated a domestic law of the country in which they were committed.

The opening session of the tribunal was held on October 18, 1945, at Berlin, and issued an indictment against the top twenty-four Nazi war criminals. They were informed that they should be ready to stand trial within thirty days after the indictment was served on them. Also indicted were seven groups or organizations. The trials would take place at Nuremberg, Germany, with Lord Justice Lawrence, of the United Kingdom and North Ireland, presiding.

The indictment split the first charge of the charter into two parts.

The judges take their places for the opening of the Nuremberg War Crimes Trial (left to right): A. F. Volchoff, USSR alternate; Major General I. T. Nikitchenke, USSR; Justice Sir Norman Birkett, British alternate; Presiding Judge Lord Justice Sir Geoffrey Lawrence, Great Britain; former Attorney General Francis Biddle, U.S.; Judge John J. Parker, U.S. alternate; Henri Donnedieu de Vabre, France; Robert Falcon, French alternate. U.S. ARMY PHOTO

THE COMMON PLAN OR CONSPIRACY: covering the formation of the Nazi party as the instrument of cohesion bringing the conspirators together; the aims and purposes of the Nazi party to resort to war to overthrow the Treaty of Versailles, to avoid the restrictions on military armament and activity of Germany, to acquire not only territories lost as a result of World War I but also the territories of other peoples so that Germany could have "living space"; specific aggressive actions from the planning in 1936 to the actual invasion of Austria on March 12, 1938; and the collaboration with Italy and Japan from November 1936 to December 1941, to wage aggressive war against the United States.

CRIMES AGAINST PEACE: covering the violation of international treaties, agreements, and assurances.

The indictment listed pages and pages of specific charges under War Crimes, ghastly, gruesome, and unbelievable, except that they had happened. Perhaps the most fantastic figures were atrocities committed in Russia. In the Lvov region the Germans exterminated about seven hundred thousand Soviet people; in the Latvian S.S.R. 577,000 people were murdered. Prisoners of war were murdered or died as a result of hunger and forced marches; hostages were shot. Essential commodities and wealth in occupied countries were despoiled; raw materials, industrial equipment, agricultural products, and currency were all plundered and sent to Germany to help further the war effort. Works of art were looted and destroyed. Cities, towns, and villages were laid waste. Civilian labor was conscripted. Occupied territory was "Germanized," and children were forced to join the Hitler Youth Movement.

But the worst crimes of all were committed under point four, Crimes Against Humanity. Chief United States Prosecutor Robert H. Jackson, in his opening statement to the court, made accusation that the lives of six million Jews were extinguished by every conceivable diabolic means.

The Nuremberg Trials of the major German war criminals began on November 20, 1945, with pleas of not guilty by all defendants except Martin Bormann, Robert Ley, and Gustav Krupp von Bohlen und Halbach, the last of whom, it was agreed, was too physically and mentally ill to stand trial.

Two of the defendants who were not in the prisoners' dock were Robert Ley, leader of the German Labor Front, who hanged himself in his cell while awaiting trial; and Martin Bormann (*in absentia*), chief of staff in the office of Hitler's deputy, secretary of the führer, and general in the SS, indicted on counts one, three, and four. Bormann had not been apprehended.

On the bench were four of the world's most distinguished jurists and their alternates. The president of the tribunal was Lord Justice Lawrence; for the United States, Mr. Francis Biddle; for the French Republic, M. Le Professeur Donnedieu de Vabres; for the Union of Soviet Socialist Republics, Major General I. T. Nikitchenko.

Justice Robert H. Jackson, chief United States prosecutor. U.S. ARMY PHOTO

It was their duty to weigh the prosecution's cases against the cases for the defendants and render for posterity a fair and just verdict. Against the criticism that judges from the victorious nations could not impartially try the Nazi defendants, the prosecution countered with the fact that judges everywhere impartially tried thieves and murderers without being connected with or condoning such themselves.

On November 21, 1945, Mr. Justice Robert H. Jackson of the United States made the opening address for the prosecution. It was a statement of historic importance. It charged both individuals and organizations with plotting and carrying out international crimes to wipe out entire peoples and nations. Since no one man could engineer such atrocities on such a mammouth scale, it followed that thousands upon thousands of willing participants collaborated to perpetrate the hideous crime of genocide. Thus, the Nuremberg Trials laid the foundations for a new concept of international justice: that whole groups and organizations, as well as individuals, could be held criminally liable for committing crimes associated with aggressive war.

As Mr. Justice Jackson said at the beginning,

What makes this inquest significant is that these prisoners represent sinister influences that will lurk in the world long after their bodies have returned to dust. We will show them to be the living symbols of racial hatred, of terrorism and violence, and of the arrogance and cruelty of power. They are symbols of fierce nationalisms and militarism, of intrigue and warmaking which have embroiled Europe generation after generation, crushing its manhood, destroying its homes, and impoverishing its life. They have so identified themselves with the philosophies they conceived and with the forces they have directed, that any tenderness to them is a victory and an encouragement to all the evils which are attached to their names. Civilization can afford no compromise with the social forces which would gain renewed strength if we deal ambiguously or indecisively with the men in whom those forces now precariously survive.

Justice Jackson then limited the scope of United States prosecution. "The case as presented by the United States will be concerned with the brains and authority behind all the crimes. These defendants were men of a station and rank which does not soil its own hands with blood. They were men who knew how to use lesser men as tools."

To forestall criticism of outside powers illegally interfering with the internal problems of a sovereign country, Jackson stated, "The purpose, as we have seen, of getting rid of the influence of free labor, the churches, and the Jews was to clear their obstruction to the precipitation of aggressive war. If aggressive warfare in violation of treaty obligations is a matter of international cognizance, the preparations for it must also be of concern to the international community." Thus,

the scope of the trials was enlarged to cover the growth of the Nazi party and all the acts of their feverish pace to prepare for the launching of an aggressive war.

Continuing his opening statement, Jackson outlined the nature of crimes and torture against prisoners of the Nazis, then continued with the international events that accompanied the Nazis' aggressive build-up. It was his task to prove the charges made against the defendants in point one of the indictment, The Common Plan or Conspiracy.

To prove the charges in point two, Crimes Against Peace, was the task of H.M. Attorney-General Sir Hartley Shawcross, chief prosecutor for the United Kingdom of Great Britain and Northern Ireland. On December 4, 1945, he began his opening statement by quoting Adolf Hitler. "I shall give a propagandist cause for starting the war, never mind whether it be true or not. The victor shall not be asked later on whether we tell the truth or not. In starting and making a war not the right is what matters but victory —the strongest has the right." He then outlined every illegal step that Germany made to take over the territories of other peoples in defiance of all treaties, covenants, and assurances.

On January 17, 1946, M. François de Menthon, chief prosecutor for the French Republic, opened the prosecution's case to prove counts three and four, War Crimes and Crimes Against Humanity, as perpetrated by the defendants. Of Hitler's race concept he charged, "In the midst of the twentieth century Germany goes back, of her own free will, beyond Christianity and civilization to the primitive barbarity of ancient Germany. She makes a deliberate break with all the universal conceptions of modern nations. The National Socialist doctrine, which raised inhumanity to the level of a principle, constitutes, in fact, a doctrine of disintegration of modern society." He reviewed the war criminality of the Nazis' forced-labor policy (including forcing persons to work for the German war effort) in the countries they overran; the seizure of agricultural and industrial products from these countries; the debasement of their currencies by outrageous indemnities. Coming to the climax of his speech, he said, "The crime which will undoubtedly be remembered as the most horrible committed by the Germans against the civilian population of the occupied countries was that of deportation and internment in the concentration camps of Germany." Next M. de Menthon stated, "Crimes committed against prisoners of war, although less known, bear ample testimony to the degree of inhumanity which Nazi Germany had attained." He gave specific policies and instances.

As a definition of crimes against persons and property, he offered the following:

The crimes against person and property, of which the defendants are guilty, are provided for by all national laws. They present an international character because they were committed in several different countries. . . . A crime of common law, the War Crime, is, nevertheless, not an ordinary infraction; it has a character peculiarly intrinsic—it is a crime committed on the occasion or under pretext of war. It must be punished because, even in time of war, attacks on the integrity of the physical being and of property are crimes if they are not justified by the laws and customs of war.

It was left to General R. A. Rudenko, chief prosecutor for the Union of Soviet Socialist Republics, to review and sum up the entire charge of the prosecution, starting on February 8, 1946. His presentation was more graphic, more descriptive of the tortures and terrible deaths, than the one his colleagues had offered. In view of the far greater magnitude of crimes the Germans inflicted on Russian civilians and soldiers, this was understandable. Addressing the judges directly, Rudenko said, "If Your Honors please, I appear here as the representative of the Union of the Soviet Socialist Republics, which bore the main brunt of the blows of the fascist invaders and which vastly contributed to the smashing of Hitlerite Germany and its satellites. On behalf of the Soviet Union, I charge the defendants on all counts enumerated in Article VI of the Charter of the International Military Tribunal." He ended eloquently, if, in the light of today's world situation, with unintentional irony.

In the name of the sacred memory of millions of innocent victims of the fascist terror, for the sake of the consolidation of peace throughout the world, for the sake of the future security of nations, we are presenting the defendants with a just and complete account which must be settled. This is an account on behalf of all mankind, an account backed by the will and conscience of all freedom-loving nations.

May justice be done!

It would be impossible to condense the more than forty-five large volumes of testimony and documents that encompassed the trial proceedings at Nuremberg. The prosecutors, their staffs, and all those who engaged in gathering evidence and witnesses to prove the guilt of the defendants had done their job well in the short time allotted them. In essence, the main defense of the accused was that they were merely carrying out orders from their superiors. Had they not, they would not now be on trial. In fact, as Göring remarked to a psychiatrist examining him in his cell, who asked if there were any men who would say "No" to the orders of the high command, "Not aboveground!"

Each prisoner had an opportunity on the

One guard is placed at each cell door. Prisoners were observed twenty-four hours a day. NATIONAL ARCHIVES

stand to state his case to the world. Each had a famous lawyer to offer his defense, then to examine him on the stand in an attempt to show his innocence. But the weight of documented evidence was too much for the defendants. After all of them had been given as long as they wanted to defend themselves, the four prosecutors presented their closing arguments.

In the course of his closing address for the United States, Justice Jackson characterized the criminal activities of each of the defendants.

A glance over the dock will show that each defendant played a part that fitted in with every other, and that all advanced the common plan. It contradicts experience that men of such diverse backgrounds and talents should so forward each other's aims by coincidence.

The large and varied role of Göring was half militant and half gangster. He stuck a pudgy finger in every pie. He used his SA muscle-men to help bring the gang into power. In order to entrench that power he contrived to have the Reichstag burned, established the Gestapo, and created the concentration camps. He was equally adept at massacring opponents and at framing scandals to get rid of stubborn generals. He built up the Luftwaffe and hurled it at his defenseless neighbors. He was among the foremost in harrying the Jews out of the land. By mobilizing the total economic resources of Germany he made possible the waging of the war which he had taken a large part in planning. He was, next to Hitler, the man who tied the activities of all defendants together in a common effort.

The parts played by the other defendants, although less comprehensive and less spectacular than that of the Reichsmarshal, were nevertheless integral and necessary contributions to the joint undertaking, without any one of which the success of the common enterprise would have been in jeopardy. There are many specific deeds of which these men have been proven guilty. . . .

The zealot Hess, before succumbing to wanderlust, was the engineer tending the party machinery, passing orders and propaganda down to the Leadership Corps, supervising every aspect of party activities, and maintaining the organization as a loyal and ready instrument of power. When apprehensions abroad threatened the success of the Nazi scheme for conquest, it was the duplicitous Ribbentrop, the salesman of deception, who was detailed to pour wine on the troubled waters of suspicion by preaching the gospel of limited and peaceful intentions. Keitel, weak and willing tool, delivered the armed forces . . . over to the party and directed them in executing its felonious designs.

Kaltenbrunner, the grand inquisitor, took up the bloody mantle of Heydrich to stifle opposition and terrorize compliance. . . . It was Rosenberg, the intellectual high priest of the "master race," who provided the doctrine of hatred which gave the impetus for the annihilation of Jewry, and put his . . . theories into practice against the Eastern occupied territories. . . . The fanatical Frank, who solidified Nazi control by establishing the new order of authority without law, so that the will of the party was the only test of legality, proceeded to export his lawlessness to Poland. . . . Frick, the ruthless organizer, helped the party to seize power . . . and chained the economy of Bohemia and Moravia to the German war machine.

Streicher . . . manufactured and distributed obscene racial libels which incited the populace to accept and assist the progressively savage operations of "race purification." As minister of economics, Funk accelerated the pace of rearmament, and as Reichsbank president banked for the SS the gold teeth-fillings of concentration camp victims. . . . It was Schacht, the façade of starched respectability, who in the early days provided . . . the bait for the hesitant, and whose wizardry later made it possible for Hitler to finance the colossal rearmament program, and to do it secretly.

Doenitz . . . promoted the success of the Nazi aggressions. Raeder, the political admiral, stealthily built up the German navy in defiance of the Versailles Treaty, and then put it to use in a series of aggressions which he had taken a large part in planning. Von Schirach . . . initiated the German youth in Nazi doctrine, trained them in legions for service in the SS and Wehrmacht, and delivered them up to the party as fanatic . . . executors of its will.

Sauckel . . . produced desperately needed manpower by driving foreign people into the land of bondage on a scale unknown even in the ancient days of tyranny in the kingdom of the Nile. Jodl . . . led the Wehrmacht in violating its own code of military honor in order to carry out the . . . aims of Nazi policy. Von Papen . . . devoted his diplomatic cunning to the service of Nazi objectives abroad.

Seyss-Inquart, spearhead of the Austrian fifth-column, took over the government of his own country to make a present of it to Hitler, and then, moving north, brought terror and oppression to the Netherlands and pillaged its economy for the benefit of the German juggernaut. Von Neurath, the old-school diplomat . . . guided Nazi diplomacy in the early years, soothed the fears of prospective victims, and as Reich protector of Bohemia and Moravia, strengthened the German position for the coming attack on Poland. Speer, as minister of armaments and war production, joined in planning and executing the program to dragoon prisoners of war and foreign workers into German war industries which waxed in output while the laborers waned in starvation. Fritzsche, radio propaganda chief, by manipulation of the truth goaded German public opinion into frenzied support of the regime. . . . And Bormann, who has not accepted our invitation to this reunion, sat at the throttle of the vast and powerful engine of the party, guiding it in the ruthless execution of Nazi policies, from the scourging of the Christian Church to the lynching of captive Allied airmen.

Now it was the judges' turn to render their

verdict. It was a lengthy one, and took the two days of September 30 and October 1, 1946. On the former day, judgments were rendered against the groups and organizations on trial; on the latter date, against individuals. Each defendant was called before the judges separately and each given his own judgment.

Göring: Guilty on all 4 counts: Death.

Hess: Guilty on counts 1 and 2: Life imprisonment.

Von Ribbentrop: Guilty on all 4 counts: Death.

Keitel: Guilty on all 4 counts: Death.

Rosenberg: Guilty on all 4 counts: Death.

Frank: Guilty on counts 3 and 4: Death.

Frick: Guilty on counts 2, 3, and 4: Death.

Streicher: Guilty on count 4: Death.

Funk: Guilty on counts 2, 3, and 4: Life imprisonment.

Schacht: Not guilty.

Doenitz: Guilty on counts 2 and 3: Ten years' imprisonment.

Raeder: Guilty on counts 1, 2, and 3: Life imprisonment.

Von Schirach: Guilty on count 4: Twenty years' imprisonment.

Sauckel: Guilty on counts 3 and 4: Death.

Jodl: Guilty on all 4 counts: Death.

Von Papen: Not guilty.

Seyss-Inquart: Guilty on counts 2, 3, and 4: Death.

Speer: Guilty on counts 3 and 4: Twenty years' imprisonment.

Von Neurath: Guilty on all 4 counts: Fifteen years' imprisonment.

Fritzsche: Not guilty.

Kaltenbrunner: Guilty on counts 3 and 4: Death.

Bormann (in absentia): Guilty on counts 3 and 4: Death.

Of the organizations on trial, the SS, the SD, the Gestapo, and the Leadership Corps of the Nazi party were declared criminal organizations; acquitted were the Reich cabinet and the general staff and high command of the German armed forces.

Those who received the death sentence were executed at Nuremberg on October 16, 1946, with the exception of Göring, who managed to cheat the hangman's noose by taking poison in his cell the day before. Those who received prison sentences were put behind bars in the Spandau jail, under the administration of the four Allied powers.

The Nuremberg Trials established a historic and momentous precedent. Here, in the case of the major war criminals, and later at the many trials of the lesser defendants, international justice against war criminals was carried out in fact, whereas after all previous wars it was carried out only by historical condemnation. As a result of these trials, the political and military leaders of any nation starting an aggressive war, ordering mass exterminations, drafting others into slave labor, and killing and torturing prisoners of war in violation of the rules of war were put on notice that they would eventually be brought before a court of international justice to answer for these crimes.

Along with a mandate to bring accused war criminals to trial, the charter of the International Military Tribunal clearly stated that each defendant would be given a fair trial, thus outlawing a drumhead court-martial of the leaders of a defeated country. The conduct of the trial itself could not have been more fair to the defendants. They received their sentences after full opportunity to defend themselves, and each was judged on the evidence alone, and not on vague charges and suspicions.

All nations are now bound by the legal precedents established at Nuremberg. As Justice Jackson stated, "While this law is first applied against German aggressors, the law includes, and if it is to serve a useful purpose it must condemn, aggression by any other nations, including those which sit here now in judgment." On December 11, 1946, the United Nations affirmed the principles of international law recognized by the charter of the Nuremberg Trials.

It would be utopian to think that the new international law laid down at Nuremberg will put an end to wars. In Vietnam, the United States has slowly withdrawn from a massive undeclared war. But it is reasonable to hope that all those participating in it were warned by the Nuremberg precedent —on conduct in the war, on the war aims of the nations involved, on the treatment of captured civilians and prisoners of war, and on the rules of modern warfare laid down in the conventions and treaties formulated between 1907 and 1928.

Nuremberg, however, leaves basic international questions unanswered, and the answers will continue to be found in the realm of political reality rather than political morality. The victors will continue to decide what crimes have been committed, and the vanquished alone will have to pay for them.

Among the aspects of the Nuremberg Trials that were precedent making and that have disturbed some social thinkers is the one that the trials presumably involved ex post facto law. Many of the crimes for which the defendants were found guilty were not, in a narrow and legal sense, crimes in their own country at the time that the acts took place. In fact, the very opposite was the essence of the accusation: that the defendants, when in power, failed to define these acts against humanity as crimes. Nuremberg established, as would the Eichmann case later, that when behavior involves acts of such enormity that they are in conflict with the nature of civilization and the elementary standards of human existence, they are crimes for which the perpetrators are responsible, even though they may contravene no written national law.

Julius and Ethel Rosenberg and Morton Sobell

1951

WERE JULIUS AND ETHEL ROSENBERG responsible for a crime which sent the world into the Korean War, proliferated the atom bomb, and gave away the greatest secrets of their country? Or were they victims of the McCarthy era of hysteria and fear, and convicted on flimsy, perjured evidence for a crime that may never have taken place? Or is there a balance of truth between these two extremes, where the accused parties may indeed have committed illegal acts, though less monstrous than charged, and received a sentence unbelievably harsh and cruel? Wherever the truth is found, those who study the Rosenberg and Sobell case are usually deeply partisan.

Called by the Columbia Law Review "the outstanding 'political' trial of this generation," the case of Julius and Ethel Rosenberg and Morton Sobell attracted worldwide attention that still lingers today.

The Second World War came to a quick end with the bombing of Hiroshima and Nagasaki. If the atom bombs that wreaked havoc on these two Japanese cities brought, in the aftermath of their tragedy, peace on earth, it was a troubled peace. For man now had a weapon so awesome in its power that the planet itself was threatened. Although atomic energy was developed in the United States, it was the culmination of the work of scientists in England, France, Italy, Denmark, Germany, the Soviet Union, and elsewhere, AND THE HOPE OF SOME AMERICANS that the secret of the atom could remain closeted within the confines of the United States was not widely shared among the world-wide scientific community.

Soon after the end of World War II, with a shaky alliance between the Western powers and the Soviet Union and with the outbreak of the undeclared yet bitter cold war, several British scientists were arrested as atomic spies. They included Allan Nunn May, a Canadian who admitted his guilt and received ten years' imprisonment. May, however, refused to divulge who his accomplices were and seems to have been motivated by ideological considerations. More importantly, Klaus Fuchs, head of the theoretical physics division at a major British atomic energy installation, who had traveled in the United States during the war, was arrested on February 2, 1950, and admitted his guilt. Exactly one week later Joseph McCarthy, with a talk in Wheeling, West Virginia, inaugurated what came to be known as the McCarthy era.

FBI agents were permitted to interview Fuchs, but how helpful he was is not certain, for he could offer no names and only the vaguest descriptions of his accomplices. Nevertheless, less than four months later the first of these alleged accomplices was arrested—Harry Gold, a thirty-nine-year-old bachelor, a chemist who during the war had held minor posts in companies far removed from work on atomic bombs.

Following Gold's there were more arrests. The public was given an impression of a chain reaction, with one person leading to the next. The most sensational of the series, and the first involving atomic energy, came when a young machinist, David Greenglass, was arrested and held on $100,000 bail. Greenglass had been stationed at Los Alamos during the war and was charged with having passed the secret of the bomb on to Gold.

Greenglass was arraigned in early June 1950, and in the middle of July the FBI announced that Greenglass had talked and had implicated his sister's husband, Julius Rosenberg. Now there was one more person held on bail of $100,000. Between the arrests of Greenglass and Rosenberg, McCarthy's influence increased, and America was facing the Communist world for the first time in a shooting war—Korea. On August 11 there came another arrest, that of Ethel Rosenberg, the sister of Greenglass and the wife of Julius Rosenberg. Finally, one week later, Morton Sobell was arrested in Texas, just across the border from Mexico. Why he had been in Mexico, and how he came to be in Texas, are issues disputed to this day.

The trial of *United States* v. *Julius Rosenberg, Ethel Rosenberg, and Morton Sobell* opened in the federal courthouse in New York City on March 6, 1951. Anatoli Yakovlev, a former Soviet consular official, was named in the indictment, although he was now in the Soviet Union. David Greenglass, a co-conspirator, had pleaded guilty; also named as co-conspirators but not being tried were Gold and Greenglass's wife, Ruth. Before the trial, the defendants had been called the atom spies in the press, often in statements that came from the FBI and the prosecution.

Julius Rosenberg and his wife, Ethel, arriving at federal courthouse, New York. WIDE WORLD PHOTOS

In his opening statement Irving Saypol, chief prosecutor, emphasized the Communist affiliations of the defendants, said that the defendants' "love of Communism and the Soviet Union soon led them into a Soviet espionage ring," and continued, "We will prove that the Rosenbergs devised and put into operation, with the aid of Soviet . . . agents in this country, an elaborate scheme which enabled them to steal through David Greenglass this one weapon, that might well hold the key to the survival of this nation and means the peace of the world, the atomic bomb."

Against Morton Sobell the prosecution presented one witness, Max Elitcher, who testified that Julius Rosenberg had admitted espionage to him and that Rosenberg, in an effort to draw Elitcher into the ring, had implicated the latter's close friend and neighbor, Sobell. But Elitcher then went on to state that Sobell had denounced Rosenberg for mentioning his name. No connection was made between Sobell and atomic spying, and only the most tenuous between Sobell and any form of spying. The defense countered by showing that Elitcher feared prosecution for perjury for having denied under oath his former membership in the Communist party, and showed that he had never been indicted.

Sobell's Communist association was clear, and his close association with the Rosenbergs threw a shadow over him. On advice of counsel he did not take the stand; counsel felt the case against him was so weak that his own testimony would be unnecessary and he might prove vulnerable on cross-examination; juries, however, notoriously draw conclusions against defendants under such circumstances. And against Sobell was his Mexican trip, which had all the earmarks of flight and panic, with inquiry about foreign ports, the use of numerous aliases, and other indications that he feared returning to the United States. Despite the protestations over the years that he had indeed planned to return, he left many signs that this was not his intention. Perhaps his lawyers would have been more convincing if they had stated that he was indeed in flight but that the flight could well have been motivated by fear rather than guilt.

This was the case against Morton Sobell. A jury found him guilty beyond a reasonable doubt, and he was sentenced to thirty years in prison.

Against Julius and Ethel Rosenberg, the case rested primarily on the testimony of Ethel's brother, David Greenglass. He claimed that Julius Rosenberg had induced him to write up secret information on the Los Alamos atomic bomb project, which Ethel typed. It was arranged that David, through his wife, Ruth, would pass other classified information on to an agent whom

Julius would send to Albuquerque. One side of a Jello box was cut into two pieces in an irregular fashion, David testified; and he was given one piece and told that a messenger would come with the second. That messenger, Harry Gold, eventually arrived and said, "Julius sent me." Gold had his half of the Jello box. When Gold left he gave David five hundred dollars, and the next day Ruth deposited four hundred dollars in her account. David Greenglass, corroborated by his wife, insisted that after the arrest of Fuchs Julius had urged him to flee from the United States, and had offered him large sums of money and assistance to go abroad.

Harry Gold took the witness stand next. He neither mentioned nor implicated Sobell, and only in an indirect manner did he implicate the Rosenbergs. Mainly he recited the story of his own espionage and of his dealings with the Soviet official, Yakovlev. But he did corroborate many parts of Greenglass's testimony—that he had been in Albuquerque, that he had met David, had turned money over to him, and had received from David an envelope which the latter said contained "the secret of the atom bomb."

For the defense, Julius and Ethel Rosenberg each took the stand, and each made a complete denial. They recounted their dealings with the Greenglasses, their business difficulties and animosities. Much of the cross-examination of the defendants had nothing to do with spying; it involved their relations with Communist and even antifascist organizations.

On Wednesday, March 28, 1951, the case went to the jury; and the following day the three defendants were found guilty. On April 5 they came before Judge Kaufman for sentencing. For the Rosenbergs it was to be death; for Sobell, thirty years, to which the judge added, "While it may be gratuitous on

Morton Sobell, Julius and Ethel Rosenberg leaving federal courthouse on March 29 after the jury was locked up for the night by Judge Irving R. Kaufman. WIDE WORLD PHOTOS

my part, I at this point note my recommendation against parole."

In the two-year period that followed, there were appeals, motions for clemency, efforts to make a deal with the prisoners whereby they would be saved in return for a confession, and steadfast reiteration of their innocence on the part of the defendants. Throughout Europe and South America, demonstrations numbering tens of thousands called for sparing the lives of the Rosenbergs. "They shall not die"—the refrain that had been heard for two Italian immigrants and some poverty-striken black youths—was heard on the streets of London, Paris, and other world capitals. Nobel Prize winners expressed their doubts of the proofs presented at the trial. Albert Einstein, the pope,

the daughter of Alfred Dreyfus, and the sister of Bartolomeo Vanzetti all urged clemency. But in vain, and on Friday, June 19, 1953, early in the evening so as to avoid a killing on the Sabbath, the Rosenbergs were put to death.

But a growing body of opinion in America has not let the case rest. McCarthyism passed and Sobell remained in jail, spending several years at Alcatraz. While those who confessed wartime treachery against the United States in the service of the enemy have eventually walked out of prison as free men, Sobell remained behind bars, although a simple admission of his guilt would have unlocked the doors. In the years since the trial, many highly placed Americans—professors, clergymen, jurists, and others—have denounced the manner in which Sobell was brought back to the United States. That he was not deported, as the American authorities contended, is apparent. He seems to have been kidnapped and brought illegally across the border in violation of the criminal laws of Mexico. This drama was to be repeated some years later by Israel in the Eichmann case.

Many aspects of the Rosenberg-Sobell case remain puzzling. They were convicted of wartime espionage, but it is generally agreed that the death penalty for espionage in wartime was meant to be used exclusively against one's enemies, not one's allies. For this ambiguity, or technicality in the wording of the law, two people gave their lives. Not since Mary Surratt had a woman been executed by the federal government; and never before had a husband-and-wife team been executed.

Although the evidence against the three was meager, it was there. Yet, as the story continues to be studied, more questions arise and fewer are settled. A tape recording of Gold's statement to his attorney, a highly prestigious Republican, reveals many discrepancies between this first statement and the testimony in court; not the least serious being his failure to mention the name Julius at any point in the tape. It may be but a slight oversight, but it is just about the only link that Gold made with Rosenberg.

Then there is the four hundred dollars that Ruth Greenglass deposited the day after Gold's visit. A study of her bank statements showed that this was only one of many mysterious cash deposits made at the time, deposits that in fact exceeded the income the Greenglasses had. Yet this information was never presented in court. Where did the money come from? Was it from a black-market operation which made David Greenglass feel even more vulnerable?

And as for Gold's visit to Albuquerque, did it ever take place at all? The prosecution entered into evidence a Hilton hotel registration card showing that Gold had been in Albuquerque at the time specified. But recent researchers have come up with serious discrepancies between this and other cards then in use by the hotel, and have cast a shadow over this evidence, suggesting that it may have been a forgery.

But nothing throws the entire case into doubt quite as much as the statements made by some outstanding authorities on atomic energy. They said that Greenglass was a poorly educated mechanic with neither knowledge of nor access to scientific material, and that the highly secret information that he allegedly passed on to Gold, at the behest of Julius Rosenberg, was practically worthless. Dr. Philip Morrison, said to be coholder of the patent on the Nagasaki bomb, called the Greenglass sketch a caricature of the bomb; and Dr. Henry Linschitz said that it was "too incomplete, ambiguous, and even incorrect to be of any service or value to the Russians in shortening the time required to develop their nuclear bombs."

Nevertheless, a judge said that "millions more of innocent people may pay the price of your treason. Indeed, by your betrayal, you have undoubtedly altered the course of history to the disadvantage of your country."

There is here a glaring and tragic inconsistency for which two people gave their lives, and another person spent a major portion of his lifetime in prison.

Jomo Kenyatta

1952

MANY OF THE BEST-KNOWN FIGURES OF THE twentieth century arose out of the struggles of colonial peoples for independence: Gandhi and Nehru in India, Sukarno in Indonesia, Luthuli in South Africa, Mboya in Kenya. Few figures among them emerge more majestic and noble than Jomo Kenyatta.

Kenya shelters many tribes in a vast rich land where numerous languages are spoken. It takes its name from Mount Kenya, a volcanic mountain that rises some seventeen thousand feet above sea level, one of the highest points on the continent. And once, only a short time ago, it was part of the empire on which the sun never set; it was but one section of British East Africa ruled by the colonial office.

The largest single tribe in Kenya are the Kikuyus, a tall, broad-shouldered people who tilled the soil, lived by hunting, and produced among their number Jomo Kenyatta. Born in the latter part of the nineteenth century (perhaps in 1893, although the exact year is not known) Kenyatta in his youth became dedicated to correcting many of the wrongs he felt had been perpetrated against the natives by white settlers and colonialists. In 1915 the Crown Land Ordinance had been passed by the British, which gave them rights to "all land occupied by the African tribes of the Colony." The Kikuyus complained that they had become tenants on their own lands, and agitation for land reform became a major issue among them.

Kenyatta traveled to England to study as a young man, and mastered anthropology under the great scholar Bronislaw Malinowski; he wrote *Facing Mount Kenya*, the story of his people, sometimes considered the best anthropological study of a primitive people written by one of its members. Kenyatta became active among African exiles and lovers of freedom, spent some time in Moscow, and then, in his mid-forties, returned to what was still British East Africa. He discovered that during the Second World War his people's leading organization, the Kikuyu Central Association, had been banned. He was unable to have the ban lifted, so he became prominent in organizing a new group, the Kenya African Union (which came to be known as KAU, usually pronounced like the English word *cow*). As president of KAU, Kenyatta agitated for the short-range goal of redistribution of land controlled by white settlers, for a greater share of power for the natives, and at the same time for the long-range goal of Kenya's freedom from Britain.

Freedom was a word sweeping the African continent in dozens, perhaps hundreds, of languages. The freedom movement took many forms: parliamentary demands, proposals at the UN, demonstrations, sabotage, and terror. Nowhere was the terroristic freedom movement more in evidence than in Kenya, where it came to be known as the Mau Mau. Terrorists struck suddenly at night, at whites and noncooperating natives. Seldom were the terrorists apprehended. The colonial office, however, hoped to reveal a link between KAU and the Mau Mau, and to halt the growing freedom movement and remove and discredit its greatest leader, Jomo Kenyatta.

Meanwhile, Kenyatta had been speaking before huge gatherings throughout Kenya. In a country in which people traveled by foot, and information was passed by word of mouth, his meetings brought tens of thousands streaming in from the countryside. On October 21, 1952, Kenyatta and five KAU confederates were detained and charged with secret membership in the outlawed Mau Mau organization.

Was there such an organization as the Mau Mau? Or was the terror simply the unorganized or amorphously organized work of individuals and small groups without central direction? And to the extent that the Mau Mau (and not merely the acts of individuals) had a real existence, was there a connection between it and KAU? These were the legal questions facing the court in the trial of Jomo Kenyatta. For, strange as it may sound, the colonial authorities had outlawed the Mau Mau without proof that the organization they were banning had ever existed.

Few had ever heard of Kapenguria, the little town which became the setting for the trial. The nearest hotel facilities were twenty-four miles away, but even there the counsel for the defense could not hold a meeting, because Asiatic and African lawyers were banned from meeting with European colleagues. Kapenguria was a town without a telephone. The nearest law library was in Nairobi, hundreds of miles and at best

Jomo Kenyatta, leader of the Kenya African Union (KAU), at the time he was on trial in 1952. WIDE WORLD PHOTOS

several days' travel away. Kapenguria was also off limits to Kikuyu who did not have passes, and a pass to come to town was not readily available for friends of Kenyatta.

Charged with management of the Mau Mau were Kenyatta and five codefendants: Kubai, Kaggia, Ngei, Karumba, and Oneko. The Mau Mau had been declared illegal on August 12, 1950, and since the defendants were not charged with any terrorist acts themselves, it seemed unlikely that a British court would hear evidence that they had managed the organization before it was outlawed. Furthermore, because the six were detained on October 21, 1952, the management would have had to exist during the intervening twenty-six-month period. Nevertheless, although twenty-one incidents purporting to demonstrate the involvement of the defendants in the management of the Mau Mau were introduced at the trial, five occurred before the organization had been outlawed.

The prosecution contended that when the Kikuyu Central Association, which had been fighting for land reform, was declared illegal, it went underground and secretly became the Mau Mau. It also contended that Kenyatta headed it, using KAU as the legal arm and the Mau Mau as the illegal arm of his movement.

The trial in the little schoolroom opened on November 24, 1952, and was postponed until December 3, to await the arrival of the chief counsel for the defense, D. N. Pritt. Aiding Mr. Pritt were attorneys from Nigeria, Jamaica, India, and elsewhere. Only one member of the defense team, H. O. Davies, was an African. Although counsel came from many parts of Africa, they were prevented from joining the trial.

When the trial convened on December 3, Deputy Public Prosecutor Somerhough made the opening statement. He said that the charge was that of managing an unlawful society, but added that he would be unable to establish a very strong link between the defendants and the Mau Mau, inasmuch as the latter was a society "which has no records."

When the trial opened for the second week, the defense was able to welcome Chaman Lall, one of the most prestigious members of the Indian bar, a member of the Supreme Court of Delhi and of the high court of the Punjab. With the arrival of Lall, the international significance of the trial became more apparent.

An African girl, Tabitha, testified that she had stood at a doorway and heard Kenyatta talk about the administering of an oath. The prosecution sought to bring in a police officer to establish that the witness had told the same story to the police, and this led to a bitter exchange between the magistrate and Mr. Pritt.

MAGISTRATE: I was hoping—Mr. Pritt will forgive me for saying so, I am quite sure—I was hoping you would by now have ceased to ask for reservation of cross-examination. You do not want to put your clients to any prejudice, of course, but I at the same time wish—you would appreciate my task is a most difficult task, and with all these reservations of cross-examination they do not make my task any easier.

PRITT: May I say this? I have reserved no witness's cross-examination longer than overnight. This is the only case I have ever heard of in my life in which the defendants on charges—serious charges—to which they might be sentenced to a sentence of seven years' imprisonment—very serious charges—it is the only case I have ever heard of in my life in which they have been prosecuted with no particulars of any description being given— particulars even being refused; and as each thing comes up, as each new incident comes up, I hear a completely new story, that I have never heard in my life, I do not know until four o'clock in the afternoon whether my clients have ever heard of it in their lives. I do not know whether they are going to tell me it is true, or a distortion, or a complete invention; and until four o'clock every afternoon, sir, I am as ignorant of it as any beggar in the streets of Nairobi

—perhaps more ignorant. Therefore, it is utterly—and, of course, the moment they tell me "Well, such and such a witness can put this right," I have set in train a series of efforts to get this witness from three hundred miles away. Consequently, sir, whilst anybody regrets any inconvenience to a court, the gross, cruel, deliberate injustices worked upon me by the government of Kenya in insisting on having this trial up here, and the most unfortunate procedure, whereby we are put in complete ignorance of the thing we have to answer until half a day before we have to answer it, makes it, of course, quite impossible for me to do any more than I am doing.

The trial continued through the first half of December, until the magistrate read an item in the *East African Standard* of December 13 in which a cable that Mr. Pritt had sent to several Labour members of Parliament was quoted. In this cable Pritt protested vigorously against the conditions under which the trial was being held, the lack of research facilities, and the exclusion of some defense counsel from the district.

The honor of a British magistrate had been touched. Counsel for the defense argued that he had intended no slight on the presiding judge, but only on the conditions and facilities in Kapenguria. But the judge was so affected that he could not continue, and had to go home and think the matter over until the next morning, at which time he returned and announced that the trial would be adjourned until a contempt case against Mr. Pritt could be settled. This was settled at the end of December in Nairobi, when the Supreme Court of Kenya acquitted

Pritt of the charge, and back he came to Kapenguria for a reconvening of the trial on January 2, 1953.

It was a bitter trial that lasted five months. The official interpreter, D. A. G. Leakey, walked out in a huff when his impartiality and ability as a translator was challenged. A hymnbook became the center of dispute when charges were made that KAU oaths in the book were actually Mau Mau oaths in disguise. Finally the prosecution concluded its case. The defense made the usual arguments for dismissal, the prosecution the usual rebuttal; the plea was rejected, and the case continued. The witness was Jomo Kenyatta, who testified in English.

Under direct examination, Kenyatta told of his career, his travels and studies in Europe, his return to Africa, and of his activities for schools, for land, and for freedom. Kenyatta, further, was asked about the policies of KAU.

Q: Is it a fact that the KAU has struggled for better working conditions, for freedom of assembly, press and movement, and for equal rights for all Africans on constitutional lines?

A: Yes, that is so.

Q: Does the KAU believe in violence?

A: No; we do not believe in violence at all: we believe in negotiation, that is, we ask for our rights through constitutional means —through discussion and representation. We feel that the racial barrier is one of the most diabolical things that we have in this colony, because we see no reason why all races in this country cannot work harmoniously together without any discrimination. That is one thing, together with many others, that we have been fighting, and we believe that if people of good will can work together they can eliminate that evil. We say that God did not discriminate when he put the people into the country. He put everybody into this world to live happily and to enjoy the gifts of nature that God has bestowed upon mankind.

MAGISTRATE: I think these answers are becoming too long; they are tending to be speeches.

LALL: Could you give us approximately the membership of KAU to date?

KENYATTA: I have forgotten exactly but I know it is over one hundred thousand members.

Q: Is there any other organization of the Africans in this country?

A: No, not as far as I know.
(Attorney Lal asked Kenyatta about the allegedly terrorist organization.)

Q: When did you first hear about the word Mau Mau?

A: The word Mau Mau came into being in 1950, I think, where we found the expression used in the *East African Standard*, and everybody was surprised. What is this Mau Mau? The word Mau Mau is not, as far as I know, and I claim to know a few of our languages, it does not belong to any of the languages that I do know.

Lall led Kenyatta to the discussion of the public meeting in which Kenyatta called upon an audience of between thirty thousand and fifty thousand for a public curse on the Mau Mau. It was a highlight of the direct examination, and might well have established Kenyatta as being free from any connection with the organization except as an opponent of it.

LALL: Public curse on?

KENYATTA: Public curse on Mau Mau.

Q: I see.

A: And hear the strongest curse we could put in public in Kikuyu. I called on the people, and asked them to say in unison, that is in Kikuyu. I do not know how to say it in English, but I said, "All those people who want to get—who agree we should get rid of Mau Mau, put up your hands." Now all these people—I mean it is not in Barazi

in this paper, but in some of the other papers, in the *East African Standard*—it shows the photograph while the people are holding up their hands. . . . Thousands of people holding up their hands. And after that I told them to repeat after me the Kikuyu curse: "Ngai Mau Mau, Irothie Na Miri Ya Mikongoe Yehere Bururi biui biui," which means to say, that is, "the Mau Mau may disappear in—abyss—or something—where you may not be recovered when you have gone, 'Irothie na miri ya Mikongoe,' You can never be recovered again."

There was here a bitter argument among Kenyatta, Lall, the magistrate, and the interpreter over the correct translation of the curse. When the interpreter agreed to accept Kenyatta's translation, he was reprimanded by the magistrate.

Kenyatta handled himself skillfully on cross-examination, avoiding every trap that sought to link him with terror or the Mau Mau, and at the same time careful never to denounce the natives who were struggling for freedom, and never to lose an opportunity to denounce the colonialists. Had he stirred up racial enmity, he was asked, and when he denied that he had, the prosecutor continued.

Q: Would you say that consistently to represent one section of the community as robbers and thieves is to stir racial dislike?

A: I will not say that—if I represent African opinion no less than European leaders represent European opinion, I do represent African opinion.

The prosecution and defense battled over the relevancy of the questions and answers, and the interrogation continued.

Q: I will put it the other way round. Have you represented consistently that the Europeans are robbers and thieves?

A: No. But I have said in that connection, and I think I have been right in saying so, that Europeans have a better share in the land. They have better position. That is, if I am qualified in a certain thing, being an African—and this is why I attack the color bar—no matter whatever qualifications an African may have, he always has a lesser pay because of his color, not according to his qualifications. That does not mean that I represent Europeans as wicked people, but I say there has been injustice, and as such I cannot be assumed to say that Europeans are bad. I say the law—

Here Kenyatta was interrupted. He was interrogated on a report of a meeting where he claimed to have denounced the Mau Mau. The report omitted any such denunciation, and he characterized the report as incomplete, as any journalistic item must be. He was supplicated to say a kind word about the British in Africa. Had they not abolished slavery? He answered that they had taken part in abolishing slavery, only to grab the land and reduce the natives to serfdom. And then the interrogation went on to the Mau Mau and the terrorists:

SOMERHOUGH: You know, do you not, that Mau Mau is anti-European?
KENYATTA: We cannot say it is anti- any particular race. It is anti-people, many people, it has killed many Africans, Asians, Europeans, so I think it is anti-society, but not anti- any particular—it would not be right to say it is anti- only one particular group of people.
Q: Yes. But its principal object is to drive the Europeans out, according to what we have heard about the oath.
A: What we have heard about the oath, yes, but in practice we do not find it so. . . . What I say, they have been anti-African and in practice they have killed Africans, they have killed Europeans, they have killed Indians, and therefore I say it is anti-

society, anti-people, as a whole, not anti-a particular group, African, European, or Asian.
Q: My question was, according to the oath, the principal object was to drive the Europeans out?
A: According to what we have heard.
Q: And do you not agree that the conditions for driving Europeans out would be considerably improved if Africans, ignorant Africans, could be persuaded that it was the English who made them slaves?
A: I do not think so, sir, unless you are anti-truth.

After seven days of cross-examination, the prosecution came up with a theory that the Mau Mau was a continuation of the banned Kikuyu Central Association, all with the same object—to drive out the Europeans, and that all of this was in the hands of Jomo Kenyatta.

Summaries by defense and by prosecution followed, and the defense stressed the weakness of the evidence linking the defendants to the Mau Mau. When did the connection take place? Where? In the presence of whom? Could a man be convicted because he had failed to denounce the terrorist group at a meeting? Or because a newspaper had not reported his denunciation?

For the prosecution there was a stronger link.

The Crown's contention, of course, is that Mau Mau, or a society like Mau Mau, can only flourish in an atmosphere of hatred between races. It is not good telling Africans to drive out Europeans if they like Europeans. . . . If you can get the idea into people's heads that they are victims of theft, the victims of ill usage, you prepare the ground, and the next step is, "Well, let us turn out the thieves, let us turn them out, let us, if necessary, kill them."

Finally, on April 8, 1953, the magistrate

brought in his decision. He briefly went over the evidence and pointed out that at no time did any of the accused utilize the court to denounce the Mau Mau. He said that he felt these defendants had organized and developed the Mau Mau and had used KAU as a cover for the terrorist group. Kenyatta then addressed the court, on behalf of himself and his codefendants.

We look forward to the day when peace shall come to this land and that the truth shall be known that we, as African leaders, have stood for peace. None of us would be happy or would condone the mutilation of human beings. We are humans and we have families and none of us will ever condone such activities as arson, etc.

Without taking up much more of your time, I will tell Your Honor that we as political bodies or political leaders stand constitutionally by our demands which no doubt are known to you and to the government of this country, and in saying this I am asking for no mercy at all on behalf of my colleagues. We are asking that justice may be done and that the injustices that exist may be righted. No doubt we have grievances, and everybody in this country, high or low, knows perfectly well that there are such grievances, and it is those grievances which affect the African people that we have been fighting for. We will not ask to be excused for asking for those grievances to be righted.

I do not want to take up more of your time, Your Honor. All that I wish to tell you is that we feel strongly that at this time the government of this country should not try to strangle the only organization, that is the Kenya African Union, of which we are the leaders, who have been working for the betterment of the African people and who are seeking harmonious relations between the races. To these few remarks, Your Honor, I may say that we do not accept your finding of guilty. It will be our duty to instruct our lawyer to take this matter up and we intend to appeal to a higher court. We believe that the Supreme Court of Kenya will give us justice because we stand for peace; we stand for the rights of the African people, that Africans may find a place among the nations.

Now came the moment of sentencing, and the magistrate addressed himself to Kenyatta, the alleged mastermind behind the plan of driving all Europeans from Kenya. "You have much to answer for and for that you will be punished. The maximum sentences which this court is empowered to pass are the sentences which I do pass, and I can only comment that in my opinion they are inadequate for what you have done."

The sentence was for seven years' imprisonment at hard labor, with a recommendation that he be restricted for the remainder of his life thereafter. "Make no mistake about it, Mau Mau will be defeated, and although there may be more crimes of violence, more murders, more arson and more terror, the rule of law and the forces of law and order will prevail in the long run, even though the way may be hard and difficult."

The other defendants received the same sentence (although one was freed on appeal), and the London *Times* announced some time later that "Jomo Kenyatta will probably spend the rest of his life in the remote northern frontier district of Kenya."

Thus the defendants went off to prison, and some of the predictions proved true, some quite false. There were more murders, more arson, more terror; the Mau Mau was not dead. The position of the British became increasingly difficult. A jailed martyr was now more revered than ever. The terror continued, and among its victims were Dr. Leakey and his wife, perhaps murdered in reprisal for the position he took at the trial. At one time there were at least fifty thousand natives in detention camps, and the

Victorious on May 27, 1963, in the Kenya parliamentary elections for the British East African Colony, Jomo Kenyatta (right) and Tom Mboya join hands and wave plumes. WIDE WORLD PHOTOS

cost of the campaign against the Mau Mau became so burdensome that millions of pounds had to be poured into the colony.

In 1957 the Kenya legislature for the first time had African and Asian members, and in the election of February 28, 1961, the Kenya African National Union won a majority of the seats. Tom Mboya, youthful leader of the party, had campaigned on the slogan, "Freedom and Kenyatta." In August 1961 Kenyatta was freed, and at a meeting in Nairobi attended by some thirty thousand Africans unrestrained in their enthusiasm,

Kenyatta was introduced as a second god. Free, and the recognized leader of Kenya, president of its leading political party, and one of the most powerful and best-loved figures on the African continent, Kenyatta called for a land without discrimination, where citizens of all races and colors would be treated as equals. The man who had been sentenced to prison by the British magistrate, and who had been expected to spend the remainder of his life in virtual confinement, became the first prime minister of the crown colony and protectorate on June 1,

1963, and was welcomed on December 12, 1963, with pomp and ceremony by Africans and British alike as the first prime minister of the independent nation of Kenya. Like Dreyfus, he returned a hero; but to his own people, unlike Dreyfus, he had never ceased to be one.

Whether there was a formal connection between the Mau Mau and the KAU is diffi- cult to establish today; that there seems to have been a division of labor, in which legal and illegal actions were developed side by side, seems apparent. That it proved effec- tive in Kenya seems to be the verdict of his- tory; whether nonviolence would have been equally successful will long be argued by those who followed the career and trial of Jomo Kenyatta.

Adolf Eichmann

1961

IN THE TRIAL OF ADOLF EICHMANN, PERHAPS more than in that of any other defendant in the history of criminal trials, the People themselves were the accusers and the prosecutor was speaking for them. Adolf Eichmann was one of the publicly little-known figures in the Nazi regime during the rise and fall of the Third Reich. Overhadowed by Ribbentrop, Goebbels, Göring, Heydrich, and many others, he remained in the background, careful to protect his obscurity.

An Austrian by birth (and with some Jewish relatives on his mother's side, a not uncommon experience for members and even leaders in the Nazi movement), Eichmann joined Hitler's party in 1932, and from 1933 to 1939 he rose in the hierarchy, gradually becoming a specialist in what the Nazis euphemistically called the Jewish problem. When Germany invaded Poland, an organized attack on Jews began. Forced-labor camps, expulsions from territory on which Jews and their forebears had lived for centuries, and forcible separation of able-bodied men from their wives and children developed into the death camps of Buchenwald and Auschwitz. As the German war machine made its progress on the European continent, the leaders of the Third Reich set for themselves no less a task than the extermination of millions of Jews.

Some of the leaders responsible died in the final days of the war. It is almost certain that HITLER WAS AMONG THEM; A FEW, LIKE Martin Bormann, may have escaped; others were brought to trial and were hanged for their war crimes or sentenced to years in prison. In the interrogations before and during the Nuremberg trials, the name of Adolf Eichmann arose with great frequency, and the belief that Eichmann was perhaps as responsible as any other single person for the tragedy that had befallen the Jewish community was confirmed.

Eichmann had been interned by the Americans in a prisoner-of-war camp, where his identity was unknown. First he used the name Barth, and then later adopted the name Eckmann, in the belief that, if recognized and addressed as Eichmann, anyone would fail to detect his true name and identity.

Later, fearing identification and apprehension, he escaped from the American camp, and made his way to Austria and then to Italy, and soon after the end of the war was befriended by a Franciscan priest in Rome (who evidently knew his identity) and by some people in the Vatican (who did not). With their aid he was able to obtain false papers and passage to Argentina, which he entered illegally in 1950. He traveled under the name of Ricardo Klement, and under that name settled near Buenos Aires, where he received a job and made contact with the German community. In early 1951 he wrote to his wife under the name of Ricardo Klement, rather than stating his identity directly, hoping that his handwriting would disclose his identity, in case anyone intercepted the mail. The children's other uncle, he wrote, would like to have the entire family come to Argentina. Mrs. Eichmann waited several months, obtained a passport in her own name, and in the spring of 1952 left Austria; several months later she joined her husband in South America.

After arriving in Buenos Aires, Mrs. Eichmann soon took on a "second" husband, became Mrs. Klement, and her children likewise changed their name, taking on the name of their "stepfather." Mrs. Eichmann's own identity became fairly well known in German circles in Argentina, but she adhered strongly to the fiction of a remarriage. From this second marriage, in fact, she eventually had another son, named Francisco Klement.

Despite the name change, Eichmann was identified, apprehended, and spirited out of Argentina. He was brought to Israel, where David Ben-Gurion announced to the Knesset that "the greatest of Nazi war criminals" had been found and "was under arrest in Israel." It soon became known that he had been captured in Argentina, the violation of whose territorial integrity led to a sharp debate. After an apology by Israel and a reprimand of her by the UN Security Council, and following recall of ambassadors for a period of two months between the new Jewish nation and the Latin American sanctuary, the episode was closed.

Meanwhile, much criticism of Israel centered upon the kidnapping itself. Many friends of Israel, including some Jewish leaders, contended that it was an act so repulsive and so violent that it could not be condoned. The discovery of Eichmann in hiding should have been followed by exposure and by the demand that he be extradited, to Israel or to Germany, in order to stand a war-crimes trial, if not a trial in Argentina. But the Nuremberg courts had been disbanded; Germany did not ask that Eichmann be extradited; there was in existence no international UN tribunal, and so the task fell to Israel.

On April 11, 1961, exactly eleven months after the abduction, the trial of Adolf Eichmann began. The defendant sat in a bullet-proof glass-enclosed cage, protected from the angry survivors of the holocaust. At his side were two guards, and he wore earphones bringing him the proceedings, often after their translation from Hebrew into German. The court awaited his plea, but it did not come. Instead, Dr. Robert Servatius, his German counsel, arose to challenge the entire proceedings.

There were several grounds for challenges. The defendant was before this court as a result of kidnapping, and hence this court lacked jurisdiction in the case. Against this, Gideon Hausner, chief prosecutor, cited numerous precedents, in America, England, Germany, and other countries, to justify holding the trial before this court in Jerusalem.

Dr. Servatius contended that the alleged crimes charged against the defendant had not been crimes in the land in which these acts were committed. This was all ex post facto, or retroactive, law. This reasoning had been the major argument of the defense at Nuremberg, and now Nuremberg was the precedent. It is one thing, the court stated, to hold a person responsible for an act that, at the time of its commission, was not only legal but moral and ethical; it is quite another when that act, although sanctioned by a constituted governmental authority, was

General view of the trial of Adolf Eichmann. Eichmann is in the bulletproof glass cage. Before the judges are Dr. Robert Servatius, chief defense counsel (seated), and Gideon Hausner, chief prosecutor (standing). WIDE WORLD PHOTOS

inherently so abhorrent, immoral, and outrageous that the legality of the act itself was open to question.

The counsel argued that these acts were committed in another land, and hence the defendant could only be tried in that country. That country, the court ruled, had not asked for the defendant; and although the acts were committed in Germany, as well as in Hungary, Poland, and elsewhere, only Israel had made herself available for the purpose of this trial.

Against this, the German attorney argued that Israel could not be a party to the proceedings, since she was not a state at the time the alleged crimes were committed. Therefore, these crimes could not have been ones against the state of Israel.

Dr. Servatius contended that a fair trial was impossible because witnesses could not be obtained from Germany. They feared traveling to Israel, where they might suffer arrest on setting foot in the country or upon testifying for Eichmann. It was a delicate and convincing point, and in an effort to demonstrate to the world that Eichmann could and would receive a fair trial, the judges gave serious consideration to this matter. It was finally agreed that testimony of the would-be witnesses would be taken before a court in Germany, or in whatever land wherein they resided, and that such persons would be subjected to cross-examination by deposition before foreign courts. Of six witnesses who eventually made deposition, two were granted immunity, while four were warned that in Israel they would be subject to arrest.

Actually, the problem raised was not as unique as it might appear, for in ordinary criminal cases, involving no international matter, defendants are often unable to convince colleagues, friends, or co-conspirators to appear as witnesses because of the latter's fear of self-incrimination; and the fact that such fear acts to impede a defense could not seriously be considered a justification for granting immunity to a witness or for throwing out the entire trial as unfair.

As a final argument Dr. Servatius declared that the judges were incompetent because they were prejudiced; they themselves might have suffered in the holocaust, or might have had relatives who suffered there, and since they were directly involved, they could not be fair and impartial. In a broader sense, this meant that no Jew should sit in judgment on Eichmann, and hence no Israeli court could try him.

To this last argument Hausner rose with indignation. It was true that the judges were not neutral with regard to the crimes; but it is not expected that in a robbery trial a judge be impartial with regard to honesty. The crimes themselves were not on trial; if they were, no trial would be necessary. The only issue was whether the defendant committed them—at issue was the degree of his guilt.

The arguments were over, and the contentions of the defense attorney had been rejected. A twelve-count indictment was submitted by the court.

Up to the moment of the indictment, some believed that Eichmann would admit his guilt, and would perhaps attempt to diminish the extent of his involvement, state that he deserved any punishment, and throw himself on the mercy of a forgiving court. Just the opposite took place. Eichmann pleaded not guilty, and tenaciously clung to the story of his innocence.

Nevertheless, scores of witnesses came forth for the prosecution. A woman told of being lined up and shot at with other victims and of being thrown into a mass grave, only to find herself breathing; then rising up from the grave in which she was surrounded by corpses and making her way stealthily to freedom. A novelist who as a young man had been interned in Auschwitz became so involved on the witness stand that he fell into a faint as he was telling his story. From America came Judge Michael Musmanno, who thirty-five years earlier had defended Sacco and Vanzetti, and who had sat as a judge in some of the Nuremberg cases. Mus-

While giving testimony against Eichmann, Polish-born Yehiel Dinur faints. WIDE WORLD PHOTOS

173

manno testified to Eichmann's involvement, his responsibility, his personal guilt, as he had learned it in the Nuremberg Trials. And if most of the testimony showed a ruthless and brutal bureaucrat who sent literally millions to their death, and who opposed any compromise at every step, any softening of the Nazi line toward the Jews, at least one witness, Abraham Gordon, placed the man as a personal murderer. In Hungary Gordon had been present when Eichmann and one of his henchmen had walked into the woodshed behind the house with a Jewish boy; he had heard screams and then had seen the two men walk out, blood on their shirts, dragging a newly slain corpse.

The direct examination of Gordon included the following:

Q: When you first saw Eichmann where was he?

A: The first time I saw him he was sitting on the balcony sipping a drink. The second time I saw him was during an air raid and he was then walking about the courtyard. We went on working and he screamed at us and said, "Get into the trenches."

Q: How many times in all did you see Eichmann?

A: The next time I saw him was when I was in one of the trenches and, all of a sudden, I heard screams. Eichmann's chauffeur, whose name was Teitl, went up to one of the Jewish boys who was working with me, whom I knew as Solomon, and who was not more than seventeen years old.

Q: Will you tell the court in your own words what happened then?

A: I saw Teitl walk up to the boy and shout at him. Then Eichmann's bodyguard, whose name was Slavic, joined them and I heard them shout at the boy, "You stole cherries from the tree." I then saw that Eichmann was standing on the balcony having some kind of conversation with Slavic who was down below. The boy began screaming,

"I didn't do it, I am innocent." I then saw Slavic and Teitl leading the boy away in the direction of the toolshed. He resisted and had to be forced. They pushed him into the toolshed and locked the door and then I saw the driver, Teitl, walk away and I never saw him [the boy] again that day. Then I saw Slavic return. He went round the back of the toolshed and shortly afterward he reappeared with Eichmann. Both entered the toolshed.

Q: What did you see or hear after that?

A: I saw Slavic and Eichmann enter the toolshed and the door was closed behind them. Then I heard frightful screams and beatings, thuds and weeping.

Q: Could you identify the voice?

A: It was the voice of the boy Solomon. The screams lasted for about ten or fifteen minutes, and then for the first time they stopped. The door then opened and Eichmann came out of the toolshed. He was rather disheveled. His shirt was sticking out. I saw stains which I thought were bloodstains. When he had entered the shed he was dressed properly. When he came out, as I have said, he was disheveled and looked exhausted. A few minutes after Eichmann had left the toolshed Slavic came out and shouted for the driver. Teitl arrived and together they entered the toolshed and dragged out the body of the boy. They dragged him by his feet and he gave no signs of life.

Q: Can you describe what you saw?

A: Well, I could not see his eyes but his face was swollen and bleeding. It is very difficult for me to describe what I saw. The driver went away and came back with a car.

Q: Did the car belong to Eichmann?

A: We saw it every day. It was always parked at the villa.

Q: What happened then?

A: After the car arrived I saw the body of the boy being placed in the back seat. I could not see exactly but I thought that they put it under the back seat. Then the car was driven off but returned about half an hour later. In the meantime we had been ordered to carry on with our work. The driver of the car was a Hungarian, but he also spoke German. He said, "I threw the stinking corpse into the Danube and your fate will be the same as that of the boy, so beware."

With all this, there were documents that the Nazis had failed to destroy, carrying Eichmann's name, remarks by him, and his signature, and giving orders, always for a final solution: extermination of the Jews.

Through six weeks of such testimony the defendant sat in his bulletproof cage, his face twitching, occasionally whispering to his attorney. Then came the defense.

Yes, Dr. Servatius had obtained six depositions from people in Germany. For the most part they exonerated Eichmann and told that he had actually played only a small part and had no authority, although one deposition, ironically, stated the very reverse. Finally, the defendant was placed on the stand, figuratively speaking. Actually, he was examined and cross-examined in his cage; Israel did not wish to risk the possibility that he would be killed by an avenger while the trial was still in session. He would not take an oath on the Bible (though offered the

Atrocity pictures being readied for an exhibit illustrating the Nazi persecution of Jews. They are being examined by American newsmen who are in Jerusalem for the Eichmann trial. WIDE WORLD PHOTOS

Adolf Eichmann takes the stand (inside his bulletproof cage) in his own defense. WIDE WORLD PHOTOS

New Testament for this purpose), but he was sworn without benefit of Scriptures.

Day after day, hour after hour, Eichmann was examined by Dr. Servatius. He traced his entire career and life from the time that he had been a young man until his apprehension in Argentina. He had joined the Nazi party because it was against Versailles, the cause of all the trouble, and not because it was anti-Jewish. In fact, he himself had never been anti-Jewish. He had always, throughout his career, during the heyday of Nazi victories and in the period of extermination, been a friend of the Jewish people.

He had been almost a Zionist; he had wanted to see the Jews get some solid ground under them; he had planned to make a Jewish colony in Madagascar.

The incident of the boy in the shed was a lie; it could not have happened and did not. As for the trains that had sent Jews to their deaths in Europe—he was only the transportation clerk, nothing more. He was taking orders, had nothing to do with policy, often opposed it; he was only doing his small part in the job. One of the questions that Dr. Servatius asked his witness concerned a statement that Eichmann had made during interrogation by the Israeli police.

DR. SERVATIUS: You said during the police interrogation that you carried a burden of guilt. Could you tell the court how you now regard this question of guilt?

EICHMANN: Some sixteen to twenty-four years have elapsed since all these events took place: what existed then exists no longer. It is difficult to say what constitutes guilt, and I must make the distinction between guilt from the legal point of view and from the human aspect. The facts in respect of which I am answerable to this court concern the role which I played in connection with the deportations. When they took place they were in pursuance of an order given by the head of the state and the guilt must be borne by those who were responsible for political decisions: when there is no responsibility there can be no guilt or blame. The responsibility must be examined from the legal point of view, and as long as human beings go on living together in society, no global solution can be found except the government of a state based on law and order and abiding by these orders. ... In order to safeguard the security of a state, it must find means to bind the individual, and this was done in Germany by making him take the oath. The question of conscience is a matter for the head of state. One must trust and be loyal to the sovereign power. He who is led by a good head of state is lucky. I had no luck. The head of state ordered the deportations, and the part I played in them emanated from the master at the top, the chief of the SS and the police. He was the man who passed on the orders to the chief of the SIPO and SD, and he, in his turn, passed them on to Müller, my immediate superior, who passed them on to my department. ... In the criminal code of the SS, it was laid down that the punishment for disobedience or insubordination would be death. I did all I could by legal means to obtain a transfer to other duties, but I did not succeed, and when in the autumn of 1939 I was transferred to the SIPO and SD this was done against my will and by order from above. I had to obey. I was in uniform at the time and there was a war on. When I went abroad in 1950 it was not because I was afraid of being brought to justice, but for political and family reasons.

My position was similar to that of millions who had to obey. The difference lies only in that my assignment was the most difficult and I had to carry it. All those who say here that it was easy and did not require an effort to disobey orders give no reasons, and do not say what they would themselves have done. It is said that one could have feigned illness. This may have been a way for generals, but not for their subordinates. If it had transpired that the illness was simulated the result would have been extremely serious, and the binding chains of one's oath should be borne in mind. Himmler said in his famous speech at Poznan that SS generals could ask to be transferred, but that applied only to generals. The small man could not have followed that course, especially when he was the recipient of secret orders. He could have shot himself, but he could not protest. Ethically I condemn myself and try to argue with myself. I wish to say, in conclusion, that I have regret and condemnation for the extermination of the Jewish people which was ordered by the German rulers, but I myself could not have done anything to prevent it. I was a tool in the hands of the strong and the powerful and in the hands of fate itself. That is what I have to say in answer to your question.

Gideon Hausner pointed an accusing

finger when he rose to cross-examine Eichmann; it was the finger of all the victims and all their suffering survivors. He presented Eichmann with document after document, witness after witness, event after event, which had placed Eichmann in conferences, making policy, demanding stronger anti-Jewish action, rejecting compromise. For two weeks the defendant answered, "I don't remember." "I can't recall." "This is not so."

Hausner quoted Eichmann's statement to the police. "I am aware that I shall be found guilty as an accomplice to murder. I am aware that I face the death penalty and I am not asking for mercy because I don't deserve it." He interrogated the accused further on it. "You said that you were ready to hang yourself in public as an atonement for these terrible crimes, and this has been recorded, from your own mouth, on page 360 of your statement."

ATTORNEY GENERAL: Are you ready to repeat those words now, here in court?

EICHMANN: I confirm what I said during my interrogation and again this morning, in answer to my counsel's last question. I have read what I said again and I do not deny it.

ATTORNEY GENERAL: So you confess to being an accomplice to the murder of millions of Jews?

EICHMANN: That I cannot admit. So far as my own participation is concerned, I must point out that I do not consider myself guilty from the legal point of view. I was only receiving orders and carrying out orders. . . .

ATTORNEY GENERAL: Please answer my question. Answer briefly "Yes" or "No." If an explanation is required you can give it afterward. My question is not a legal question. In your heart do you feel yourself guilty as an accomplice in the murder of millions of Jews?

EICHMANN: Yes, from the human point of view, because I was guilty of carrying out the deportations.

Mr. Hausner ended his summation by saying that

multitudes of the Jewish nation are gone and they cannot be brought back to life. To lament their death and their suffering, and to bewail that part of the nation which has been struck down, a new writer of *Lamentations* must arise. But there must be justice for the crime that was perpetrated. I am proud of the fact that the day has come when a man of Israel can speak the language of justice to a captured evildoer. Here in this state, we do not speak to him with pleading and importunity. There is no need to beg for his mercy, no need to bribe him. We do not flee from him, or have to wander in terror from one country to another. Here law and justice prevail. In this period of the return of the exiles of Judea and Jerusalem, justice is being done here; the trial is taking place here for the blood of the righteous that was spilled, as the prophet Joel foretold. And again I ask you, judges of Israel, render a just and truthful verdict.

For Servatius the accused was but a minor bureaucrat.

All those who dealt with these problems were of higher rank than the defendant. They received the political directives directly from the political authorities. The accused's department would only deal with police measures and

Adolf Eichmann listens tight-lipped in the Jerusalem courtroom on May 29 as Israel's Supreme Court rejects his appeal from the death sentence. WIDE WORLD PHOTOS

would also prepare certain technical matters with regard to the implementation of the purely technical aspects of these orders.

The accused had no influence whatsoever on these problems. The concentration of ghettos in the east was only the concern of the local authorities where the ghettos were situated. The accused took part in the meeting deciding on the liquidation of the Lódz ghetto, but he was there only as a representative of Himmler. Therefore it is absolutely impossible to draw any conclusion with regard to his personal competence and authority there.

On December 15, 1961, Eichmann was found guilty, a verdict anticipated by all. But what would happen to the man? Some had suggested that he be made to work the Israeli soil, to spend his remaining years at hard labor helping in some small way to build the land of the people whom he had almost destroyed. He would not have survived long in such a task; Israel would have had to expend great labor to guard him. Most importantly, such a sentence would have given no satisfaction to the still-suffering survivors of the war.

Some suggested that Eichmann be spared to demonstrate Israeli magnanimity. Martin Buber, the philosopher, spoke out against the proposed execution of Eichmann.

Servatius pleaded for mercy, Hausner for the death penalty. In sentencing Eichmann to be hanged, the court declared:

Even had we found that the accused acted out of blind obedience, as he alleges, we would still have said that one who had participated in crimes of such dimensions, for years on end, must undergo the greatest punishment known to the law, and no order given to him could be a ground even for mitigating his punishment. But in fact we have found that in acting as he did, the accused identified himself in his heart with the orders received by him and he was actuated by an ardent desire to attain the criminal objective. The court sentences Adolf Eichmann to death for the crimes against the Jewish people, the crimes against humanity, and the war crimes of which he has been found guilty.

Hannah Arendt, in her controversial book on the trial, is critical of the court and prosecution and often views the defendant as being a puppet in a system of evil rather than as a creator and instigator of it. Nevertheless, she finds that the death penalty was necessary, and suggests that the court might have stated its reasons for passing such a sentence in some form such as this:

Let us assume, for the sake of argument, that it was nothing more than misfortune that made you a willing instrument in the organization of mass murder; there still remains the fact that you have carried out, and therefore actively supported, a policy of mass murder. For politics is not like the nursery; in politics obedience and support are the same. And just as you supported and carried out a policy of not wanting to share the earth with the Jewish people and the people of a number of other nations—as though you and your superiors had any right to determine who should and who should not inhabit the world—we find that no one, that is, no member of the human race, can be expected to want to share the earth with you. This is the reason, and the only reason, you must hang.

After appeals had been denied, Eichmann went to the gallows on May 31, 1962. He saw his wife on the last day and said good-bye, refused the solace of a Protestant minister, and to the end would not admit what he had so readily admitted in Argentina—his guilt and sorrow for the untold tragedy that he had inflicted upon humanity. Instead, with arrogance, he hurled his final words, "Long live Germany. Long live Argentina. Long live Austria. These are the countries with which I have been most closely associated, and I shall not forget them. I greet my wife, my family, and my friends. I had to obey the rules of war and my flag."

The Trial of the Chicago Eight: Who Became the Chicago Seven

1969-1970

THEY CAME TO CHICAGO BY THE THOUSANDS, mainly young people, but some older as well; they were the army of the new politics —angry, disillusioned, demanding to be heard. They had come for the national convention of the Democratic party. Primarily concerned about an unpopular and seemingly endless war, they would stage a festival of life to contrast with the dance of death of Vietnam.

This was August 1968. The President of the United States, elected to office in 1964 on the promise that he was not going to send American boys to fight a land war in Asia, had dropped in popularity to the point where he had decided not to seek reelection or even make a personal appearance at his party's convention. Some who converged on Chicago were hopeful that the democratic process might offer them an opportunity to work within the system, and that meaningful changes could be made by those who would correct rather than overturn American institutions. Others were disillusioned; the war had continued and leaders in whom they had placed trust and hope had been assassinated.

It is difficult to say how many of those crowding Chicago had come as activists, to make their presence felt and to have some influence on platform and ticket. Leaders of industry and of farm blocs and unions had always had their lobbies at conventions. At the 1968 DEMOCRATIC CONVENTION, people came representing groups that had not before been heard: migrant farm workers pressing for a grape boycott, welfare recipients, poor blacks, and many men and women who were united by their desire to end the war. They were there not to lobby in back rooms nor to make deals, but to influence the convention by marching, by slogans and waving banners, and by a show of numbers.

But it did not work out this way. The Chicago police force and other city officials denied the antiwar group a permit to march. They refused to allow a demonstration close to the convention itself, prohibited use of the public park as sleeping grounds for the visitors, and sought at every turn to keep the protesters where few would see or hear them. The protesters were determined to be both seen and heard, however. The police met them in a head-on collision. Tear gas was hurled at a throng of marchers, many became ill (inevitably including some innocent bystanders and watchers), clubs were swung, people were arrested, and the Democratic party convention going on inside the hall itself became a sorry shambles, a mirror reflection of the events without. The convention nominated Vice-President Hubert Humphrey as its presidential candidate amid anger and confusion.

Several months before, in Memphis, where he had gone to support striking

Chicago city police and antiwar demonstrators clash during the Democratic national convention of 1968. UNITED PRESS INTERNATIONAL

garbage workers, Dr. Martin Luther King, Jr., a civil rights leader and Nobel Peace Prize winner, was assassinated. A wave of indignation had swept America, and as a result a civil rights bill that had been floundering in Congress for months gained strong support. This bill was to be America's response to King's murder, and opposition to the new legislation had to be muted. To appease their conservative constituencies, opponents of the civil rights legislation appended new clauses to the bill. These clauses formed the basis of federal anti-riot legislation which came to be known variously as the Stokely Carmichael or Rap Brown laws, which made it a federal crime to enter into a conspiracy and cross state lines with the

intent of inciting a riot. It was a supreme irony that a bill was passed as a tribute to Martin Luther King that, had it been law during his lifetime, could well have been used to imprison him.

Tucked away as part of the civil rights legislation, the anticonspiracy law might well have been forgotten if indictments had not been handed down against eight people who had been, in one way or another, associated with the leadership of the demonstrations at the Democratic party convention.

The indictments charged that the eight had conspired to come to Chicago at the time of the trial to incite a riot. Actually, several policemen had also been charged with inciting the same riot, but had been found not guilty, after a trial which many claimed was not vigorously prosecuted. In fact, a board of inquiry set up by the President of the United States to investigate the disturbances during the convention had concluded that there had been a police riot, not an antiwar riot.

The eight defendants were an unconventional group. All were involved in the antiwar movement. All had indeed been in Chicago, playing major or minor roles, when the riots occurred. But other than that, they had never met as a single group and had exchanged no letters. Several had never met before, and one knew none of the others. It was an unusual conspiracy indeed: people conspiring without a single meeting, without an exchange of plans or ideas.

The case is officially known as *United States of America, Plaintiff,* v. *David T. Dellinger* et al., *Defendants.* Dellinger, the oldest of those on trial, had been a peace activist for many years. Rennie Davis and Tom Hayden, also active in the antiwar movement, had been founders of Students for a Democratic Society, or SDS. Abbie Hoffman and Jerry Rubin were among the best-known spokesmen of the counterculture that was developing in America; their movement was known as the Youth International Party, or Yippies. John Froines was an assistant professor of chemistry at the University of Oregon, Lee Weiner an instructor in sociology at Northwestern University. Both were activists, though lesser known than the other defendants. The eighth of the accused was Bobby Seale, a black mili-

The eight defendants in the "conspiracy" trial (top, left to right): Jerry Rubin, Abbie Hoffman, Thomas Hayden, and Rennie Davis; (bottom, left to right): Bobby Seale, Lee Weiner, John Froines, and David Dellinger. UNITED PRESS INTERNATIONAL

tant and a leader of the Panther movement. All but Froines and Weiner were charged with crossing state lines with intent to incite a riot. The two professors were accused of teaching and demonstrating the use and application of incendiary devices.

Pacifists, militants, Yippies, and professors—together they had a sense of the comic as well as the tragic. Summoned to Chicago for trial, they all came as free men, except for the Panther leader, Bobby Seale. He was under arrest in California and was fighting extradition to Connecticut, where he would be tried for the murder of Alex Rackley, said to have been a police informer in the Panther ranks.

Bobby Seale had had skirmishes with the law before, and his attorney had been Charles Garry of California. Garry was supposed to head up the defense team in Chicago. But Garry was undergoing an operation and could not appear, and all of the eight defendants but Seale had agreed that William Kunstler, a lawyer for a variety of radical causes and particularly known for his activities in many civil rights cases, should head the defense team. Assisting him was a large staff, of whom the most active in the courtroom procedures to follow was Leonard Weinglass. Thomas Foran, federal attorney general for the area, was the government prosecutor. He was assisted by Richard Schultz.

Julius Hoffman was the presiding judge. From the first day of the trial, it proved to be a great ordeal for him. It started on an alarming note. Bobby Seale came into court and asked that his trial be severed from the others, because his lawyer, Garry, could not be present. After an angry interchange in which this request was denied, Seale demanded the right to defend himself, for otherwise he was completely without counsel. He declared that he had fired Kunstler

and any other lawyer who purported to represent him. Foran argued that Seale's self-defense should not be permitted, as an untrained layman in a case of this type might make statements or ask questions improper enough to result in a mistrial for the other defendants, thus jeopardizing the ongoing proceedings.

During the pretrial period, Kunstler had signed a notice of appearance for Seale. Judge Hoffman ordered that Kunstler remain as Seale's attorney, and declared that a change of attorneys after a case has begun was not permitted—although technically the case had not yet gotten under way.

Four other lawyers had been involved in pretrial representations, and had notified the court by telegram that they were no longer associating themselves with the case. Again, this was a technical procedure usually taken for granted. To the amazement of the legal profession not only in Chicago but throughout the country, Hoffman issued warrants for the arrest of the attorneys. A law professor was awakened by federal authorities and whisked from California to Chicago, photographed and fingerprinted, and was among the attorneys summarily charged with contempt. There was to be no argument, trial, or bail pending appeal. The indignation that arose over the jailing of the attorneys was instantaneous, and a higher court lost no time in freeing them.

From this point on, the trial became a spectacle in which either the judge or the defendants provoked outrage, indignation, or ridicule. The courtroom seemed to be a theatre. For five months the trial dragged on, and it consumed some twenty-two thousand pages of transcript.

For the early period, much of the theatrics involved the case of Bobby Seale. He sat in court ignoring the entire proceedings, except when his name was uttered by a witness, at which time he would rise and demand the right to cross-examine the witness himself, insisting that he had no lawyer in court since Charles Garry was ill, and insisting he had a constitutional right to act as counsel for himself. He would be admonished and ordered to keep quiet and sit down, and when he would persist the marshals would be told to put him in his place. All this was to no avail, for soon he would hear his name again and ask why he could not act as his own lawyer. At one point he accused the judge of using a courtroom where pictures of slaveholders adorned the walls, referring to George Washington and Thomas Jefferson. Time and again, arguments over Seale's defense took place; each time the jury left the courtroom and returned as soon as the decision against Seale had been made.

Julius Hoffman did not have patience for these arguments and for interruptions from the defendants. He could not ban Bobby Seale from the courtroom and proceed with the trial. Yet Seale's daily demands for self-representation were so disturbing to Judge Hoffman that he finally ordered Seale bound in his chair, tied with tight shackles, and gagged. As the gag was being imposed upon him, Seale threatened to bite the fingers of the marshals. Reporters looked on with dismay and spectators with a sense of horror; none could believe that this was taking place in an American courtroom. The jury was brought in and saw the gagged Seale squirming and trying to make himself heard.

With Seale bound and gagged, the other defendants and their counsel protested.

KUNSTLER: Your Honor, are we going to stop this medieval torture that is going on in this courtroom? I think this is a disgrace.

RUBIN: This guy is putting his elbow in Bobby's mouth and it wasn't necessary at all.

KUNSTLER: This is no longer a court of order, Your Honor; this is a medieval torture chamber. It is a disgrace. They are assaulting the other defendants also. . . .

Your Honor, this is an unholy disgrace to the law that is going on in this courtroom and I as an American lawyer feel a disgrace.

FORAN: Created by Mr. Kunstler.

KUNSTLER: Created by nothing other than what you have done to this man.

A. HOFFMAN: You come down here and watch it, Judge.

FORAN: May the record show that the outbursts are the defendant Rubin.

SEALE: You fascist dogs, you rotten, low-life son-of-a-bitch. I am glad I said it about Washington used to have slaves, the first President—

DELLINGER: Somebody go to protect him.

FORAN: Your Honor, may the record show that that is Mr. Dellinger saying someone go to protect him and the other comment is by Mr. Rubin.

RUBIN: And my statement, too.

As the shouting continued, Kunstler said to the judge, "I feel so utterly ashamed to be an American lawyer at this time," to which Julius Hoffman replied, "You should be ashamed of your conduct in this case, sir." By this time, there was chaos and a recess was called.

A week later, early in November, the gag was removed and Seale demanded the right to cross-examine a witness.

SEALE: I would like to approach the lectern.

HOFFMAN: You may not cross-examine, sir.

SEALE: Well, I think I have a right to cross-examine.

HOFFMAN: No, you have no right in the circumstances of this case.

SEALE: Why did you follow me, could you please tell me, Mr. Witness—

HOFFMAN: Mr. Seale—

SEALE: —at the airport?

HOFFMAN: Mr. Seale, I ask you to sit down.

SEALE: Have you ever killed a Black Panther party member?

HOFFMAN: Mr. Seale, I will have to ask you to sit down, please.

SEALE: Have you ever been on any raids in the Black Panther party's offices or Blank Panther party members' homes?

HOFFMAN: Mr. Seale, this is the last time I am asking you to sit down, as courteously as possible.

SEALE: Why don't you let me cross-examine the witness and defend myself?

HOFFMAN: Because you are not entitled to. You have a lawyer of record who signed his appearance in his own handwriting.

SEALE: This man was fired. He was not my lawyer before the jury heard one shred of evidence, before one witness even raised his hand to be sworn in the trial. The trial had not started until that happens.

It was clear that the judge had lost his struggle with Seale. Whatever was now done, whether Seale remained gagged, was allowed to defend himself, or had his case severed from that of the others, Hoffman had jockeyed himself into defeat. He capitulated and severed the Seale case from the others, thus ridding himself and his courtroom of the young militant who had stood up and called him a racist and fascist. Hoffman called Seale before him, ordered a mistrial in his case but in none of the others, held him in contempt, and offered him the opportunity to speak before being sentenced on the contempt charge.

"How come I'm allowed to talk in my own defense now but I couldn't before?" Seale asked. But Hoffman was in no mood for such a conversation, although there was a logical answer: that he was being invited to speak as one about to be sentenced, something accorded every prisoner in an American courtroom, and not as counsel for himself, a right that has some debatable aspects to it. Instead of entering into a discussion with Seale, the judge summarily sentenced him to four years in prison on various contempt charges.

Public attention seemed to focus on the elements of spectacle and theatre in this trial, rather than on the proceedings that were supposed to determine significant points of law as well as the guilt or innocence of the accused. Seldom has a court seemed so openly one-sided, reminiscent in many ways of the Sacco-Vanzetti case and Southern courts in the times of the Scottsboro case. If Judge Hoffman seemed aligned with the prosecution, that in the long run benefited the defendants. They would have been pleased to win their case, but they were for the most part involved in laughing at the American establishment, in showing the decadence and absurdity of the system, and they were able to use Julius Hoffman as their straight man.

Judge Hoffman chose the jury by himself, not permitting the defense counsel to question the talismen. This was no violation of federal rules, but he refused to ask these prospective jurors even the most elementary questions that the defense submitted. Nevertheless, some four or five of the 12 seated seemed to the defendants to be the kind of people who might rule in their favor. The trial hardly had begun when the families of two jurors reported the receipt of letters threatening that the Black Panthers were watching. One letter came to a juror whom the defendants were anxious to retain, but since she had not seen the letter (the jury had been sequestered), it was possible to keep it from her. The judge made the contents of the letter known to her, and then asked if she could still render an impartial verdict, to which she replied in the negative, and was dismissed and replaced by an alternate. At this Kunstler protested vigorously, noting that she had not seen the letter until shown it by the judge, who had himself been responsible for her disqualification. In the view of the defendants, the entire episode of the letters to the jurors appeared to be a plot—by the government—to replace at least one woman who might have leaned toward the defense. Although it could not be proved that agents of the prosecution had sent the letters, it appears plausible enough on the face of it to constitute one of the most serious aspects of a trial that had many astounding features.

Willam Kunstler's chief defense assistant, Leonard Weinglass, was ridiculed by the opposition and even by the judge. They poked fun at him by pretending to have forgotten his name, calling him Feinglass, Weinrob, Weinruss, Weinramer, and other variations of Weinglass. Early in the trial there was a luncheon recess and Weinglass was scheduled to speak immediately thereafter. Nicholas von Hoffman (no relation to either Julius or Abbie), a reporter for the *Washington Post*, stated that he heard Julius Hoffman say, in the elevator coming up to the courtroom, "Now we are going to hear this wild man Weinglass." It was ominously reminiscent of the judge's remark about those "anarchist bastards" in the Sacco-Vanzetti trial. All motions for a mistrial and for disqualification of the judge were denied.

No one in the court acted as a model of

Federal District Judge Julius J. Hoffman (right). UPI Telephoto

decorum. The defendants shouted obscenities, put on demonstrations, and openly displayed the low esteem in which they held the judge. The prosecution not only ran the show, but gave demeaning lectures to the defense counsel, and hurled epithets at Kunstler and Weinglass with no admonishment from the court.

For the defendants, who still hoped for a hung jury, there was at least the public forum that they attained through the five long months. They were frequently interviewed, offered speaking engagements, and when they were not expressing their indignation at Judge Hoffman, they could at least express their disrespect. Some observers felt the judge provoked it. One day the defendants came into court with a birthday cake for Bobby Seale; on another occasion they draped the defense table with two flags, one from the U.S.A. and another from North Vietnam, and at another time they walked into court dressed in judicial robes.

Through it all, some two hundred witnesses came forth, some with more success than others. The government made no serious attempt to prove a conspiracy: there was never proved to be a gathering, not even an exchange of telephone calls and letters, that linked the eight to each other. At most, five knew each other, had been active in similar antiwar movements, and were cooperating, together with hundreds and perhaps thousands of others, in mobilizing to present a festival of life, as the counterconvention had been called. That they crossed state lines was conceded; but the crux of the matter was to determine their states of mind: did they cross state lines with intent to incite to riot?

Much of the government's case was based on the testimony of Chicago officials who had conferred with some of the defendants and had refused their requests for permits. There were police informers, FBI and police agents who had penetrated into antiwar and other militant movements, who now came forth to charge that the defendants had sought to inflame and incite.

The defense that Kunstler and Weinglass attempted to make was thwarted at every turn. Some defendants took the stand, but were not permitted to state their intentions in coming to Chicago, although that was what the trial was all about.

Where do you reside, Weinglass asked defendant Abbie Hoffman when he was on the stand, testifying in his own behalf.

A. HOFFMAN: I live in Woodstock Nation.

WEINGLASS: Will you tell the court and jury where it is.

A. HOFFMAN: It is a nation of alienated young people. We carry it around with us as a state of mind in the same way the Sioux Indians carried the Sioux nation around with them. It is a nation dedicated to cooperation versus competition, to the idea that people should have better means of exchange than property or money, that there should be some other basis for human interaction. It is a nation dedicated to—

J. HOFFMAN: Excuse me, sir. Read the question to the witness, please. (The question was read) Just where it is, that is all.

A. HOFFMAN: It is in my mind and in the minds of my brothers and sisters. We carry it around with us in the same way that the Sioux Indians carried around the Sioux nation. It does not consist of property or material but, rather, of ideas and certain values, those values being cooperation versus competition, and that we believe in a society—

SCHULTZ: This doesn't say where Woodstock Nation, whatever that is, is.

WEINGLASS: Your Honor, the witness has identified it as being a state of mind and he has, I think, a right to define that state of mind.

J. HOFFMAN: No, we want the place of residence, if he has one, place of doing business, if you have a business, or both if you desire to tell them both. One address will be sufficient. Nothing about philosophy or India, sir. Just where you live, if you have a place to live. Now you said Woodstock. In what state is Woodstock?

A. HOFFMAN: It is in the state of mind, in the mind of myself and my brothers and sisters.

The defense had one witness so powerful that even the most hostile jury would have to be influenced by his testimony: the man who had been attorney general of the United States at the time of the demonstrations, Ramsey Clark. He had discussed with Chicago officials the protest plans, and was prepared to recount these discussions. Against Clark the prosecution and judge had a unique weapon: to determine in advance that he had nothing to say relevant to the case, hear him out of the earshot of the jury, decide that he could not testify, and finally forbid the defense lawyers from making all this known to the jury. Newspapers throughout the country expressed their outrage, and even conservative lawyers were left in utter dismay as they witnessed the biased procedures used in the trial. There was now nothing left but to act out the charade. No guilty verdict could possibly be upheld on appeal.

Norman Mailer came to the stand, and provided a few words of trenchant social criticism. Witnesses for the defense included a member of the British Parliament who had been in Chicago at the time of the riot, the popular young black political leader Julian Bond, author William Styron, and the civil rights leader and comedian Dick Gregory. Allen Ginsberg held the court in awe as he chanted the Hare Krishna mantra and A-u-u-m-m-m, and defended the concepts of his mystic and often homosexual poetry. After Kunstler declared that he had no more witnesses except a cameraman, but before any closing statements or

motions had been made, he discovered that Ralph Abernathy, close associate of the late Dr. King, had returned to America and was in Chicago, ready to appear. Kunstler asked for the routine courtesy of being allowed to hear the witness; it was a courtesy similar to and smaller than innumerable ones granted to the prosecution throughout the trial, but it was rebuffed.

When Abernathy was banned as a witness, Kunstler made what was probably his strongest statement of the case. Addressing Julius Hoffman directly, he said:

You have violated every principle of fair play when you excluded Ramsey Clark from that witness stand. *The New York Times*, among others, has called it the ultimate outrage in American justice.

I am outraged to be in this court before you. Now because I made a statement on Friday that I had only a cameraman, and I discovered on Saturday that Ralph Abernathy, who is the chairman of the Mobilization [or MOBE, the antiwar group that had been the prime mover in the Chicago demonstrations] is in town, and can be here, and because you took the whole day from us on Thursday by listening to this ridiculous argument about whether Ramsey Clark could take that stand in front of the jury, I am trembling because I am so outraged. I haven't been about to get this out before, and I was saying it now, and then I want you to put me in jail if you want to. You can do anything you want with me, if you want to, because I feel disgraced to be here, to say to us on the technicality of my representation that we can't put Ralph Abernathy on the stand. He is the cochairman of the MOBE. He has relevant testimony. I know that doesn't mean much in this court when the attorney general of the United States walked out of here with his lips so tight he could hardly breathe, and if you could see the expression on his face, you would know, and his wife informed me he never felt such anger at the United States government as at not being able to testify on that stand. . . .

I know that this is not a fair trial. I know it in my heart. If I have to lose my license to practice law and if I have to go to jail, I can't think of a better cause to go to jail for and to lose my license for than to tell Your Honor that you are doing a disservice to the law in saying that we can't have Ralph Abernathy on the stand. You are saying truth will not out because of the technicality of a lawyer's representation.

The closing statements were like the rest of the trial: the prosecution was permitted to make any charge it wished, the defense was interrupted and warned on many occasions. Only the charge to the jury was a change of pace: cut and dried, and unimaginative.

After the jury retired to consider the case, and without its knowledge, the defendants were handed contempt sentences for their behavior during the five-month ordeal. One by one they were called up, and told how many times they had been in contempt, and were given sentences ranging from two to twenty-nine months. Not satisfied, Hoffman then called Kunstler and Weinglass, and each of them was sentenced for so-called contempt in the conduct of the trial, for periods of four years and twenty months, respectively. Ordinarily, no sentence of more than six months is permitted for contempt in a federal court, without a trial by jury. Hoffman gave out short sentences of only a few days to a few months, but on many different counts, and the sentences would run consecutively.

The two sides lined up against each other in the jury room, a majority for conviction, a minority for acquittal. For several days they were hopelessly deadlocked, and so informed the judge, but he insisted that they continue the deliberations until unanimity was reached. Expecting a hung jury, the defense was not unhappy; it would be saved the cost of an appeal (except for the contempt sentences); and a retrial, after the expensive and farcical theatrics of the past five months, seemed most unlikely.

Inside the jury room, one juror set herself up as negotiator, seeking to reach a compromise. Unexpectedly, she was successful, and a verdict was brought in. On the charge of conspiracy, all were found not guilty. The five accused of crossing state lines with intent to incite to riot were found guilty, though Froines and Weiner, charged with teaching the use of incendiary devices, were acquitted. The irony of the verdict was that the case against Froines and Weiner had been far stronger than that against the other five.

Kunstler made one last effort for acquittal by asking the judge to poll the jury to see if each agreed with the verdict and to determine whether a compromise had been reached (compromise verdicts are illegal, because they run counter to the principle of guilt beyond a reasonable doubt). But no, there would be no polling of the jury.

Without awaiting presentence reports, which are for advising a judge in such matters, Julius Hoffman handed down maximum prison terms and fines, to which he added an unprecedented feature: the defendants would stay in prison until they had paid for the cost of prosecuting them!

There were final statements by the defendants. Rennie Davis said that he would come out of prison to move next door to Tom Foran and organize his kids into the revolution. "We are going to turn the sons and daughters of the ruling class in this country into Viet Cong." Jerry Rubin said that they were on trial because they had been trying to wake up America, "and the only way we can wake it up is by screaming, yelling, standing on our heads, doing what-

William Kunstler (right) speaking outside the Federal Building after he was sentenced to four years and 13 days for contempt of court. UNITED PRESS INTERNATIONAL

ever we can do. That's what we tried to do during this trial. That's what our defense was."

Abbie Hoffman pointed to the pictures of the leaders of the American Revolution on the courtroom wall and said, "I know those guys on the wall. I know them better than you, I feel. I know Adams. I mean, I know all the Adams. They grew up twenty miles from my home in Massachusetts. I played with Sam Adams on the Concord Bridge. I was there when Paul Revere rode right up on his motorcycle and said, 'The pigs are coming, the pigs are coming. Right into Lexington.'"

Then they were all whisked away, declared by the judge to be dangerous men who could not be allowed freedom on bail pending appeals. A few days later, a higher court reinstated bail.

Not long after the trial, Thomas Foran was quoted as saying, "We have lost our kids to this fag revolution, and we've got to reach out for them. Our kids don't understand that we don't mean anything by it when we call people niggers. They look at us like we're dinosaurs when we talk like that." Foran never denied the quote, and when he was criticized for the insensitivity of the remark, he said that he did not mean a "fag revolution" but a "Fagin revolution."

The war in Vietnam was still going on, though drawing to what appeared to be its last stages, when the verdicts in the Chicago trial as well as the contempt sentences were finally set aside. On November 21, 1972, the United States Court of Appeals for the Seventh Circuit reversed the convictions, citing among other reasons the judge's "antagonistic courtroom behavior." *The New York Times* commented that "Judge Hoffman and the prosecutor, former United States Attorney Thomas A. Foran, were rebuked in today's findings in language rarely directed by an appellate court at another jurist." The constitutionality of the anti-riot law itself was upheld, by a vote of 2 to 1. No plans for a retrial were mentioned.

However, the contempt cases against the two lawyers and several of the defendants were still being tried in 1973. A new judge was appointed to hear them. The public interest had waned, attention was on the alleged Watergate conspiracy and not on the alleged Chicago conspiracy. The prosecution called no witnesses. It presented the record of the previous trial and rested its case. The government seemed to be expressing its wish that the memory of the Chicago case would be effaced forever.

A combination of the personalities and the wit of several of the defendants, the hostility to the war in Vietnam around which so much of the trial centered, and the attitude of the judge had made the Chicago event a highly political criminal trial.

Philip Berrigan
and the Harrisburg Seven

1972

BY THE END OF THE 1960s, MAJOR TRIALS no longer involved one or two individuals in what has come to be known as "ordinary crime," but rather men and women with strong ideological convictions, whose violations of the law, real or suspected, were politically motivated. It was an era of political trials. In the United States, two themes dominated these trials—race and war. The Chicago trial was a confrontation between the old order of things and the new (or as one might say, between the old and the young). The Angela Davis trial (see following chapter), like those of the Panthers and other black militants, was a confrontation between a member of an oppressed group and those considered to be the oppressors. And the case of Philip Berrigan and the Harrisburg Seven, for all its legal technicalities, was a meeting between those considered by some to be symbols of goodness and righteousness, and their accusers, who were in turn sometimes cast as evil. For the government it was a question of whether a kidnapping had been planned and nipped in the bud; for the defendants, it was an opportunity to turn the accusation around and place the government on the defensive because it continued to wage the war in Vietnam.

The Catholic left was in some ways an unexpected development on the American social and political scene. Traditionally, the Catholic population of the United States has practiced conservative politics, although it often clustered in urban centers of power which became focal points for liberal reform. It did, however, have a radical tradition going back to the Molly Maguires and the struggle for unionism. In the period of the 1950s and 1960s a small but vocal sector of priests, nuns, and others with strong associations with the Catholic Church emerged as militant civil rights workers, anti-poverty workers (particularly in Latin America), and later, activists in the antiwar movement. They spoke with the voices of morality as part of the conscience of America, upholding the heritage of the Prince of Peace. In addition they had the cloak of protection that so frequently surrounds religion when it defies civil government.

Among the leaders of this new Catholic left were Daniel and Philip Berrigan. They lectured, gave sermons, wrote poetry, journeyed to Vietnam, and sought ways to confront the warmakers without resorting to the violence they deplored. On May 17, 1968, in an effort to escalate the antiwar movement dramatically, the Berrigan brothers and seven other activists (including an expriest and an exnun, as well as former missionaries) raided a draft board office in Catonsville, Maryland. They had given advance notice of their intentions to a select group of newspapermen. In the draft board office they found a file of people classified 1-A who were eligible for an early call to military service, burned the file with napalm that they had made themselves, and then prayed—all in full view of cameramen and reporters.

The Catonsville Nine, as they came to be known, were arrested, tried, found guilty, and sentenced. Free on bail, their appeals were rejected, and they were ordered to surrender to the authorities. But on April 9, 1970, the surrender date (the numerous appeals had taken considerable time), the Berrigans were not to be seen. They had decided that they were needed for the continuing antiwar resistance, and that nothing would be served by their passively submitting to imprisonment. More than that, they probably already realized that during the period they were fugitives, anything they said would be most newsworthy. Finally, the American government would be embarrassed by its inability to apprehend the fugitive priests.

The hunt for the Berrigans proved more embarrassing to the FBI than anyone had foreseen. The brothers were seen by many activists, gave interviews, and even appeared at public meetings. At one peace meeting at Cornell, Daniel Berrigan's appearance was announced in advance. The rally was attended by many students and faculty, but how many FBI agents were in the audience one can only conjecture. It looked as if Dan Berrigan had courted danger a little too closely but at one point the lights went out, and by the time they came on again he had slipped away. For Phil Berrigan the fugitive life came to an end when he was caught in a rectory closet. For Dan the flight continued through the late spring and early summer. On August 2 he delivered a sermon in a church in Germantown, near Philadelphia.

Although the sermon had not been announced in advance, and hence agents were not among the parishioners, it received wide publicity after the event, leaving the FBI further humiliated. Publicity on the Berrigans continued and heightened. A play written by Dan on the Catonsville trial opened, although he was not present on opening night. Then, on a small island off the coast of New England, he was found with friends on August 11. He had never made the Ten Most Wanted list, but in a sense his name must have led all the rest.

When Phil Berrigan was arrested, he was sent to the federal penitentiary at Lewisburg, Pennsylvania, where he remained for approximately four months, until the end of August, when he was transferred to Danbury, Connecticut, joining his brother Dan. In the lonely days at Lewisburg, disheartened by the inability of the antiwar movement to mount a successful campaign, Phil Berrigan was aided by relationships he developed in prison and by continued contact with the outside world. One individual whom he met, a prisoner named Boyd Douglas, Jr., was in a position to assist the imprisoned priest by taking uncensored letters out of prison and bringing others back. Boyd was a man with privileges that no other inmate at Lewisburg had. Each day he was freed from the penitentiary to go to nearby Bucknell University, under a student-release program. Thus, Phil Berrigan could learn what was going on among his friends, could even hear indirectly of his brother from those who were in touch with him, and could learn of the activities of a group that called itself the East Coast Conspiracy to Save Lives. Particularly important, he could remain in touch, through uncensored mail, with his close friend and colleague, Sister Elizabeth McAlister, professor of art history at Marymount College in Tarrytown, New

Reverend Philip Berrigan waves a "peace sign" from behind bars. UNITED PRESS INTERNATIONAL

York. She was a dynamic figure in the anti-war movement.

The Catholic left, deprived of two of its outstanding leaders, still continued to be active. It issued proclamations, carried out small actions, and fought against the sense of frustration that seemed to be engulfing the antiwar movement. Perhaps if one could plan an event infinitely more dramatic than any yet carried out, not violent and yet of a character that would awaken the entire world to the war's evil, it would place the morality of the resistance in confrontation with the immorality of the warmakers. Raids on draft boards no longer seemed to be effective. A group of activists talked and

pondered, and finally someone suggested that they might make a citizen's arrest of a high government official, intercepting and holding him, then give him a mock trial for war crimes, culminating in a demand to end the holocaust in Southeast Asia, finally followed by his release. Henry Kissinger was mentioned as the ideal person to arrest. Then someone suggested that the entire government could be paralyzed by sabotaging the heating system in mid-winter in Washington. There was talk of calling on large numbers of people to make telephone calls to Washington, all at the same time, in order to tie up the telephone apparatus; and other talk of inundating Wall Street with numerous tiny orders so that the financial exchanges would break down.

Some of this was written by Sister McAlister in a letter to Phil, embellished no doubt, to buoy his spirits and imbue him with a sense that the resistance was alive and well. She sent the letter to her mail drop at Bucknell, a young lady who duly passed it on to Boyd Douglas for delivery to Phil Berrigan. Boyd did just that, but not before he had a copy made, as he had done with each of the previous letters. In Lewisburg that night, alone in his cell, Father Philip Berrigan read the letter. Sister McAlister had written, in part, as follows:

Eq called us up to Conn. last night along with Bill Davidon who, in case people have not told you, has become one of our better people. Parenthetically someone with a knowledge of the scene, a keen sense for tactic & detail & little fear of risk for himself. He's the most central fig. in the Phila. scene & went into the Boards in Georgetown with those kids. Eq outlined a plan for an action which would say—escalated seriousness & we discussed pros and cons for several hours. It needs much more thought & careful selection of personnel. To kidnap—in our terminology make a citizen's arrest of—someone like Henry Kissinger. Him because of his influence as policy maker and yet sans cabinet status, he would therefore not be as much protected as one of the bigger wigs; he is a bachelor which would mean if he were so guarded, he would be anxious to have unguarded moments where he could carry on his private affairs—literally & figuratively. To issue a set of demands, e.g. cessation of use of B52s over N. Vietnam, Laos, Cambodia, & release of political prisoners. Hold him for about a week during which time big bigs of the liberal ilk would be brought to him—also kidnapped if necessary (which for the most part it would be)—& hold a trial or grand jury affair out of which an indictment would be brought. There is no pretense of these demands being met & he would be re-

leased after this time with a word that we're non-violent as opposed to you who would let a man be killed—one of your own—so that you can go on killing. The liberals would also be released as would a film of the whole proceedings in which, hopefully, he would be far more honest than he is on his own territory. The impact of such a thing would be phenomenal.

The impact of the letter was phenomenal, also, not only on Phil Berrigan, but on the FBI. On November 27, 1970, after the Berrigan brothers had been reunited in the Danbury prison, J. Edgar Hoover appeared before a Senate subcommittee, where he had a particularly urgent message to deliver. There he told the committee, as part of his annual request for funds to safeguard America against its internal enemies, that a plot was afoot to kidnap a high government official and hold him for ransom, and also to blow up the pipes that delivered heat to the government offices, all this masterminded by the East Coast Conspiracy to Save Lives. The radical priests, the Berrigan brothers, were involved, together with many others, in the kidnap and sabatoge conspiracy. A press release that had already been prepared was distributed, and it reiterated what Hoover had told the senators.

Hoover's statement was met with considerable skepticism and ridicule. It was pointed out that the Berrigans were not even members of the East Coast group, although they certainly supported its aims; their anti-violence stand was emphasized; and finally a United States congressman, William R. Anderson of Tennessee, challenged Hoover to produce evidence and obtain indictments, or make a retraction. Within the resistance, although no one took the discussion seriously and there had been no plans that could be seriously labeled a conspiracy, there was some dismay. For such a discussion had been held, the idea thrown around, and it seemed strange that the FBI had learned of it. That it had been elevated from idle conversation to conspiracy may have had its humorous side; but among the inner circle of activists it was inconceivable that anyone was not trustworthy, or even that someone was talking without normal circumspection. Sister McAlister recalled her letter to Phil Berrigan and suspected that Boyd Douglas was the leak.

The FBI had made its accusation; now it had to pursue its charge. A few days after the accusation, newspapers learned that Henry Kissinger was to have been the victim of the alleged kidnapping.

Obtaining an indictment was not easy. Yet, Hoover's statement and the challenge to it by a disbelieving public was as embarrassing to the FBI as the manhunt for Dan and Phil had been. President Nixon was asked at a press conference if he approved of what Hoover had done and evaded the question by talking about the patriotism of the FBI leader.

In Harrisburg, Pennsylvania, the grand jury met and subpoenaed many witnesses. Several refused to cooperate. One rose in the middle of being questioned and said that she was going to mass! In the end a seven-point indictment was drawn up accusing six persons of conspiring to commit the kidnapping and sabotage. Indicted were Philip Berrigan, Sister McAlister, Reverend John Wenderoth (publicly identified with the East Coast Conspiracy to Save Lives), Reverend Neil McLaughlin (an antiwar and civil rights activist and friend of Wenderoth), Anthony Scoblick (a former priest, now married, and publicly known for militant activities), and Eqbal Ahmad (neither Catholic nor an American citizen, a fellow at the Adlai Stevenson Institute for International Affairs). In addition, seven persons,

including Dan Berrigan, were named as nonindicted co-conspirators. This prosecution strategy gave the government an opportunity to introduce against the defendants evidence which would otherwise have been inadmissible.

The difficulty with the indictment from the prosecution's viewpoint was that it rested almost entirely on the McAlister letter, hardly enough evidence to prove a serious conspiracy. As for the alleged plan of blowing up the heating pipes, a government worker whose older sister was active in the Catholic antiwar movement but who was apparently not involved himself was an FBI suspect, although this suspicion appeared to be solely based on the sister's political activities. It was expected that if he could be frightened or intimidated, he would confess to having shown some members of the conspiracy around the tunnel system. But he denied this with such vigor that one has only to read the testimony to be convinced it was all a "fishing expedition": that is, with no information and just a hunch based on his family association, he was being questioned in the hope that something incriminating might turn up. He was being accused so that, however slightly involved, he would confess and implicate others. He did not.

Even with Douglas ready to testify that he had taken the "kidnap letter" and others into prison, there was nothing on which to hang a conspiracy—no meetings, no plans, no real acts. To many it appeared that the indictment was a mechanism to appease Hoover and help him save face after he had overstepped himself with the dramatic announcement. Since the pro-Berrigan forces would not let the matter be forgotten quietly, the government had to prosecute. To some insiders the affair began to look silly.

When William S. Lynch was assigned to prosecute the case for the government, he studied the grand jury minutes, the indictment, and the evidence, and was clearly dissatisfied. However, he devised a remarkable way to save what appeared to be a lost cause. He reopened the case and obtained a new indictment to supersede the old one. The new charge named eight conspirators. These included the original six plus Mary Cain Scoblick, whose husband was already named in the first indictment, and John T. Glick, an activist whose case was later severed from the others. There were still co-conspirators, but Dan Berrigan was not among them. There had been six conspirators, then eight, and now seven. So it remained.

The indictment was a detailed one in which the seven who eventually went to trial were accused of entering into a conspiracy to commit many acts—raid draft boards, interfere with selective service functions, kidnap a government official, sabotage government installations in Washington, and do other illegal acts. They were all bundled together in one conspiracy and one accusation against one group. Then, additionally, Phil Berrigan and Sister McAlister were accused of illegally smuggling letters in and out of prison.

As reporters immediately recognized, Lynch had effected a clever coup. If a jury were convinced that the group had entered into a conspiracy to raid draft boards (not an unlikely conclusion), they might find the whole group guilty, and in this way it would look as if Hoover's accusations were justified, although nothing would be proven with regard to the kidnapping matter. Reporters and defendants might see the new indictment as trickery to salvage the prestige of the FBI director, but this did not mean that it would fail to convince a juror or the country at large.

The trial of the Harrisburg Seven opened on January 24, 1972, before Judge R. Dixon Herman. The defense had a remarkable array of legal talent, attesting to the serious purpose the defendants wanted to launch through the courtroom. Among others there were Ramsey Clark, former attorney general of the United States; Leo Boudin, one of the nation's most highly regarded constitutional lawyers and a man long identified with liberal causes; Paul O'Dwyer, active in New York politics, an outspoken critic of the war, a supporter of the Catholic left, and later to run successfully for president of the New York City Council; and Tom Menaker, a prominent local attorney.

Much of the early jockeying for position concerned jury selection. Each defendant was given four peremptory challenges (without cause), an advantage over the prosecution, which had a total of only six such challenges. After considerable interrogation, a jury of nine women and three men was chosen. One woman, a Catholic, expressed antiwar sentiments; another, a Protestant, had four sons who were conscientious objectors. A black woman had a husband in the American Legion, and several of the jurors expressed reservations about the propriety of an alien participating in antiwar activities, a matter of interest since Eqbal Ahmad was one of the defendants.

From the beginning, the prosecution sought to keep the war out of the case, but the defense wanted both to establish that there had been no conspiracy, and also to use the courtroom as a forum to reach millions with an antiwar message. For Lynch, the chief prosecutor, the main concern was the question of breaking the law, which no one had a right to do, no matter what motive, and he ridiculed as arrogant the idea that Catholic priests had a higher-than-law morality to guide them.

He maintained that these were ordinary crimes of which the defendants were accused, not political ones.

After a few minor witnesses, the star witness for the prosecution came to the stand. Boyd Douglas's story began to unfold, although much of it was to come out later under relentless cross-examination. He had been a many-time loser, had had a difficult childhood, and was in trouble with the law from early adolescence. His record included an undesirable discharge from the army, counterfeiting, impersonation, and international check forgery, with the sums far from trifling. He had used many aliases in his day, some only for writing bad checks. At one time, probably anticipating that he would be apprehended in a certain bank he had entered to obtain funds after depositing worthless checks, he had a gun on him. Later he would claim that he had not intended to use it at all, or at least not against anyone except himself.

While serving one of his prison sentences, Boyd Douglas had volunteered for a medical experiment conducted by the National Institutes of Health, and as a result had been left with ugly scars. He brought suit against the government for two million dollars, but there was some question as to whether or not he had deliberately induced the affliction that caused the scars. At any rate, the matter was settled for about fifteen thousand dollars and he received about two-thirds of this sum, the rest going to his lawyer.

In Lewisburg he had already served the greater part of his sentence when he was permitted daytime freedom for the study-release program. The federal government and penologists had great hope for this program, in which a select group of trustworthy and qualified prisoners prepare for reentry into the outside world by attending a university not far from the penitentiary, re-turning each evening to spend the night in their cells. It was a program similar to, but on a smaller scale than, one that was being tried with employment, a work-release or work-furlough experiment.

At Bucknell, where Douglas at the time was the only student-release convict, he had made the acquaintance of other students, who knew that he was a prisoner and accepted him nevertheless. He courted several girls, usually without success it appears, and told them fanciful stories about his own background.

Douglas had evidently not been an agent for the prison authorities when he first became a student under the release program, nor even when he first developed a relationship with Phil Berrigan and offered to be the courier. Undoubtedly he saw himself gaining from the prestige of being able to boast to students and faculty of a close relationship with the imprisoned priest. Nevertheless, he seems to have had letters hand-copied or photostated before he was recruited for the informer job, and he had been safeguarding these copies. Perhaps he himself had no clear-cut advance notion of what he would do with them; he may just have had a sense of self-importance. In cross-examination the defense hinted that blackmail was in his mind, but Douglas would not make such an admission. He did admit, however, that he recruited students for antigovernment demonstrations, boasted of a knowledge of explosives, strongly suggested that this was a knowledge that the antiwar movement could utilize, and probably had committed other acts that clearly fall into the realm of the agent provocateur.

A routine check of Phil Berrigan's room had disclosed a contraband letter, and a little interrogation by prison authorities led them to realize who the courier was. From that point on it was not difficult to recruit

Douglas into their ranks. But though he claimed he worked for only patriotic reasons, because he wanted to help his country against the antiwar people who were out to destroy it, his motives appeared more mercenary than that. He was constantly urging that the government give him large sums of money for his undercover work, and at one time collected for some minor expenses from more than one source. He was several days on the stand.

The government presented a feeble case, except for the fact of the smuggled letters, and the peculiar wording of the superseding indictment. For there *had* been draft board raids, although that did not mean that there

had been conspiracy; and the entire prosecution seemed to carry a suggestion of double jeopardy. With so weak a case, the defense showed its opinion of the entire matter by resting, without calling a single witness and without troubling to present a single document. The case went to the jury.

The jury argued, questioned the judge regarding conspiracy law and with regard to what verdicts were required if the defendants had conspired to commit one of the acts but not others, and finally there was a partial agreement. The priest and his friend, Phil and Elizabeth, were guilty of the letter-smuggling charge. After further deliberation, the jury became deadlocked and was finally

Sister Elizabeth McAlister being escorted from Federal Building by defense attorney Paul O'Dwyer after the jury found Sister McAlister and Reverend Philip Berrigan guilty of smuggling letters from Lewisburg Prison. UNITED PRESS INTERNATIONAL

Seven members of the "Harrisburg Eight" at a news conference (left to right): Mary and Anthony Scoblick, Eqbal Ahmad, John (Ted) Glick, Reverend Joseph Wenderoth, Reverend Neil McLaughlin, Sister Elizabeth McAlister. United Press International

dismissed. Following dismissal and the declaration that there had been a mistrial, the jury revealed that it had finally voted 10 to 2 in favor of acquittal on the conspiracy charge, and further revealed that one of the holdouts for a guilty verdict was the mother of the four conscientious objectors!

The entire trial for conspiracy to kidnap and sabotage had been built on a very tenuous thread, and the case had probably been prosecuted only because of the premature and ill-timed announcement by J. Edgar Hoover. It was now over, and there would be no retrial.

The letter-smuggling charge raised an interesting legal issue. Such an act was indeed against the law, but there had never been a prosecution for it before the Berrigan-McAlister case; previously, such transgressions had always been handled by a reprimand or a mild administrative type of punishment visited upon the prisoner. The defense charged that this was selective prosecution because of the antiwar activities of Berrigan and McAlister, and as such it amounted to persecution, not prosecution.

In the end, the Harrisburg Seven seemed to have won a double victory: exoneration on the specific charges that were leveled against them, and a moral confrontation with their prosecutors. For their admirers theirs had been a conspiracy to end the war in Vietnam by holding its immorality up for all to see.

Angela Davis

1972

ANGELA DAVIS WAS A PHILOSOPHY TEACHER at the University of California in Los Angeles who leaped into prominence during the last months of the sixties, when a movement arose to dismiss her from her professorial post. She was black, articulate, highly educated, extremely militant, and a member of the Communist party of the United States. In California a law had long been on the books prohibiting the state college system from employing a Communist. Using this law, a sharply divided board of regents dismissed the assistant professor, setting off widespread protests that included voices beyond those of young radicals and outraged blacks. The American Association of University Professors threatened legal action. The director of the Afro-American Studies Center at UCLA asked for permission to discuss the case with the regents, and was refused.

It did not take long for Angela Davis to become a heroine. A lecture she gave at UCLA was attended by two thousand cheering students, and a faculty movement was started to withhold all grades as a form of protest. In her first round in court she was victorious. The court ordered UCLA to accept enrollment in her classes for credit, and a short time later a higher court ruled that the 1950 ban on Communist teachers was unconstitutional. Faced with this judicial defeat, the regents changed tactics,

UPHOLDING THE DISMISSAL ON THE BASIS OF what they claimed to be her poor teaching. To many it looked as if Ronald Regan and the conservative majority on his board of regents would face a setback, since Davis received the support of her department, her faculty, professional associations, the student body, and blacks of all political persuasions throughout the country. Then, in August 1970, the case took a new and unexpected turn.

California has a vast prison system. Large numbers of prisoners are black and Mexican-American. They charge that a racist society pushes them toward crime, and that racism in prison keeps them in confinement while whites are released. The prisoners also charge the guards with racism. In 1969, in a struggle between a white guard and black prisoners at San Quentin, one of the world's largest prisons just a few miles from San Francisco, the guard had been killed.

On August 7, 1970, James D. McClain was on trial for the murder of the prison guard. The trial was being held in the Marin County Courthouse at San Rafael, five or six miles from San Quentin. While the trial was going on, a young man entered the courtroom, drew a gun, and freed McClain and a convict witness, William Arthur Christmas. Taking several hostages, including three women jurors and the judge, the young man drove away. At a roadblock a shootout ensued. Judge Harold J. Haley, McClain, Christmas, and Jonathan Jackson, the youth who had apparently led the entire plot, were killed.

At the funeral of Jonathan Jackson, Panther leader Huey Newton said Jackson had died heroically in the effort to bring freedom to others. For the Jackson family, the tragedy was particularly acute, for Jonathan's older brother, George, was a prisoner at San Quentin, having spent twelve years in captivity, serving an indeterminate one-day-to-life sentence for armed robbery. Denied parole year after year, he had won the admiration of a small coterie; his letters from prison were about to be published in book form (*Soledad Brother*) and he was already receiving national attention.

There were recriminations among officials after the shootout. Some declared that the killing of the judge had been unnecessary and, in an effort to forestall criticism, police declared that the first shooting had come from the getaway car.

About a week after the courtroom event, a newspaper reported what was probably a leak from an official investigator. One of the guns used by Jackson belonged to Angela Davis. By the time the story appeared, the philosophy teacher was not to be found. Under California law, anyone who aids and abets in the commission of a major crime is equally guilty with the perpetrator. On the basis of the report about the gun's ownership, warrants were issued for the arrest of Angela Davis, charging her with murder and kidnapping. In fact it was said that not one gun but two used in the shootout had been purchased in her name, with a hint that a third gun might have been bought by her. More than that, the purchases had apparently been made only one or two days before the killing.

One other prisoner had been in the courtroom, as a witness in the McClain case. This was Ruchell Magee, one of the men who came to be known as the Soledad Brothers, after the name of the prison. Although he had been present in court, and a sheriff or other police officer had apparently freed him when so ordered at gunpoint, Magee either had not gone or was not taken into the getaway car. Eventually he was charged, like Davis, with murder and kidnapping, under the aiding and abetting provisions of the law. But since most of the attention was on Angela Davis, Ruchell Magee was an obscure figure. Those who knew him said that he was an outstanding jailhouse lawyer, a prisoner who spends his time studying criminal law, and often becomes extremely knowledgeable in the field.

For two months law enforcement officials sought Angela Davis. She was finally apprehended in a New York motel. Her hairstyle had changed, but otherwise she looked much the same as she had in California. Held without bail and charged with unlawful interstate flight to avoid prosecution, she fought extradition, and almost immediately became a focal point for protest. A demonstration was held, and for the first time the cry was heard that would be repeated during the next year, Free Angela Davis. Black intellectuals rallied to her side, and any hope by governmental authorities that she would be seen as an accessory to a brutal and nonpolitical murder was quickly abandoned. In New York she went on a hunger strike, started a suit to be released from solitary confinement, and watched as her cause gained wide support. Even the YWCA spoke out in her behalf.

Throughout the world, the name of Angela Davis became known. Petitions were circulated in Italy in her behalf. Rumors had it that kidnapping and hijacking plots

Angela Davis demonstrators gather in a parking lot across the street from the Santa Clara County Courthouse in San Jose. UNITED PRESS INTERNATIONAL

were being hatched to secure her freedom. A wildcat strike broke out in Pittsburgh because a bus driver was not permitted to wear his Free Angela Davis button. A demonstration for her freedom was held in Bonn, Germany. In America, an explosion in an oil refinery immediately set off rumors that it was caused by her partisans. In the Soviet Union, fourteen leading scientists expressed their concern over her safety, lauded her as a selfless fighter for social ideals, and appealed to American courts to judge her with "full impartiality and humanity." Perhaps the most dramatic protest took place in front of American military headquarters in Saigon, a demonstration of about forty American soldiers demanding freedom for Angela Davis.

The American government was acutely sensitive to all of this. It invited the Soviet scientists to come to this country to watch the trial (and expressed hope that a reciprocal arrangement could be worked out for trials in the Soviet Union of international interest), and the state department and the U.S. Information Agency sent frequent lengthy reports to its outposts all over the world, giving them the government's perspective on the case.

Just before Christmas of 1970, Angela Davis finally lost her battle against extradition and was returned to California, where she was immediately visited by her family. She announced the appointment of a prominent militant black attorney from Atlanta, Howard R. Moore, Jr., as chief counsel for the defense, and asked for permission to act as her own co-counsel. The prosecution objected, but her plea was granted with warnings that the rules of the court would have to be followed. This meant that she could address the court and jury without being placed on the witness stand and therefore would not be subject to cross-examination.

The other defendant, Magee, was brought to the courtroom during pretrial motions and hearings literally in chains. He was bound to his seat, and when he demanded to be heard, he was ordered removed from the court. At one point in the preliminary skirmishes Magee produced an affidavit in which he charged that an attorney appointed to defend him had come to him in prison and, purportedly speaking on behalf of two California judges, offered him immunity if he would perjure himself by testifying against his codefendant. The attorney denied the charge, and asked for the right to withdraw from the case.

The generally conservative NAACP stated that it would watch the trial with great care, and warned that Angela Davis was not being given the benefit of a presumption of innocence. The Urban League expressed its fear that she would not be given a fair trial. She received visits in jail and expressions of support from the young Irish Catholic leader, Bernadette Devlin, and the American antiwar activist and actress, Jane Fonda.

In August 1971, just about a year after the shootout in which his brother had died, George Jackson was killed in prison, under conditions that have never been satisfactorily explained. The authorities charged that he was making an effort to escape, but many observers felt that this was an unlikely story. His death came at a time when he had achieved a national reputation for his prison writings, and during the pretrial jailing of Angela Davis it left widespread fear concerning the atmosphere in which she was to be tried.

The case being prepared against Angela Davis began to become public knowledge, in the manner that American prosecutors so often permit evidence to become known before a jury has been selected and a trial has begun. It became known that a charge would be filed that she had been seen the day before the shootout near the Marin County courthouse with a young man later identified as Jonathan Jackson, and that she would be named as the person who had purchased the guns.

Magee was not cooperating in all respects with the more prominent defendant; and probably without forewarning her attorneys, he made a charge in open court that Judge McMurray was prejudiced against him. He called upon the judge to step aside, and to everyone's astonishment, McMurray did. Moore and the other attorneys for Davis appeared to be unhappy with the judge's self-disqualification, and when a new judge was named, it was Davis's turn to charge prejudice.

In New York City a minor portion of the trial in the Davis case was being held. The man who had been apprehended with Angela Davis at the time of her arrest was David Poindexter, a mysterious, wealthy, and apparently radical black, charged with harboring a fugitive. It might appear that this would be self-evident, but there was an important technicality. One had to prove beyond a reasonable doubt that Poindexter knew that a *federal* warrant had been issued for the fugitive's arrest, and not merely that she was wanted in California. After a trial that lasted a little less than two weeks, Poindexter was acquitted, and immediately announced his intention of going on a barnstorming tour all over the United States to demand freedom, at least on bail, for Angela Davis.

With the Poindexter case disposed of, attention shifted again to the West Coast.

Angela Davis outside Santa Clara Superior Court on the first day of her trial. UNITED PRESS INTERNATIONAL

There Magee expressed his contempt for the defense lawyers who had been assigned to him, called the judge a Klansman in disguise, contended that the case should be tried in a federal and not a state court, and asked that his trial be separated from that of Miss Davis. As for her, there was a constant demand for her release on bail. The probation department of California recommended that she be freed on the posting of one hundred thousand dollars, but this was rejected. Together with the fight for bail there was a motion for change of venue, as the climate in San Marin County was said to be inimical to a fair trial. One might say the request was granted in part. Although San Marin would no longer be the seat of the trial, it was not going to be heard in San Francisco or Los Angeles, as the defense lawyers had requested, but in San Jose, a move that was loudly denounced.

By the end of 1971, with the trial not yet underway, the government said that it had already incurred expenses amounting to a third of a million dollars in the matter of Angela Davis. She had spent a year in California in jail, and it appeared that she would continue to be confined during the trial itself, but this suddenly changed when the California Supreme Court ruled that capital punishment was unconstitutional in that state. The question of bail was reopened on the grounds that Angela Davis was no longer charged with a capital crime. Judge Arnason, now in charge of the case, ordered her release, and a wealthy farmer put up the money, for which he and his family were threatened, ostracized, and subjected to many forms of harassment. Suddenly, without enough advance warning for the word to pass around, Angela walked out of jail. She was cheered joyously by about one hundred persons who had gathered to greet her, and she smiled.

In a small courtroom in San Jose, California, with the strictest of security measures, the trial of Angela Davis, severed from that of Magee, finally opened on February 18, 1972. During the jury selection, a *New York Times* reporter was arrested on a marijuana charge and his press credentials were removed, only to be restored after a short time. Later, when he refused to plead guilty even to a minor offense, he was given a trial and acquitted. Many interpreted the incident as a sign that an effort would be made to intimidate the press.

A protracted struggle over jury selection was anticipated, but after a panel of eleven whites and one black was temporarily seated, the defense took the other side completely by surprise and announced that the panel was acceptable. The prosecution was jockeyed into the position of either renouncing its unstated objectives of having an all-white jury, or raising an objection that would quite obviously appear to be racially motivated. The latter path was taken, and the lone black was removed, leaving anger among spectators and a definite impression that color alone had caused the exclusion. The defendant used the occasion to re-iterate her pessimism on the possibility of obtaining a fair trial in Santa Clara County.

In an opening statement the prosecution revealed the nature of its case. Not only would it be shown that the guns used in the shootout had been purchased by and belonged to Angela Davis, but that her motive had not been political. She was in love, it was contended, with George Jackson, and was motivated in her effort to free him in exchange for the hostages in order to fulfill that love.

As co-counsel, Angela Davis was able to speak for herself. In an opening statement she admitted that the guns were hers, pointed out that she needed them for protection, and that her love for George Jackson was one of political admiration. She had indeed been struggling for the freedom of the Soledad Brothers, but she believed in obtaining that freedom through the courts, not through violence. She reminded her audience that she had been brought up in Birmingham, where guns were traditionally needed by black people to protect themselves against violence, not to perpetrate violence.

The witnesses produced little that was unexpected. Those who had been jurors at the time of the shootout testified as to what had occurred, and particularly what had been said by those now dead. Jonathan Jackson seemed to have made it clear, they declared, that the hostages were going to be exchanged for the freedom of the Soledad Brothers, and that his own brother George would be among those freed.

On April 6, after the trial had been plodding along for several weeks, out-of-court activity again attracted attention when James Carr, a former cellmate of George Jackson, was killed in an ambush. There was speculation that the killing was connected with the case, that he was going to be a witness—for which side was not clear—and that he had been murdered to prevent his testimony. The matter was never cleared up, but in court the question arose as to whether the jury had heard of the event, and whether it had prejudiced their ability to hear the case. The prosecution had spoken to reporters about the Carr murder, and following vigorous protests from the defense about these statements, the court warned both sides to refrain from discussing the trial with newsmen.

In the trial itself, witnesses recounted the events of the San Rafael shootout. One gun that had been used was identified as having been purchased by the accused only two days before the killings. The love element was proven to exist by letters sent by Angela Davis to George Jackson, and after a vigorous struggle the letters were read in court. "All my efforts have gone into one direction —free George Jackson and the Soledad Brothers," she had written, and the prosecution was prone to read sinister connotations into those words.

Thus far, the involvement of Angela Davis had been only weakly developed. It depended mainly on the guns and her alleged love. However, prison guards identified her as a person who had accompanied Jonathan Jackson when he visited his brother in August 1970. The date of the visit was placed as two days before the shootout. An effort was made to link the defendant to a car driven to the courthouse on the day of the shootings. An attendant at a gas station remembered seeing her the day before in that car in that area. A former convict said that Davis had visited the prison, but did not enter it, on the day before the events in which Jonathan lost his life. Some of the witnesses were vague as to how they were able to recall such details and identify people with such certainty, and the defense did its best to confuse them by having a woman with a strong resemblance to Angela Davis sit next to her during a part of the trial.

Such was the case against Angela Davis, except for her flight, with whatever suggestion of guilt one wished to draw from it. For the defense, witnesses told of her whereabouts at the time of the shootout and before, of her surprise in hearing of it and her distress to learn that her guns were missing. An expert challenged the credibility of the prosecution eyewitnesses. And, in a poignant and tragic drama, Lester Jackson, the father of the slain youths, Jonathan and George, was called as witness for the prosecution's rebuttal. He refused to testify and was held in contempt. The judge was in a dilemma. Obviously, to jail the man would arouse widespread sympathies for the defendant, for this was the man who had lost two sons in the tragedy that had unfolded. But on the other hand, permitting him to refuse with impunity to take the stand would violate elementary principles of law. The matter was solved by fining the elder Jackson one hundred dollars. The fine was paid, and he left the court without testifying.

The state called for a conviction of murder in the first degree. The defense scoffed and said the entire case against the defendant was absurd. After three days of deliberation, the jury brought in its verdict. Angela Davis was found not guilty.

It was a victory for the militant and all of her supporters, but an effort was made to turn it into a victory for the American government as well. The acting director of the FBI said that he was satisfied with the verdict as an example of American democracy at work. But asked if there had been a fair trial, Angela Davis replied negatively. A fair trial would have been no trial.

Thus she emerged, martyr yet free. She was a symbol of courage, strength, and defiance of the most powerful forces in the nation. Her trial is not a record of the testimony itself, of what went on inside the court and on the stand, but of the marches, the slogans, the millions of words written about it, and the bringing of her message to people who she might otherwise never have been able to reach. This was a manifestation of the new politics in America and, in fact, in many other parts of the world.

As for the verdict, it could not have been otherwise under the rule that guilt must be established beyond a reasonable doubt. The links the prosecution made of the defendant to the planning of the murder were tenuous at best, though not nonexistent. Certainly they were insufficient to sustain a conviction. And then again, it was a jury of all-whites, not working in the obscurity of a little Southern town, but sensitive to world-wide publicity, and to the charge of racism that would inevitably come with a verdict other than exoneration. Thus, there was a constituency—youthful, disaffected, militant— of blacks and whites marching in the streets, powerless to make decisions, yet constituting a force contrary to the decision-making powers, and placing judges and juries on the defensive and the alert.

Bibliography

SOCRATES

Church, F. J. *The Trial and Death of Socrates: Being the Euthyphro, Apology, Crito and Phaedo of Plato.* London: Macmillan and Company, 1880.

Grote, George. *Life, Teachings, and Death of Socrates.* New York: Stanford & Delisser, 1858.

Phillipson, Coleman. *The Trial of Socrates.* London: Stevens and Sons Limited, 1928.

Plato. *Collected Works: The Apology of Socrates, Phaedo, Crito.* A version by Henry Cary. London: George Bell & Sons, 1890.

————. *Socrates: A Translation of the Apology, Crito and Parts of the Phaedo.* Edited by W. W. Goodwin. New York: Charles Scribner's Sons, 1878.

JOAN OF ARC

Bangs, Mary Rogers. *Jeanne d'Arc: The Maid of France.* Boston: Houghton Mifflin Company, 1910.

Barrett, W. P. *The Trial of Joan of Arc.* Translated into English from the Original Latin and French Documents. New York: Gotham House, Inc., 1932.

Ireland, W. H., ed. *Memoirs of Jeanne d'Arc.* 2 volumes. London: Robert Triphook, 1824.

Paine, Albert Bigelow. *Joan of Arc: Maid of France.* 2 volumes. New York: The Macmillan Company, 1925.

The Trial of Joan of Arc. A translation by W. S. Scott of the verbatim report of the proceedings from the Orléans Manuscript. London: The Folio Society, 1956.

CATHERINE OF ARAGON

Albert, Marvin H. *The Divorce.* New York: Simon and Schuster, 1965.

Cavendish, George. *The Life of Cardinal Wolsey.* London: Harding, Triphook and Lepard, 1825.

Claremont, Francesca. *Catherine of Aragon.* London: Robert Hale Limited, 1939.

Froude, James Anthony. *The Divorce of Catherine of Aragon.* London: Longmans, Green and Company, 1891.

Jerrold, Walter. *Henry VIII and His Wives.* London: Hutchinson and Company, 1925.

Mattingly, Garrett. *Catherine of Aragon.* Boston: Little, Brown and Company, 1941.

GALILEO GALILEI

Fahrie, J. J. *Memorials of Galileo Galilei: 1564–1642.* Leamington and London: The Courier Press, 1929.

Galilei, Galileo. *Dialogue on the Great World Systems.* In the Salisbury Translation, revised, annotated, and with an introduction by George de Santillana. Chicago: University of Chicago Press, 1953.

Holden, Edward S. "Galileo." A series of articles in *The Popular Science Monthly,* 1905.

Santillana, George de. *The Crime of Galileo.* Chicago: University of Chicago Press, 1955.

Wegg-Prosser, F. R. *Galileo and His Judges.* London: Chapman and Hall, 1889.

CHARLES I OF ENGLAND

Abbott, Jacob. *History of King Charles the First of England.* New York: Harper &

Brothers, 1848.

Belloc, Hilaire. *Charles the First—King of England*. Philadelphia: J. B. Lippincott Company, 1933.

Coit, Charles Wheeler. *The Life of Charles the First: The Royal Martyr*. Boston: Houghton Mifflin Company, 1926.

Lockyer Roger, ed. *The Trial of Charles I*. A Contemporary Account Taken from the Memoirs of Sir Thomas Herbert and John Rushworth. London: The Folio Society, 1959.

Wedgwood, C. V. *A Coffin for King Charles*. New York: The Macmillan Company, 1964.

Williamson, Hugh Ross. *The Day They Killed the King*. London: Frederick Muller Limited, 1957.

Salem Witchcraft Trials

Beard, George M. *The Psychology of the Salem Witchcraft Excitement of 1692*. New York: G. P. Putnam's Sons, 1882.

Levin, David. *What Happened in Salem?* New York: Harcourt, Brace, and World, Inc., 1960.

Mather, Cotton. *Wonders of the Invisible World*. London: John Russell Smith, 1862.

Perley, M. V. B. *A Short History of the Salem Witchcraft Trials*. Salem, Mass.: M. V. B. Perley, 1911.

Records of Salem Witchcraft. Copied from the original documents and privately printed for W. Elliot Woodward, Roxbury, Mass.: 1864.

Robbins, Rossell Hope. *The Encyclopedia of Witchcraft and Demonology*. New York: Crown Publishers, Inc., 1959.

Starkey, Marion L. *The Devil in Massachusetts*. New York: Alfred A. Knopf, Inc., 1949.

John Peter Zenger

Brown, James Wright. *Life and Times of John Peter Zenger*. A Statement of Facts Chronologically Arranged—as gathered from Rutherford, Konkle, Cheslaw, Sheehan, Cooper and Robb. New York: *Editor and Publisher*, March 14, 21, 28; April 4 and 11, 1953.

Buranelli, Vincent, ed. *The Trial of Peter Zenger*. New York: New York University Press, 1957.

Rutherford, Livingston. *John Peter Zenger: His Press, His Trial and a Bibliography of Zenger Imprints, also a Reprint of the First Edition of the Trial*. New York: Dodd, Mead and Company, 1904.

The Story of John Peter Zenger. John Peter Zenger Memorial, Federal Hall Memorial, New York: 1953.

The Impeachment Trial of Andrew Johnson

Clemenceau, Georges. *American Reconstruction 1865–1870 and the Impeachment of President Johnson*. New York: Lincoln Mac-Veagh and Dial Press, 1928.

De Witt, David M. *The Impeachment and Trial of Andrew Johnson, Seventeenth President of the United States: A History*. New York: The Macmillan Company, 1903.

Franklin, John Hope. *Reconstruction: After the Civil War*. Chicago: University of Chicago Press, 1961.

Lomask, Milton. *Andrew Johnson: President on Trial*. New York: Farrar, Straus & Giroux, 1960.

Stampp, Kenneth M. *The Era of Reconstruction, 1865–1877*. New York: Alfred A. Knopf, 1965.

Stryker, Lloyd Paul. *Andrew Johnson: A Study in Courage*. New York: The Macmillan Company, 1929.

Trial of Andrew Johnson, President of the United States, Before the Senate of the United States, on Impeachment by the House of Representatives for High Crimes and Misdemeanors. Published by order of the Senate. 3 volumes. Washington, D.C.: Government Printing Office, 1868.

Oscar Wilde

Brasol, Boris. *Oscar Wilde: The Man, the Artist, the Martyr*. New York: Charles Scribner's Sons, 1938.

Bibliography

Croft-Cooke, Rupert. *Bosie: The Story of Lord Alfred Douglas, His Friends and His Enemies.* London: Witt, 1963.

Douglas, Lord Alfred. *The Autobiography of Lord Alfred Douglas.* London: M. Secker, 1929. (Published in U.S.A. under title *My Friendship with Oscar Wilde.* New York: Coventry House, 1932.)

———. *Without Apology.* London: M. Secker, 1938.

Harris, Frank. *Oscar Wilde: His Life and Confessions.* New York: Covici, Friede, 1930.

Holland, Vyvyan. *Son of Oscar Wilde.* London: Hart-Davis Limited, 1954, and New York: E. P. Dutton & Company, 1954.

Hyde, H. Montgomery. *Oscar Wilde: The Aftermath.* New York: Farrar, Straus & Giroux, 1963.

———, ed. *The Trials of Oscar Wilde.* London: William Hodge and Company, 1948.

CAPTAIN ALFRED DREYFUS

Byrnes, Robert F. *Antisemitism in Modern France.* Vol. 1: *The Prologue to the Dreyfus Affair.* New Brunswick, N.J.: Rutgers University Press, 1950.

Derfler, Leslie, ed. *The Dreyfus Affair: Tragedy of Errors?* Boston: D. C. Heath and Company, 1963.

Halasz, Nicholas. *Captain Dreyfus: The Story of a Mass Hysteria.* New York: Grove Press, Inc., 1957.

Schwartzkoppen, Max Von. *The Truth About Dreyfus.* From the Schwartzkoppen Papers. New York: G. P. Putnam's Sons, 1931.

Tuchman, Barbara. *The Proud Tower.* New York: The Macmillan Company, 1965.

EDITH CAVELL

Got, Ambroise. *The Case of Miss Cavell: From the Unpublished Documents of the Trial: The Property of a Former Commissioner of the German Government.* London: Hodder and Stoughton, 1920.

Hoehling, A. A. *A Whisper of Eternity: The Mystery of Edith Cavell.* New York: Thomas Yoseloff, Inc., 1957.

Whitton, Lt. Col. F. E. *Service Trials and Tragedies.* London: Hutchinson & Company, 1930.

NICOLA SACCO AND BARTOLOMEO VANZETTI

Ehrmann, Herbert B. *The Untried Case: The Sacco-Vanzetti Case and the Morelli Gang.* New York: Vanguard Press, 1933.

Felix, David. *Protest: Sacco-Vanzetti and the Intellectuals.* Bloomington: Indiana University Press, 1965.

Frankfurter, Felix. "Case of Sacco and Vanzetti," *Atlantic Monthly,* March, 1927.

———. *The Case of Sacco and Vanzetti: A Critical Analysis for Lawyers and Laymen.* Boston: Little, Brown & Company, 1927.

Joughin, Louis, and Edmund M. Morgan. *The Legacy of Sacco and Vanzetti.* New York: Harcourt, Brace, 1948.

Musmanno, Michael A. *After Twelve Years.* New York: Alfred A. Knopf, 1939.

Russell, Francis. *Tragedy at Dedham.* New York: McGraw-Hill Book Company, Inc., 1962.

Sacco, Nicola, and Bartolomeo Vanzetti. *The Letters of Sacco and Vanzetti.* Edited by Marion D. Frankfurter and Gardner Jackson. New York: Viking Press, 1928.

The Sacco-Vanzetti Case. Transcript of the Record of the Trial of Nicola Sacco and Bartolomeo Vanzetti in the Courts of Massachusetts and Subsequent Proceedings 1920–7. 6 volumes. New York: Henry Holt & Company, 1928.

JOHN THOMAS SCOPES

Allen, Leslie H., ed. *Bryan and Darrow at Dayton: The Record and Documents of the "Bible-Evolution Trial."* New York: Arthur Lee, 1925.

Darrow, Clarence. *The Story of My Life.* New York: Grosset & Dunlap, 1932.

Ginger, Raymond. *Six Days or Forever? Tennessee v. John Thomas Scopes.* Boston: Beacon Press, 1958.

Levine, Lawrence W. *Defender of the Faith: William Jennings Bryan: The Last Decade, 1915–1925.* New York: Oxford University Press, 1965.

Tompkins, Jerry R., ed. *D-Days at Dayton.* Baton Rouge: Louisiana State University Press, 1965.

Weinberg, Arthur, ed. *Attorney for the Damned.* New York: Simon & Schuster, 1957.

General Billy Mitchell

Aviation Magazine, September 14, November 23, December 28, 1925.

Burlingame, Roger. *General Billy Mitchell: Champion of Air Defense.* New York: McGraw-Hill Book Company, 1952.

Levine, Isaac Don. *Mitchell: Pioneer of Air Power.* Revised edition. New York: Duell, Sloane and Pearce, 1958.

Mitchell, Ruth. *My Brother Bill: The Life of General "Billy" Mitchell.* New York: Harcourt, Brace & Co., 1953.

Mitchell, William. Unpublished diary. Library of Congress.

The New York Times, October 29 to December 19, 1925.

The Scottsboro Boys

American Civil Liberties Union. *Report on the Scottsboro, Alabama, Case.* New York, 1931.

Belfrage, Sally. "The Scottsboro Boys Today." *Fact,* Nov.–Dec., 1966, pp. 58–64.

Carter, Dan T. *Scottsboro: A Tragedy of the American South.* New York: Oxford University Press, 1971.

Chalmers, Allan K. *They Shall Be Free.* Garden City, N.Y.: Doubleday & Company, 1951.

Four Free, Five in Prison—on the Same Evidence. What the Nation's Press Says About the Scottsboro Case. New York: Scottsboro Defense Committee, 1937.

Fraenkel, Osmond K. *Ozie Powell (and Others), Petitioners vs. The State of Alabama.* New York: Court Press, 1933.

Leibowitz, Samuel. *Haywood Patterson, petitioner, against State of Alabama.* New York: Ackerman Press, 1937.

———. *(Brief for) Haywood Patterson, Appellant.* 1937.

Patterson, Haywood, petitioner. *Transcript of record.* Supreme Court of the United States. Washington, D.C.: Judd & Detweiler, Inc., 1937.

———, (with Earl Conrad). *Scottsboro Boy.* Garden City, New York: Doubleday & Company, 1950.

Scottsboro: A Record of a Broken Promise. New York: Scottsboro Defense Committee, 1939.

Scottsboro: The Shame of America: The True Story and the True Meaning of the Famous Case. New York: Scottsboro Defense Committee, 1936.

The Nuremberg Trials

Bernstein, Victor H. *Final Judgment: The Story of Nuremberg.* New York: Boni and Gaer, 1947.

Gilbert, G. M. *Nuremberg Diary.* New York: Farrar, Straus and Cudahy, Inc., 1947.

Harris, Whitney R. *Tyranny on Trial: The Evidence at Nuremberg.* Dallas: Southern Methodist University Press, 1954.

International Military Tribunal. *Trial of the Major War Criminals Before the International Military Tribunal: Nuremberg, 14 November 1945–1 October 1946. Official Record of the Proceedings.* Volume 1. Germany: published at Nuremberg, 1947.

———. *The Trial of German Major War Criminals: Opening Speeches of the Chief Prosecutors.* London: His Majesty's Stationery Office, 1946.

Jackson, Robert H. *The Case Against the Nazi War Criminals: Opening Statements for the United States of America.* New York: Alfred A. Knopf, 1946.

Musmanno, Michael A. *The Eichmann Kommandos.* Philadelphia: Macrae Smith, 1961.

Woetzel, Robert K. *The Nuremberg Trials in International Law.* New York: Frederick A. Praeger, Inc., 1960.

Julius and Ethel Rosenberg and Martin Sobell

Moorehead, Alan. *The Traitors.* London:

Hamish Hamilton Limited, 1952.

Nizer, Louis. *The Implosion Conspiracy.* New York: Doubleday & Company, 1973.

"The Rosenberg Case: Some Reflections on Federal Criminal Law," *Columbia Law Review*, February 1954.

Schneir, Walter and Miriam. *Invitation to an Inquest.* Garden City, N.Y.: Doubleday & Company, 1965.

Sharp, Malcolm. *Was Justice Done? The Rosenberg-Sobell Case.* New York: Monthly Review Press, 1956.

The Testament of Ethel and Julius Rosenberg. New York: Cameron & Kahn, 1954.

U.S. vs. *Rosenbergs, Sobell, Yakovlev, and David Greenglass.* Transcript of trial, published by Committee to Secure Justice for Morton Sobell, New York.

Wexley, John. *The Judgment of Julius and Ethel Rosenberg.* New York: Cameron & Kahn, 1955.

Jomo Kenyatta

Baldwin, William W. *Mau Mau Man-Hunt: The Adventures of the Only American Who Has Fought the Terrorists in Kenya.* New York: E. P. Dutton & Company, 1957.

Cox, Richard. *Kenyatta's Country.* New York: Frederick A. Praeger, 1966.

Delf, George. *Jomo Kenyatta: Towards Truth About "The Light of Kenya."* New York: Doubleday & Company, 1961.

Holman, Dennis, *Bwana Drum.* New York: W. W. Norton, 1964.

Mboya, Tom. *Freedom and After.* Boston: Little, Brown and Company, 1963.

Adolf Eichmann

Arendt, Hannah. *Eichmann in Jerusalem: A Report on the Banality of Evil.* New York: Viking Press, 1963.

Friedman, Tuviah. *The Hunter.* Garden City, N.Y.; Doubleday and Company, 1961.

Hausner, Gideon. *Justice in Jerusalem.* New York: Harper & Row, 1966.

Pearlman, Moshe. *The Capture and Trial of Adolf Eichmann.* New York: Simon and Schuster, 1963.

Reynolds, Quentin, with Ephraim Katz and Zwy Aldouby. *Minister of Death: The Adolf Eichmann Story.* New York: Viking Press, 1960.

Robinson, Jacob. *And the Crooked Shall Be Made Straight: The Eichmann Trial, the Jewish Catastrophe, and Hannah Arendt's Narrative.* New York: The Macmillan Company, 1965.

Russell, Lord, of Liverpool. *The Record: The Trial of Adolf Eichmann for His Crimes Against the Jewish People and Against Humanity.* New York: Alfred A. Knopf, 1963.

The Trial of the Chicago Eight: Who Became the Chigago Seven

The New York Times, Washington Post, and other newspapers for August 1968 and for September 1969 through February 1970.

Contempt: Transcript of the Contempt Citations, Sentences, and Responses of the Chicago Conspiracy 10. Foreword by Ramsey Clark. Introduction by Harry Kalven, Jr. Chicago: Swallow Press, 1970.

Epstein, Jason. *The Great Conspiracy Trial: An Essay on Law, Liberty and the Constitution.* New York: Random House, 1970.

Hayden, Tom. *Trial.* New York: Holt, Rinehart and Winston, 1970.

Lukas, J. Anthony. *The Barnyard Epithet and Other Obscenities: Notes on the Chicago Conspiracy Trial.* New York: Harper & Row, 1970.

Sadock, Verna. *Verdict: The Exclusive Picture Story of the Trial of the Chicago Eight.* New York: Third Press, 1970.

Stein, David Lewis. *Living the Revolution: The Yippies in Chicago.* Indianapolis: Bobbs Merrill, 1969.

The Tales of Hoffman. Edited from the Official Transcript by Mark L. Levine, George C. McNamee, and Daniel Greenberg. Introduction by Dwight Macdonald. New York: Bantam Books, 1970.

The "Trial" of Bobby Seale. With Special Contributions by Julian Bond, Norman Dorsen, and Charles Rembar, and a Personal Statement by Bobby Seale. New York: Priam Books, 1970.

Walker, Daniel. *Rights in Conflict: Convention Week in Chicago, August 25–29, 1968*. A Report to the National Commission on the Causes and Prevention of Violence. Special Introduction by Max Frankel. New York: Dutton, 1968.

PHILIP BERRIGAN AND THE HARRISBURG SEVEN

Berrigan, Daniel. *America Is Hard to Find*. Garden City, N.Y.: Doubleday, 1972.

———. *No Bars to Manhood*. Garden City, N.Y.: Doubleday, 1970.

———. *The Dark Night of Resistance*. Garden City, N.Y.: Doubleday, 1971.

———. *The Trial of the Catonsville Nine*. Boston: Beacon Press, 1970.

Berrigan, Daniel, and Robert Coles. *The Geography of Faith: Conversations Between Daniel Berrigan, When Underground, and Robert Coles*. Boston: Beacon Press, 1971.

Berrigan, Daniel, and Lee Lockwood. *Conversations with Daniel Berrigan*. New York: Random House, 1972.

———. *A Season in Jail: And Other Felonious Conversations*. New York: Random House, 1972.

Berrigan, Philip. *Prison Journals of a Priest Revolutionary*. Compiled and edited by Vincent McGee. New York: Holt, Rinehart and Winston, 1970.

Casey, William van Etten, and Philip Nobile, editors. *The Berrigans*. New York: Praeger, 1971.

Nelson, Jack, and Ronald J. Ostrow. *The FBI and the Berrigans: The Making of a Conspiracy*. New York: Coward, McCann and Geoghegan, 1972.

O'Rourke, William. *The Harrisburg Seven and the New Catholic Left*. New York: Thomas Y. Crowell, 1972.

ANGELA DAVIS

Davis, Angela, et al. *If They Come in the Morning: Voices of Resistance*. Foreword by Julian Bond. New York: Third Press, Joseph Opaku Publishing Company, 1971.

Jackson, George. *Blood in My Eye*. New York: Random House, 1972.

———. *Soledad Brother: The Prison Letters of George Jackson*. New York: Coward, McCann and Geoghegan, 1971.

Nadelson, Regina. *Angela Davis*. New York: Peter H. Wyden, 1972.